SOMETHING ABOUT
THOSE EYES

"No eye has seen; no ear has heard and no mind has imagined what God has prepared for those who love Him."

1 Corinthians 2:9

Debbie Wheeland

A True Story of Healing, Redemption, and Grace

Something About Those Eyes
Copyright © 2018 by Debbie Wheeland

The stories in this book reflect the author's recollection of events. Some names, locations, and identifying characteristics may have been changed to protect the privacy of those depicted. Dialogue has been re-created from memory.

This book was printed in the United States of America

ISBN (Print): 978-1-54393-499-1
ISBN (eBook): 978-1-54393-500-4

Foreward

Something About Those Eyes by Debbie Wheeland is a written chronicle of her life. As a child, she describes the sexual and emotional abuse she suffered and as an adult, she endured physical abuse. Even though the consequences of her childhood mistreatment plagued her into adulthood, she survived by diligently working to understand how her past affected her which has led to healing and redemption. God has "made up for the years the locusts have eaten," (Joel 2:25) for Debbie and her family.

Jeenie Gordon, M.S. M. A.
Licensed Marriage & Family Therapist
Prolific Author

Foreward

In her book, the author describes her life growing up with alcoholism, sexual, physical, and emotional abuse as well as dysfunctional relationships. As you journey with her she will show you how she has risen above her circumstances in this poignant and powerful tale of loss, recovery, hope, love, forgiveness, healing and redemption.

As you enter her world you will come to love her personal stories written with humor, wit and passion. I guarantee the reader will experience a pivotal of emotions. You'll find yourself laughing, crying, reacting with anger and sharing in her joy as Debbie takes you through the trials and triumphs of her life.

"As I entered each room, memories of the abuse flooded my mind. I could see myself as a little girl and it brought me to tears. I finally became aware that the little girl inside of me still needed to be healed."

As a therapist, I recommend Debbie's personal story. Her memoir is instrumental in teaching the victim how to become the victor and live life to the fullest, while leaving the past behind.

Sharie Stines, PsyD, CATC-V

Praise for:

SOMETHING ABOUT THOSE EYES

5 STARS for this spellbinding, tear-jerking, thought-provoking, awe-inspiring, mind-blowing, charismatic, captivating, gripping, heart-wrenching inspirational triumphant, rags-to-riches book.

Something About Those Eyes, is a real-life memoir of Debbie's courageous journey through her life. Her captivating story will leave you on the edge of your seat. You will not be able to put the book down. Her descriptive, touching account of her life sweeps you in with a whirlwind of emotions ranging from laughter to tears to exasperation. Debbie speaks of her childhood and the incestuous sexual abuse she had to endure, two failed marriages, where she encountered physical and emotional abuse. Finally, she was able to find peace through her devout faith in God and finding her Prince, who swept her off her feet. Her book speaks of faith, hope, love, acceptance, forgiveness, healing and triumphing over adversity.

"You watched me as I was being formed in utter seclusion as I was woven together in the dark of the womb. You saw me before I was born. Every day of my life was recorded in your book. Every moment was laid out before a single day had passed." Psalm 139: 15-16

Karen Barber, Blue Ridge Mountain Book, North Carolina

Debbie is an outstanding mother and wife. She has been a close friend for over fifteen years. Her book is inspiring. It is a must read for any woman whose life has been affected by abuse. My friend's memoir helps you to believe in redemption and restoration. There actually is love and light at the end of the tunnel.

Debbie's story is proof there is hope for women who have been victims of abuse and living with addiction.

Lisa Moore, friend and neighbor, CA

My aunt writes a truly inspiring story. I spent two days reading her book. It was amazing, and I've been on a roller coaster of emotions since. I truly loved her story and was honored to read it. Debbie, you are an incredible woman with an amazing family!

Kristina Canada, niece - Director of Marketing Universal Studios, CA

My friend's book brought me into a closer relationship with God; it was sad, happy, inspiring, hopeful and at times funny. I couldn't put it down. I highly recommend it.

Lois Roth, friend for over 30 years, CO

Something About Those Eyes is a riveting memoir from my aunt. Through her many struggles, she perseveres with a love for life and her family, a steadfast faith and a forgiving nature. She is an inspiration for all who have experienced and overcome abuse. Despite the difficulties that she faced, she was able to find joy and laughter in every day. The stories of her childhood are full of life's simple pleasures and humor. You will laugh and you will cry as you read her journey from abuse to meeting and marrying her real-life Prince Charming.

Melissa Furgison, niece, CA

Debbie and I met some years ago when our children were very young. Through the years we have been a part of each other's lives. Our children are now grown with children of their own. We have shared many tears, and sometimes the pain was so deep but it led us to the One who hears the cry of the broken-hearted, our Precious Lord Jesus Christ. I was blessed to play a part in her healing. Thank you, my friend, for giving others hope by sharing your story.

Rosa, friend and mentor for forty-two years, CO

Something About Those Eyes, takes you on a roller coaster of emotions. The book not only opened my eyes but also my heart to what many women suffer behind closed doors, yet for many years remain locked in silent pain. Debbie's memoir although heart-wrenching and often unimaginable will leave you inspired and hopeful, knowing that in all things God works for the good of those who love him.

Renee Caloca, friend and Elementary teacher, CA

Debbie's life has been one of vulnerability, violation, quiet suffering, unspeakable hopelessness and significant challenges. Yet, it has also been one of forgiveness goodness of heart and Spirit. And one of God's mercy, grace, and redemption resulting in a dynamic, victorious life lived to the glory of God. (Ephesians 3:20)

Bobbie Bailey
friend for over 20 years and mentor for unwed mothers, CA

In a culture inundated with alcoholism, sexual and emotional abuse, Debbie's *Something About Those Eyes* depicts these everyday issues throughout her own life. While taking you back to your own childhood it will inspire and give you hope as you see God's faithfulness to heal and restore her. This is a must read for those of us who have not begun the healing process and those who appreciate a hilariously entertaining story! Debbie has been a dear friend for over twenty years.

Annette Camareno, friend, CA

Something About Those Eyes tells the true story about a little girl's journey through life, inflicted with the worst kinds of pain and abuse by the people who were supposed to love her the most. The man who proves that fairy-tale endings are indeed possible and that Prince Charming does in fact exist. Reading Debbie's journey, my emotions ran the gamut of fear, sadness, anger, pain, and ultimately joy that left me in utter amazement of this woman. She shares her story with a simple, unpretentious honesty that grabs a hold of your heartstrings. Through her beautiful eyes Debbie sees the world in a positive and hopeful light looking for the best, the good in all in everyone. She sees the face of God and his love for his children despite the ugliness those same eyes have seen in her worst years. Her story is inspiring and gives hope that through Him all things are possible. She is courageous for sharing her story. She is brave for actually putting it out there. And she is my hero for having survived to become a better person in spite of her abusers.

A fan for life, Gina Adams, friend

Chapters

1

Terror in the Night

"Fathers, do not provoke your children to anger by the way you treat them." Ephesians 6:4

When I was young I had frequent nightmares. Maybe they were from the science fiction shows I liked to watch, *The Twilight Zone* and *The Outer Limits*. Mom didn't know I was afraid to go to sleep at night, fortunately, my little sister Monica and I shared a twin size bed. One side of our bed was shoved against the wall, which is where I slept. I believed if a stranger came in he would grab my sister and I would have time to run away. Later we joked as adults and Monica shared her version of the story, I liked sleeping on the end because I thought if a stranger came in I would roll onto the floor and slide under the bed and he would grab you then I would have time to run away. My sister and I were only a year apart and we were always close and the truth is we would have tried to protect each other.

Sometimes before going to bed, Dad wrestled with us kids on the carpeted living room floor, tickling us until we'd all erupt in giggles. Later, after a warm bath, naked and dripping, Monica and I would dive under the covers. I loved the feel of cool, crisp, clean sheets on my body. Dad would gently pull us out by our ankles and dry us off. "Come on girls, it's time to get your pajamas on." Afterwards, I'd fall asleep with a smile on my face, listening to my father walk around the house singing silly, childish rhythms he'd made up. He brought fun and laughter into our home.

One night, as I lay sleeping, no noises were heard and dreams danced around in my head. My heart beat slowly as my chest rose up and down. Suddenly, I felt a shift in weight as the mattress moved, and I heard heavy breathing. With my eyes tightly closed, I sensed a presence. I did not want to see the stranger who had laid down next to me. No sounds, no words, no face, just a nameless shadow. My heart began to beat rapidly. It felt like it would explode and tear me to shreds from the inside out.

I lay there frozen, as if dead, too petrified to move, too scared to open my eyes, not daring to see, not wanting to know, afraid even to breathe, trying to force myself to go back to sleep. It was as if I rose above my body and watched what was happening down below. *Don't think, don't look, just pretend it's not happening. It's all a dream; I hope it's over soon. I can't wait for daytime to come and bring an end to the eerie, silent, scary darkness.*

My eyelids fluttered as light slowly drifted into the shadows. Opening my eyes, I began to focus on familiar patterns in the room as the brightness of the early morning sun streamed through a slight opening between the curtains. Sitting up and rubbing my eyes, I caught sight of my little sister lying next to me near the wall on our twin-sized bed, strands of dark brown hair falling around her tiny face. *There is nobody here but us. I must have had another bad dream. It must have been my imagination playing tricks on me.*

The cool morning air touched my body and I shivered. As I sat up, eager for the new day, I realized I was on the edge of the bed. *How did I get here? I always slept near the wall.* I looked down and saw my nightgown and lace underwear in a heap on the floor. *Those are my panties.* All of a sudden, I realized my nakedness and gasped! Quiet tears streamed down my face. *I hate the night time. I hate it when the sun goes down. I wish my grandmother was visiting she always slept with us girls.*

Hurry, can't let my sister see me without any clothes on. Please don't wake up Monica. I can't let her know about the faceless intruder who comes in the darkness of the night. Stepping barefoot upon the cold, floor, reaching down, I grab my panties and pulled them up around my waist. Throwing my nightgown over my head, I quietly ran to the bathroom down the hall and wiped the wetness from between my legs, all the while grimacing in pain.

But then the house felt abnormally quiet and fear settled around me. Too afraid to walk back into the small room I shared with my sister, I sat petrified on the closed toilet lid desperately trying to forget the events of the night before. Tears clouded my eyes. *Can't let anyone know. Must forget. Must not remember.* Silently, I tiptoed into the living room and turned on the 25-inch black and white television set. Tears turned into laughter watching Saturday morning cartoons although I still felt afraid.

Soon Mike and Monica ran quickly from their bedrooms. Then I heard the pounding of footsteps from the rest of my siblings, Dave and Rob, the two little ones, were close on their heels and I could hear baby Steve stirring in the other room.

Glaring at me, my older brother reached out and changed the knob on the TV.

"I'm going to tell Mommy on you. I was watching *The Roadrunner.*"

Mike looked at me smugly daring me to turn the channel back. "Mom's not here and I can do whatever I want."

Apprehension began to well up inside of me. "You're a liar. Who's watching us then?"

Mike waved a note in front on my face. "Says here the babysitter is coming over 'cause Mom had to go to work. And I'm going to watch MY favorite cartoons until she gets here."

Good. Daddy must be gone too, instantly the fear left me. I didn't care about watching cartoons anymore. Walking into the kitchen, I poured myself a bowl of Cheerios with three heaping teaspoons of sugar. Afterwards I fixed a bottle and went to get baby Steve out of his crib.

I pointed to my older brother, "Is Debbie the one coming over?"

"Of course, she is the one."

"Oh goody, she is my favorite babysitter."

"You just like her because you both have the same name."

"So, what! Debbie likes me better than she likes you."

Mike laughed and chased me. All us kids piled on top of each other and soon forgot about the cartoons. Wrapped in blankets we rolled around the floor, bodies sprawled on top of one another, laughing and having fun.

By the time Debbie came over, we were again glued to the television. As soon as she walked in she promptly shut off the cartoons and turned on the radio. Soon the sound of rock & roll drifted through the room.

"Come on kids, we're going to get this house cleaned. The sooner we get it done the sooner you can watch your shows again."

Although we were momentarily angry with her, she made chores fun. And sometimes afterwards, she'd let us help her bake cookies or make crafts.

During the Christmas season a few months earlier, I had accidentally broken an ornament and some blood oozed from my little finger. Running to Debbie, I showed her my cut. She picked up a piece of the broken glass, jabbed her own finger and smeared our blood together. "Now we are blood sisters."

I never forgot it and I always felt like we had a special bond.

"Please don't leave," I said a few hours later after my father came home.

"Your dad is here now and your mom will be home soon," Debbie turned to close the door behind her.

After she left, I caught a glimpse of Dad strolling in the kitchen, wearing nothing but his white underwear. Something about his near-nakedness bothered me. Debbie would tell me years later, he frequently walked around the house like that and she always felt uncomfortable whenever he was there.

Later that day, I passed the bathroom. My dad always left the door ajar when he used the toilet. I turned my head quickly and walked even faster to stay out of his sight. *Why didn't he shut the door?* Mom finally returned home from her job at the factory where she had started working shortly after her last baby was born.

Soon she prepared dinner and it was time for bed. Usually after we ate, all us kids watched television or played outside until it was time to go to bed. I'd beg Mom to let me stay up with promises of helping bathe the younger kids or help clean the kitchen, hoping to prolong bedtime, I hated the dark. But unfortunately, bedtime always came too soon. As I lay in bed shuddering, fear permeated me but I could no longer hold my eyes open. I'd try talking to Monica as long as I could, but eventually darkness would envelope the room.

As I got older, and the nighttime visits became more frequent, the stranger's face became familiar to me, and my beloved daddy would whisper in my ear, "Shhh, honey, you know I'd never hurt you. I know you want to make Daddy feel good now, so here is what I want you to do to me."

Other times he would murmur, "Remember this is our secret. If you tell your mother she'll put me in jail and I'll have to leave. You don't want me to go away, do you honey?"

At six years old, I didn't know what jail was but it sounded bad to me, and I knew I didn't want to be responsible for him leaving. I would do anything I could to make sure that didn't happen. My father's weekly or monthly visits—I can't recall how often—went on for several years. It became our secret, and it ruled my life. I got used to being awaken in the middle of the night. Keeping my eyes tightly shut, I couldn't wait for it to end; yet other times I even enjoyed how he made me feel.

Whether my young mother was at work, or dead tired from the sleeping pills she ingested, she never woke up, nor did anyone else during his nighttime visits. Throughout the years while this was happening, my sister seemed to be nowhere in sight, even though we both shared the same bed, and the ironic thing was, I never wondered where she was.

As I got older and realized what Dad was doing to me was wrong, I began to feel guilty and ashamed. Sometimes I tried to protest in the darkness of my room. Then he began to threaten me. "If you don't do this with me I will do this to your sister." I was determined to protect my sister at any cost, I did not want her to go through the horror I was experiencing.

My father spoke things to me and masterfully manipulated me into thinking it was all my fault. The words he used were meticulously chosen and I believed him and blamed myself for the terror in the night.

2

I Was Chosen

"You watched me as I was being formed in utter seclusion as I was woven together in the dark of the womb. You saw me before I was born. Every day of my life was recorded in your book. Every moment was laid out before a single day had passed." Psalm 139: 15-16

Throughout my childhood, my daddy wasn't home much. He spent long hours at work and even longer hours gambling at the casinos in Las Vegas. Being a full-time homemaker meant Mom was home alone with us in the hot, desert town of Henderson, Nevada, where I was born in 1955. She kept busy with her then four children. Looking forward to Daddy coming home to eat dinner with the family was the highlight of my young mothers' day. Mom would spend hours preparing delicious, homemade meals, then she'd dress us in our finest clothes and seat us at the dining room table. Hence, the waiting would begin.

"I'm so hungry. Can we eat?" I asked, as I licked my tongue against my lips, salivating over the fried chicken at the table.

"No, let's wait just a little longer for Daddy to come home."

"But we're so hungry," whined my siblings.

"Just a little longer," Mom walked back and forth glancing out the front window, holding the baby in her arms.

Suddenly a car drove up. Flinging open the front door, my mother watched sadly as it turned around in our driveway and kept going down the street.

"Please, Mommy can't we eat. I don't want to wait for Daddy anymore," cried my older brother, Mike.

Reluctantly, she would dish out our servings. Sitting at the table, watching us eat, Mom was determined to share supper with her husband, no matter what time he showed up. Usually it was hours later, after all us kids had fallen asleep. Rarely did he return home while we were still awake. The loneliness my mother felt during her marriage must have begun at this time.

When I was almost four our family moved to Fontana, California where my dad got a job with Kaiser Steel and within months our mother was pregnant with her fifth child. A year later her sixth, and final, child would follow.

Shortly after arriving in California, my youthful parents drove us kids to the mountains to see snow for the first time. We pulled over on the way to Big Bear and stopped at a nearby gas station. Bundled up in my warm, furry coat, I reached out my little hands and watched, fascinated, as the cold, white flakes cascaded onto my tiny fingers. Mesmerized with the snow, I put it to my lips and felt its chill on my warm tongue. "It's freezing Daddy," I shivered.

Smiling at my father whom I adored, I listened as he patiently explained to me all about the snow.

We called our new home "the spider house," they seemed to be everywhere. I loved hanging out at the house next door after my brother went to school. My mother said I missed him terribly and cried every day after he left. The little boy that lived next door, Greg, was my age and had lots of freckles. We played while our mothers drank coffee, gossiped, and watched the younger children.

One morning while I was at Greg's house, Mom called from across the street. "Debra come here, I want you to help our neighbors, they locked themselves out of their house." Pointing to a small garage window she said, "I need you to crawl in and run through the garage, then go in the house and unlock the front door."

I wanted desperately to please my mother. Hoisting me up, she pushed my body through the small, daunting window. Suddenly, I froze and started screaming, "No, I don't want to go in Mommy. I'm afraid; it's so dark in here. I can't see anything. Take me out!"

While I was halfway in and halfway out, my mother tried to coax me into moving forward but I continued screaming. Finally, she pulled me out and I noticed her face--she stared at me with that disappointed look!

"Debra was scared of the dark, but you're not afraid to go through this window are you Greg?"

Jumping up and down, eager to get started he bragged, "I can do it. I'm not a scaredy-cat."

Greg ran through the dark garage and into the house. Proudly, he opened the front door, the adults applauded him. *That should have been me.*

After that experience my father, took advantage of my unwarranted fears, and sometimes at night he and Mom would load us kids into the family station wagon. Shutting off the headlights, he purposely drove down the lane with walnut trees that lined both sides. It was the darkest and scariest street in the whole town.

"Open your eyes, there's nothing to be afraid of," he'd taunt me.

"Stop it, turn the lights back on. Please let's go home," I'd wail, as my siblings and parents laughed.

It was probably just a harmless family game. Maybe it was his way of teaching me not to be afraid of the dark, but I felt like such a coward. *Why was I so afraid of the dark? Why couldn't I be brave?*

Even though I was temporarily angry with my dad it was all forgotten in the morning when I would hear my father singing nonsensical songs while preparing our breakfast. *"Cream of Wheat is so good to eat and it makes you feel so fine."* Each of us kids would roar with laughter as we tried to keep in tune with him. When Dad was around, which wasn't often, he liked to cook, and he'd make a big deal out of preparing a meal. Adding a little bit of beer to the spaghetti sauce, he'd raise the bottle up to his lips and drink the rest. All us kids were his audience and we loved standing around the kitchen hearing our father's laughter. Often times he would set out small bowls and spoons on the kitchen table at night. The next morning all we had to do was pour our cereal and milk before we set out for school. He was thoughtful that way.

My father had other ways of amusing the family. Early one Saturday morning, Mom motioned to our dad. "Bob, go to the swap meet and get a washing machine. The dirty clothes are piling up."

Hours later Dad returned home in a friend's borrowed truck. He walked around to the back, opened the latch and led out a darling, brown and white spotted calf.

My mother was livid. "Where's my washing machine?"

"Oh, Inez I couldn't resist. Look at those big brown eyes. Isn't he cute?"

My siblings and I roared with laughter but Mom was furious. "Bob, that cow has to go."

"Okay, I will return him tomorrow."

We spent the whole day paying attention to our new pet. Early the next morning we couldn't wait to visit him. Opening up the garage door, the smell of a sewer rushed out at us. Yuck! That adorable, little calf made a nasty mess all over the garage floor during the night. Dad promptly loaded him on the truck and took him back to the swap meet and returned home with Mom's new washing machine.

3

Neighbors, Friends and Fights

"He who brings trouble on his family will inherit only wind, and the fool will be a servant to the wise." Proverbs 11:29

I was just about to start kindergarten when we moved from the spider house to our first house on Ceres Drive, in a low-income neighborhood in Fontana. One day, while I was standing out back looking through the chain link fence that separated us from the people next-door, I noticed a short, brown-haired girl playing in her backyard. "Hey, what's your name?"

"My name is Theresa. What's yours?"

"I'm Debbie. I'm five, how old are you?"

"I'm five, the same as you."

Then I met Theresa's older sister, who was named Debbie, she was ten.

When Debbie got a little older she became our regular babysitter when Mom started working on Saturdays. Our father's absence was a regular occurrence; no one seemed bothered by that because we knew

13

Debbie would come over and watch us. Saturday mornings were the highlight of the week for my siblings and me. Whoever woke up first was careful not to awaken the others because the first kid to the TV set was king of the television and was able to pick their favorite cartoon. I'd forgo breakfast to have the TV all to myself even if for only a few minutes. *Tom and Jerry, Roadrunner, Felix the Cat, and Bugs Bunny* were some of my favorites. On evenings when my parents went out we could always count on Debbie to babysit us. She'd fix dinner and give us our baths, and put us to bed.

Sometimes, after tucking us in for the night I'd feel a light tap on my shoulder, "Deb, you're old enough to stay up late. Want to get back up and watch a movie with me?"

"Yea!" I'd start to yell excitedly.

"Shhh… you'll wake up your sister. Come on let's go."

I felt so special because Debbie picked me to stay up with her.

Years later my older brother, Mike and I shared stories. "Debbie always woke me up and let me watch TV with her while everybody else slept," I bragged.

"Silly girl, Debbie would get me up on the nights you were still in bed. Ha! Ha! And you thought you were the only one."

Debbie and our mom had a close relationship. They were more like mother and daughter. Mom taught Debbie how to cook and the two of them frequently sat at the dining room table having heart-to-heart talks. As the years went by they'd sip coffee and Debbie would divulge her boy troubles and family problems to my mom.

Most of the adolescent kids in the neighborhood enjoyed spending time with our mother. The teenage girls often confided in her, and the boys called her Sofia. Mom resembled the actress, Sofia Loren with long, thick, dark hair, big brown eyes, wavy lashes, and olive skin. (Although

Sofia Loren was Italian, while Mom was Spanish.) Our mother looked young for her age and acted youthful. She enjoyed kidding around with all our friends, especially the teenage boys in the neighborhood. Mom made everyone laugh but often at home she was moody, bossy, unkind and opinionated.

The sixties were a time when the neighborhood ladies went from house to house with their cups of coffee in hand to visit each other. We'd follow Mom and play with their kids. Every Thursday night the housewives would get together and watch their favorite singer, Tom Jones. We could hear them swooning over his songs and watch them blowing kisses at the television set.

One of my mom's neighborhood friends, Amelia, had two children. I would often tag along with my mom when she hung out with her. On one of these visits, I overheard Mom say to Amelia, "I just know I'm going to die before I turn thirty-five."

For years after I had overheard her, I lived in constant fear afraid her prediction would come true. Whenever Mom was sad, depressed or angry, which seemed fairly often, I did whatever I could to comfort her. Whether it meant taking care of my siblings, cleaning the house, making dinner, keeping the kids quiet, or bringing Mom her prescription drugs, I was consumed with ways to make her happy so she would want to live. Every year, I was relieved when her birthday would come and she was still alive.

My mother and father fought incessantly and as time went on the fights between them escalated. Even though we kids were supposed to be sleeping, the house was so small and the walls were so thin, we would hear bits and pieces of their conversations as they yelled at each other. Sometimes we would hear the words pills, affairs, or booze, but at the time they made no sense to us. We just tried to drown out the screams, holding our pillows over our ears.

"Steve is not even my kid," Dad would scream.

"Why do you keep throwing it in my face. I made one mistake." Mom yelled back.

Of course, we didn't understand what they were talking about, but we later found out our mother and Uncle Sam, my dad's baby brother, had had an affair and my youngest brother was the result.

Some days we'd come home from school and catch Dad, his eyes red from crying, reading the large family Bible. Grumbling and blaming my mother for everything, he'd try to get us kids to sympathize with him. I had never seen a grown man cry like a baby, and I despised my dad for it. Even at my young age, I knew he was not taking responsibility for his wrong actions, but was trying to make my mother look like the bad one. His performance only reinforced my feelings about my dad, he was a coward and a crybaby. And I was terrified of turning out just like him.

4

Siblings

"Love each other as brothers and sisters. Be tenderhearted and keep a humble attitude." 1 Peter 3:8b

As I got use to those incidents with my dad, life went on as normal. Somehow, I kept the nighttime activities separated from the daytime. The September I turned seven, our mother planned one big birthday party for my older brother Mike, my sister Monica and me. We were all born in the same month and were only a year apart. Most of the neighborhood kids showed up as we celebrated in the back yard. Mom hung balloons on the clothesline and taped pink and blue crepe paper around an old-fashioned wringer washing machine that stood outside. Then she set out bowls of potato chips and warm chocolate chip cookies on top of our red and black-checkered ironing board. The smell of grilled hot dogs and hamburgers filled the air. After lunch was eaten, Mom put candles in our cake and sang happy birthday to each of us. Later on, she served us a piece of birthday cake with our favorite, strawberry, chocolate and vanilla Neapolitan ice cream. I remember that day because it was the first and last time we celebrated our birthdays together.

A couple years later my mother taught me how to bake from scratch. It wasn't long before I was the one making the birthday cakes for all five of my siblings, Mike (10), Monica (8), Dave (6), Rob (5), and Steve (4). They'd hang out in the kitchen with me while I prepared their favorite treats.

My little brothers watched me intently, "can I lick the bowl?"

"Of course, and you can each taste a spoonful of the mix." I motioned to Mike and Monica; I didn't want anyone left out.

Holidays came and went while we were young and my father was still a part of our lives. The highlight of our Christmas season was attending the annual Christmas party at Kaiser Steel. Before going to bed the night before, Monica and I sat cross-legged on the floor while Mom put soft, pink sponge rollers in our hair. We wanted to look extra special the next day.

In the morning, Mom dressed us in our best clothes. Excitedly, we looked forward to receiving our red, nylon net stockings, filled with penny candy and small trinkets that Santa Claus would hand out.

I had a bad habit my mother called rocking, which I did before falling asleep at night. Leaning on my knees and forearms with my head smashed in my pillow, I would rock back and forth until I fell asleep. One time, the night before the annual Christmas party, with my hair curled tightly around pink sponge rollers, I rocked the bed so hard which caused it to move in front of the bedroom door. Sadly, all the rollers fell out. The next morning when I noticed the curlers on my pillow, I ran to my mother sobbing. "Please, curl my hair again and let me sit in front of the swamp cooler, I don't want to look ugly for the party."

"No, that is just too bad, young lady. You're the one who rocked all the rollers out of your hair. It's your own fault. I've asked you time and time again to stop rocking. Maybe now you'll listen."

"I promise I will stop." I hated it when my mother was angry with me and I hated myself for my bad habit. Along with rocking I also sucked my thumb. Over the years Mom tried putting hot sauce on my thumb, bandaging it, or screaming at me every time she saw it in my mouth. Nothing worked and it would take many years before I stopped.

At a young age our mother gave Monica and me the responsibility of pretending to be the tooth fairy and Easter bunny to our younger siblings. When my little brothers started losing their teeth we would quietly sneak in their rooms take their teeth and replace them with nickels and dimes. It was so much fun, we both loved pretending.

Although we rarely had extra money we didn't realize how poor we were. Sometimes Mom took in ironing to make ends meet. Since Dad was a tightwad, he handled our lack of funds in a different way. Loading us into the family station wagon, he'd direct us to get into the car, "I don't want any of you kids to wear shoes."

We'd stop at Pic N Save, Kmart, Penny's Department store even the grocery market, and our father would march all six of us into the store. "Try on a pair of Zorries (which later were referred to as flip flops.) Here put on these tennis shoes."

Admiring our brand-new shoes, we'd walk out the door, right past the cash registers, without paying. Other times we would strut out with new outfits. One time, Dad proudly marched with his offspring into Sears and picked out a pair of expensive sunglasses. "Here Dave, see how these look on you."

My little brother walked out to the car thrilled with his new possession. As soon as we were safely inside, Dad reached over and yanked them off Dave's face. "Thanks for my sunglasses, buddy." Our father always made sure his six kids had new clothes and shoes without spending a dime!

Every year Dad waited until Christmas Eve to get us a tree, knowing the day before Christmas, the trees would be free. We didn't care when we got the tree, we were just glad to get one. We'd happily decorate hours before Santa Claus was due to arrive.

Most of the people in our neighborhood also had lots of kids and hardly any money, but each family was generous with their food. Our mom always prepared a big dinner for us. She regularly included vegetables, meat, and potatoes. She was great at making homemade tortillas and homemade bread. Two houses down, Mrs. Leo always had a huge pot of piping hot pinto beans simmering on the stove. Up the street, Mrs. Kinzer's home was filled with the smell of scrumptious homemade tamales. Our growing family stopped growing when my baby brother, Steve was born in the late spring of 1960. With six kids in tow, we thought we had a monopoly in the neighborhood until we counted Mrs. Kinzer's kids; there were ten of them.

There was never a dull moment in the Griswold household. We experienced many amusing escapades, thanks to Mike, who we thought of as our hero. We all counted on him and looked up to him with awe in our hearts. Because of this, there was never any animosity for our cherished oldest sibling even though we all somehow knew Mike was Mom's favorite.

From the time he was little, he was the mischievous one. Our mother had a pet peeve; we couldn't ask her anything while she was half asleep. But that didn't stop Mike. On Saturday mornings, (after Mom quit her job) he would wake at the crack of dawn, come into our bedroom and proudly announce in a booming voice, "Today is bread ball day, get up, hurry get up!"

"You better ask Mommy's permission," I said, being the obedient one and always afraid to break the rules.

Tiptoeing into Mom's room, Mike stood next to her bed, "Mom, can we make bread balls this morning?"

Waving her hand, with one eye open, she sighed, "I don't care. Now get out of here."

"She said okay. Let's get started," Mike waved us kids into the kitchen.

All six of us would march into our small kitchen where Mike would grab soft, squishy, pieces of white bread and pass them to each of us. Tearing off the crust, we'd sprinkle granulated sugar on top and roll our delicious creations into little white balls. Of course, they didn't stay white, as our dirty hands soon turned the round dough spheres into a dingy grey. Hungrily, we'd cram our delicious delights into our mouths, and throw the remaining balls at each other. Pretty soon the whole loaf disappeared. What a mess awaited our mother when she'd finally drag herself out of bed.

Six pairs of innocent eyes would be staring up at her, as she'd scream, "Who did this?"

All fingers pointed to Mike.

"I asked you and you said we could make bread balls today."

"No, I didn't," yelled Mom.

"But you opened your eye and looked at me, I thought you were awake," grinned Mike..

"All of you get in the kitchen and clean up this mess right now!"

At other times, our imaginative brother would entertain us with his funny, made-up stories. Proudly, he'd pull out the reel-to-reel tape recorder.

"Tell us the story of Froggy Toad and Lily Pad again," we'd beg.

Sticking out his tongue as if to catch a fly, Mike would change his voice and make frog sounds, "Ribbit, Ribbit!"

Rolling on the floor, chuckling loudly, our laughter filled the house. We'd kick each other and jump around like little frogs. Mom would sit back and watch us, obviously enjoying the fun. Jerry Lewis was my brother's favorite television character and he would trip and fall, just like Jerry. Other times we'd holler, "Mike, do your frying bacon imitation."

Standing with his arms straight down at his sides he would shake furiously, throw his self on the floor and tremble spastically, moving every part of his body as if he were sizzling.

Mike wasn't the only entertainer of the family. I'd make up songs and pretend to be various television characters. My favorite song was from the movie, "Damn Yankees" and I pretended to be the main star, Lola. I'd dance around the house wearing a towel around my shoulders singing, "Whatever Lola wants Lola gets." All the kids and our mother would roar with laughter. "Debbie, you're so dramatic. You should become an actress," Mom would often say.

We all loved hanging out with our big brother. During the summer months we'd spend most days walking the short distance to the orange grove around the block. Back in the sixties there were acres of orange trees and grape vineyards growing everywhere. Us kids would spend our weekends collecting branches, old tires, large rocks, dried tumbleweeds, and anything else we could use to make forts. When our stomachs growled with hunger, none of us wanted to head home and end our fun. We'd pick fresh, ripe oranges off the trees, or stuff juicy, purple grapes in our mouth then we'd run to the nearby YMCA to use the bathroom or get a drink of water. Back then there were no water bottles, or cell phones, and certainly no fear of strangers to accost us. We always felt safe with our big brother even though he was just a year older than me and small in stature.

While we were still in elementary school Dad enrolled us all in the local YMCA and we were fortunate enough to take swimming lessons there. Luckily, it was a short walk from our house. Throughout the summer on Saturday afternoons we'd all swim in the YMCA's enormous indoor pool. Monica and I had vivid imaginations and along with our friends we'd pretend to be mermaids or pirates hunting for buried treasure. Most of the kids in our neighborhood hung out at the Y and we were like one big happy family. There was teasing, fighting, making up, sleepovers and fun adventures.

I was the family caretaker and I took care of my little brothers. Playing with them pretending to be a horse while they rode on my back was a favorite game we often played. Other times we played Hide and Seek and I'd chase them through the house while they howled with laughter. When my little brothers started school, I was the one who made sure they had clean clothes to wear, got their cereal ready for them, and packed them a lunch.

For whatever reason, our mother didn't seem to be around. Often she'd retreat by spending hours hiding away in her bedroom or getting in her car and driving away somewhere. She was emotionally unavailable to us kids, of course we did not realize it at the time.

I considered Monica my best friend, although we had our share of arguments and fights. Outwardly, Monica seemed like a sweet little thing, but she had a mean streak. When she wanted to intimidate me, she'd make herself appear tough and scary and I always fell for it. One time when I was nine and Monica was eight, I saw her in the kitchen standing still with her back towards me.

Being the bossy big sister I was, I poked her in the back. "You're supposed to be washing the dishes. I'm telling Mommy on you."

Monica slowly turned to me, with a large butcher knife in her hand raised at me, and her face smeared with black eyeliner. Glaring at me though frightening half-slit eyes, she shrieked, "I'm going to kill you," while slowly heading towards me.

Terrified, I screamed, "I can't believe you want to kill me! I'm your sister!" I started running from her.

She put the knife down and laughed. "You're so gullible. Of course, I don't want to kill you. I was just teasing you. I even got mom's makeup and put it on my face to make myself look evil. I made sure no one else was in the house, because I didn't want to trip and accidentally hurt you or myself."

"I thought you really hated me. You hurt my feelings."

"I didn't really mean it. Why do you have to take everything so seriously?"

Monica prided herself on giving me a good scare and once I got over it we both had a good laugh over it.

Our mother regularly accused Monica of being lazy while I was occasionally praised for being the helpful one. Cleaning the whole house, I was always trying to prove to Mom how good I was. Regretfully, I tattled on my sister, because she didn't do as much as I did. When Mom walked through the doors I'd greet her with, "I cleaned the whole house and Monica didn't do nothing!" *Maybe Mom would love me more because I always cleaned without being asked!*

Monica often threw horrible fits. Sadly, our mother took out her frustrations on my little sister and she'd frequently get a spanking. Grabbing her by her pony-tail, Mom would smack her over and over while screaming cruel things to her. "You're so lazy. You don't do anything around here. I'm sick of your fits. You act like a crazy person."

Monica had long wavy, beautiful dark brown hair. It was always longer than mine. My hair was stringy, straight, thin and shorter than hers. She was short and petite while I was tall and gangly. Since I didn't believe I was pretty, I thought my sister was beautiful and was occasionally envious of her. Our hair always seemed to be full of knots, but we loved having long hair. Our mother would sit us down, grab a hairbrush and try and comb through our headful of tangles. If we'd squirm, or fidget, she'd bop us on the head or shoulder with the brush to quiet us down. I remember the time Mom let the neighborhood teenager cut our hair short just like the Beatles. It took us a long time to forgive our mother for that. Mom felt bad and she never cut our hair short again.

When my sister was a teenager, people used to say she looked like Valerie Bertinelli from the sitcom, *One Day at a Time*, while I was told I resembled Susan Dey from the *Partridge Family*. Sadly, neither of us grew up believing we were pretty, confident or feeling good about ourselves.

Monica and I often played house, she usually pretended to be the father or her favorite actor, Tony Curtis. I was always the family dog. Us three oldest kids would put on shows for our siblings and the neighborhood children. Finding old clothes, scarves and mismatched socks we'd dress crazy and we'd act out comedy routines, causing rippling laughter amongst everyone. In those days, there were no video games or DVDs, and we always found fun ways to use our imaginations.

Mom never went out of the house without her makeup on and all six of us would gather in our small bathroom and watch her meticulously line her eyes with black liner, color her cheeks with pink rouge and put on red lipstick. Joking with her we'd try unsuccessfully to get her to close her mouth while putting on mascara. She never did. Pulling the curlers out of her hair she'd hold it up high and tease it with a comb before brushing it out. Mom would raise her arms above her head, "look at me I'm a witch," and sometimes she'd even chase us throughout the house.

You could always find our mother outside tossing a ball with the boys, or working in the yard. Throughout their childhood the boys were usually involved in baseball. Some of the best times we had were watching our brothers play games at the park on warm, summer evenings. We bought penny candy at the snack bar and walked around with our neighborhood friends while cheering on our siblings. No matter what was going on with Mom, she always went to the games, either volunteering or sitting in the audience supporting our brothers with screams and hollers.

My three younger brothers were uniquely different from each other and they were all a year apart. Dave, who was the fourth child, always told tall tales and amused us with his funny stories. I will never forget the time when Dave was five, Mom and Dad threw a huge adult party. The next morning Dave woke up early and walked in the garage. He proceeded to drink all the half empty glasses of orange juice. Unbeknownst to him the glasses were also filled with vodka. We teased him for years about getting drunk at such an early age.

Dave often walked and talked in his sleep. Once, when Mom was out and we three older kids were still up watching television, Dave walked down the hallway after he had been in bed a few hours. He stood in the living room then knelt down and began to flick his fingers against the hard floor.

"What are you doing Dave?" We snickered.

He continued to flick his fingers on the floor. "I lost my marbles."

Rolling on the floor, we exploded with laughter. Afterwards I quietly led my little brother back to his bed. The next morning, he had no remembrance of his antic from the night before. Another time while we older kids were up late, Dave strolled out of his room, opened the front door, walked out, and slammed it shut. We waited a few minutes for him to return. Then Mike, Monica, and I ran outside in search of our brother. We found Dave curled up in a fetal position in the middle of the street, fast asleep on the cold, hard, asphalt. We always got a good laugh over Dave. Since he was the only one with blond hair (mine had already darkened,) we'd often gang up on him and tease him, unmercifully. "You're not really a Griswold, you were adopted. Mom found you on the doorstep."

He'd cry at first but when he got older he was the first one to play jokes on us. And now he tells people. "I'm not really a Griswold. I'm adopted."

Rob liked to whine and grumble. We found him to be an easy target to make fun of because he had asthma and occasionally had wheezing attacks. Luckily, he only landed in the hospital a couple times from his condition. To his detriment we'd mock him unmercifully by holding our throats and repeating, "I can't breathe, I can't breathe," which caused him to whine and cry even louder. Of course we didn't understand how serious asthma was and we didn't realize how cruel and insensitive we were being. We could hear Mom screaming in the background, "You kids better stop that!" Mom was a yeller and she rarely knew what was going on, which only encouraged us to torment the younger ones.

Rob recalled we had a big box of mismatched socks. Each morning while getting ready for school we'd run to the box and look for identical socks. Rob also remembers our family always being out of toilet paper. To this day he keeps no less than thirty rolls of extra paper and he prides himself on buying plenty of socks. Interesting how our childhood habits define us!

Steve, the baby of the family, was the skinniest and scrawniest one, although now he is the biggest one of the bunch. When Steve was born, Mom remarked about how cute and adorable he was. "He's so pretty he could be a girl." She kept his hair long, and before his second birthday, she put a dress on him and called him Michele. We still have the picture to prove what a pretty boy Steve was.

Our babysitter spoiled Steve and he became a first-class brat. He would holler and cry a lot and we teased him and made him cry even more. We also ganged up on him and made him believe he was adopted, too. This caused him to wail even louder. It was music to our ears!

Halloween was Steve's favorite holiday. After hours of trick-or-treating, Mom would empty all our treats into one large pillowcase, roll it up and hide it away. Somehow, our baby brother always found those tasty candies and every year we could count on our brother to gobble up most of our Halloween candy. Steve had an overactive imagination. When he was three he would say to us, "Remember the time I was a policeman or a fireman?" We would bait him and keep asking him questions because he loved the attention and we enjoyed laughing at his stories.

Most of the time I thoroughly enjoyed taking care of my younger siblings. When Steve grew up and got married he'd often say to his wife, "I prefer it when you burn my hotdogs, that's the way my sister, Debbie always cooked them. And that's the way I like them."

Even though there was much teasing, we all truly loved each other and we banded together to protect one another. I don't remember any sibling rivalry when we were little, or to this day. My mom drilled it into our heads while growing up, "Stay close to each other, you're all you have."

5

God and Cops

"For I know the plans I have for you." Declares the Lord,
"plans to prosper you and not to harm you, plans to give
you hope and a future." Jeremiah 29:11

I grew up attending St. Joseph's Catholic Church in Fontana, my parents thought it was important us kids went while they slept in on Sunday mornings. On Saturdays, we three older kids went to Catechism. I was afraid of the nuns, with their black dresses down to their ankles and their hair completely hidden inside their head-coverings. My sister says she remembers learning about Jesus. But the only thing I remember is learning about Mary and I thought she was wonderful, I adored her. I watched a movie about St. Bernadette who claimed she saw the Virgin Mary. Afterwards, I'd spend countless hours daydreaming she would appear to me. Faithfully, I said prayers to Mary and often visited the statue of her in the church's courtyard. One October I even put some of my Halloween candy at Mary's feet as a sacrifice to her.

God was always an angry god to me. I constantly worried that he would take his giant club and beat me over the head when I made a mistake. I felt like I had to be perfect to receive his love. I viewed God the same way I saw my mother, someone I couldn't please, no matter how hard I tried. Each Sunday morning, I'd rush around the house begging my siblings to go to church with me, while my stomach growled because we weren't allowed to eat breakfast until after we'd had our small, round white communion wafer. There was something so pure and sacrificial about that wafer melting on my tongue. Usually Mike and Monica would accompany me, but often times I'd walk five blocks alone. I needed to assuage the guilt, shame, and self-hatred that haunted me. I didn't want God to be mad at me, and I just knew in my child's mind that if I didn't go to church on Sundays bad things would happen to me or one of my family members. I had to protect everyone and I hoped to keep God at bay, make him happy and avoid being punished by him.

I can vividly remember my First Communion. My mother clothed my sister and me in matching, frilly, snow-white dresses. I can still recall the hand-made lace veil my grandmother made just for me. I was so proud and I felt like a princess. I didn't understand what I was doing, but I knew it was a happy occasion and I was to become a bride!

Confession, on Saturday afternoons, was something to be dreaded by my two siblings but I looked forward to it. Mike, Monica, and I would slowly make our way to the church. One time the three of us were kneeling at the pew and it was time for Mike to go into the little booth and confess his sins to the priest.

"Bless me Father for I have sinned, it's been one week since my last confession. I got in a fight with my sister, I…"

Mike talked so loudly; soon I began to feel guilty over hearing his private sins. Instantly covering my ears, I whispered Hail Mary and The Lord's Prayer as loudly as I could to drown out my brother's sins.

I could hardly contain my excitement as I waited for my turn. I felt so clean after talking to the priest. Of course, I never told him what was really happening in our home, and almost immediately, as I'd leave the church and head home, the dirtiness and shame I felt about myself would settle over me like a dark cloud.

I thought everything bad that happened to me or my family was somehow the result of the secret I lived with. I truly believed it was my fault and I tried so hard to be compliant, doing what I was told without arguing, cleaning the house, making dinners, teaching my siblings manners, being the good little mother to the younger kids.

When I was about to enter the fifth grade Mom and Dad moved into a brand new, contemporary home on the other side of town, 1450 Holly drive would become our new address. It was much nicer than our old house it had wall-to-wall carpeting, a fireplace, central air-conditioning and heating, two bathrooms, a patio, and modern appliances, including a dishwasher, which we'd never had before. We were all thrilled to move into our new home.

Mom had quit the factory job that had taken her away from the family on Saturdays but the fighting between my parents didn't end, even though the residence changed. In fact, their loud quarrels grew even louder. The name-calling and accusations continued to spiral out of control. By that time, I had stopped going to church because it was too far from our new house.

One Friday night a loud banging on the front door awakened all of us. Running into the front room, we were blinded by the bright lights coming from outside. It was if the brilliance of the sun was shining right in our living room in the middle of the night. *Where was the light coming from?*

"Mommy, who's at the door?" One of my brothers asked.

"Go on, you kids, get back to bed now!" Mom screamed.

Quickly, I took my younger siblings back to their bedroom then snuck back into the living room. Hiding behind a chair with my sister and older brother we watched in horror as the front door was kicked open. Looking outside we could see several black and white police cars pointing towards the front of our house. Each had the high beams of their headlights on. The officers cuffed my dad and escorted him to the car. I watched in horror. *It's my fault; they are taking my father to jail. How did they find out about our secret?*

As soon as morning came we couldn't wait to go outside and play and put aside the events of the night before. I don't know how long our dad was gone, or why the policemen came and took him away. We didn't ask any questions and we never did get a new front door.. Feeling guilty but relieved, I quickly realized how happy I was to have my dad out of the house.

It didn't take us long to make friends in our new neighborhood. Monica and I met a girl named Molly, who lived around the corner. "Come in and meet my Daddy," she said one day.

"Daddy these are my new friends, Monica and Debbie." Her father was sitting in a Lazy-boy chair. He reached down, unscrewed his leg, pulled it out from his shorts and leaned his freaky artificial leg against the chair. I ran out of the house screaming. My sister and Molly dragged me back into the house, and after that I grew used to her dad's scary, wooden prosthesis.

While playing at Molly's house one day, her dad promised us animal crackers with icing and sprinkles on top if my sister and I would help her clean the house. Little red sugar ants were everywhere, but we didn't care. With six kids, we rarely bought store bought cookies. The thought of those delectable treats made the afternoon chores go quickly.

I would watch our new friend climb up on her daddy's lap and he would cuddle and kiss her cheeks. They would laugh together and smile at each other. *Is that what dads are supposed to do with their daughters?* It seemed so foreign to me! I wondered if they had secrets, too.

There were other happy memories at our house on Holly drive too. Just around the block there was an orange grove, so we were able to resume building forts. We hung out all day that summer with our new friends, walking the streets, reaching for the fresh, tangy oranges that grew plentiful on the overhanging branches. We were never alone, a group of us would walk unafraid miles from our house to pick plump purple grapes from nearby vineyards and pop them in our mouths. One of our favorite things to do was explore old, abandoned houses around the neighborhood. I loved picturing how other people lived in the olden days. One time we found a bird's nest with a fresh, blue egg in it. Running all the way home we couldn't wait to show Mom our treasure. But by the time we got home, the egg was cracked and most of the bird's nest had come apart.

We loved our adventures, spending time with each other, discovering new things, and being away from the house. It must have given us a feeling of independence and control over our often-chaotic lives. My mother never asked where we went all day. She didn't care as long as we had gotten our chores done. Mom never had restrictions on when we had to come home, and she usually had a home-cooked meal ready for us. Since we often skipped lunch, the thought of Mom's crunchy tacos and tasty bean burritos always lured us back to the house by dinnertime.

Much later, Mom finally told us older kids that our dad had been arrested for selling drugs and that was the reason the cops kicked our door in. He was released from jail a few months later, and showed up at our house. Shortly thereafter, my mother disappeared for a while. When we were all grown up, she told us she had been arrested for selling speed and the police had locked her up for a few months also. Afterwards she moved to an apartment above the local neighborhood bar called The Sugar Shack.

While Mom was away, Dad moved his nineteen-year-old girl-friend, Glenda, into our home. I hated the new arrangement and I missed my mom. We kids didn't like the new rules my dad and Glenda implemented. I was ten and in the fifth grade and my dad decided to give us an allowance for the first time in our lives. The catch was each time we failed to do one of our chores he deducted twenty-five to fifty cents. It didn't affect me as much as my siblings because not only did I do my chores but I often did theirs as well.

One time my dad's girlfriend took my sister and I to the mall to do some window-shopping. We had never been there before. Glenda ordered us a warm piece of gingerbread cake with a dollop of whip cream on top from the food court. It melted in our mouth my sister and I had never tasted anything so good. Although we experienced fun times with Glenda, we missed our mom terribly and we resented the way she tried to act like our mother.

When it came to school, at first, I hated going there and I despised my teacher, Mr. Bollinger. He deliberately sat me between two boys, Terry and Arthur. I was afraid of boys and those two were best friends and they both had a crush on me. They always tried to talk to me at my desk or when we lined up. I was so embarrassed and I blamed my teacher that's why I disliked him.

Mr. Bollinger had a strange ritual; every day before lunch all thirty kids had to line up and scrub our fingernails before eating lunch. I couldn't stand waiting in that line with the boys on either side of me teasing me and brushing up against me. I just wanted to hurry up and get to the cafeteria. At some point during the school year I began to feel guilty for hating my teacher and forgave him for seating me between Arthur and Terry. I started looking forward to going to school and eventually began to like him. It felt sad when I had to say goodbye at the end of the fifth grade. Now whenever I hear Roger Miller songs, I'm reminded of Mr. Bollinger who played those songs on his 45 records in the classroom.

Towards the end of fifth grade we had to take the California Achievement Test. Raising my hand high Mr. Bollinger could see I was visibly upset. Walking over to my desk, he discretely asked, "What is it Debbie? Why aren't you starting the test?"

"I don't know what to check for my nationality," I knew my mother was Spanish, mixed with American Indian and other things and my father was English, German, and Irish.

"What do you mean? You're white, aren't you?"

"No, I'm a wetback!" I answered, proudly.

Hiding a laugh my teacher said, "Who told you, you were a wetback?"

"My father calls me one all the time."

"Do you know what a wetback is?"

"What do you mean?" I said with a confused look on my face.

Mr. Bollinger kindly explained, "A wetback is someone who swims the Rio Grande River from Mexico in order to come into the United States illegally. You are not a wetback."

Over the years I have laughed about that memory. My dad must have said it so often that I believed that's what I was. I did not realize he was insulting me and my brothers and sister and heartlessly making fun of my mom because of her nationality. I was too young to know about verbal abuse. And while we often heard the "N" word growing up, at the time I did not realize my dad was being racist. Not only did we grow up hearing Dad belittling our mom but he also referred to us as little bastards and he'd pop us in the head with his open hand. Finally, one day my mom put a stop to it and screamed at him, "Bob, don't ever touch my children again."

He never hit us after that.

While still in the fifth grade, I had made a new best friend, who was in my class. I always looked forward to going go to her house after school. She had a dream bedroom, a white canopy bed took up almost the entire room. I had only seen a bed like that in the Sears and Roebuck catalog. I spent many afternoons at her house and from my observations she seemed to come from a normal family. Her mother would greet us after school and fix us a snack while asking about our day. That never happened in my home.

I had hoped, with my dad's young girlfriend living in our home, that the nighttime visits would end. When the sun was shining, I felt safe! On a warm, summer afternoon, while Mom was still living out of the house, my dad locked all of my siblings outside and ordered me to go in my bedroom. *Where was Glenda? I wondered.* Promptly, he pulled down the shades and proceeded to undress me. This had never happened in the daylight hours. Shaking, I knew what was going to follow. My brothers and sister were right outside my bedroom window laughing and playing and I longed to be with them. I begged my father to stop and let me go outside. I was furious with him for bringing the secret of the night into the daytime. Anxiety filled me, knowing that everyone I loved was still awake. I was sure they all knew what was occurring and hated me for it. I tried to shut my mind off, but all I could think about was how mad I was at him. *Why is this happening to me? I am such a bad girl!*

Later when it was over I hoped my siblings wouldn't ask me what I had been doing while they were all outside. I had been directed to lie if they inquired and I hated lying. They never asked me anything. Boy, was I relieved. Thankfully, it would be the last time my dad ever touched me.

After that it wasn't long before our mother came back to live with us, then my father left with his young girlfriend. I found out later that it had been my dad who would not let Mom come home. Peace welled inside me as I sat next to my mother on the living room couch that evening.

"Come here and listen. I have something to tell you kids."

All eyes turned towards her.

6

Where's Dad?

"I will strengthen you, though you have not acknowledged me." Isaiah 45:5b

The six of us watched Mom intently as she spoke. "Your father and I are getting a divorce."

"What is divorce?" asked five-year old, Steve.

"Your dad won't ever live with us again and It is not your fault, we both love you. But we do not love each other anymore. If you ever want to talk about it, I want you to know I care about your feelings. We will have to move out of this house."

"Mom, are we going to move back to our old house on Ceres drive?" Mike asked.

"No, but we will be moving back to Ceres, to a different house"

"When are we moving?" I asked.

"You guys can all finish the school year out so we will be here a few more months."

I didn't care about leaving our new house. I hated what had happened there, although I had made several friends that year. I couldn't wait to move back to our old street where all of our old friends still lived. Divorce was not a common occurrence at that time and we didn't know anybody else whose parents were divorced, I worried that people wouldn't like us anymore.

Even with my dad gone, turmoil continued to escalate in our lives. At first Mom was good about trying to explain things. But even though she kept the door open for us to question her, rarely did we take her up on it. It was a nice gesture, but Mom failed to realize we were afraid to really tell her how we felt. After all, we grew up hearing Mom's favorite saying, "Children are to be seen and not heard." And while the laughs around our house were often frequent, Mom had unknowingly taught us to bury our feelings. The minute we showed any anger, annoyance, or irritation we were threatened and sent to our room.

Another thing was we all grew up knowing our mother preferred boys to girls. She often commented, "I don't like girls who are sissy and whiny, and my daughters will not turn out like that." So, Monica and I learned to keep our thoughts and feelings to ourselves.

After the divorce, it seemed like my mom was not carefree like she had been before. Her dependence on drugs had increased, although we didn't realize it at the time. We only knew Mom was spending more time brooding in her room and her moods were often volatile.

She had extreme angry outbursts or bouts of depression, and then she'd be laughing and telling jokes. We never knew which mood she'd be in.

Mom started going out at night and she brought home her first boyfriend, one of many. I was furious with her, but I was glad she and my dad were no longer a couple. Nevertheless, the thought of her being with another man bothered me.

Debbie no longer babysat for us. Mom tried out several of her new friends' teenagers to watch us. Unfortunately for my sister, one boy tried to molest her.

Later when my mom returned she asked, "How did you like the new babysitter? Is he going to work out for you kids?"

My sister didn't have the courage to tell our mother what really happened and she somehow knew our mother wouldn't validate her feelings so she gathered all us kids and we all agreed to tell Mom we hated our new babysitter.

"I promise you I will never let him in our home again." Mom reassured us.

Although that didn't stop her from going out to the bars, only now, she simply left us on our own. She must have figured my eleven-year-old brother was old enough to take care of things.

We rarely saw our mother drink. Occasionally she'd sip a chilled can of beer but we never saw her drunk. Mom would always do her drinking at the bars. Before going out, she would make sure we were all in bed. Then just before she'd leave, she would come into my room, and lightly tap me on the shoulder to wake me. "Debbie, I'm going out now. If your brothers and sister wake up take good care of them. I'll be home soon. Go back to sleep now.

"No, Mom, don't go, please don't go out again. I just know something bad is going to happen to you and you'll get into an accident and die and never come back!"

"Don't be silly. Nothing's going to happen." She'd try and reassure me, anxious to depart.

No matter how many tears I shed, no matter how many times I'd plead with her to change her mind, she always went out. Lying awake in the darkness, staring at the open bedroom door, afraid to go to sleep, and afraid to stay awake, I would think about my mom dying. Remembering back to her conversation with Amelia, that I had overheard a few years earlier.

I was sure that when I would wake up, Mom would still be gone, or worse yet, she would not be home at all because she'd been killed! Hours later, I would fall into a fitful sleep. Thankfully, she was usually in her bed when I woke up in the mornings. But that still didn't stop me from being afraid for the next time.

I had been nicknamed "Mother MaCree," by my siblings because I had taken care of my brothers while they were still in diapers. I cleaned and cooked and I took it upon myself to teach my siblings manners during the dinner hour. "Dave, get your elbows off the table. Mike, don't talk with your mouth full. Steve, chew your food before swallowing."

All I had wanted was to make sure my family didn't act like barbarians. But inevitably, all the kids would chant, "Deb's, Mother MaCree, Deb's, Mother MaCree." When Mom was home, she ignored us and didn't come to my rescue while the other kids teased me. Usually, I would end up crying, but it didn't deter me, I still tried to mother my siblings and I continued to be called Mother MaCree.

A lot went on after Dad left. One thing was, I experienced my first crush. Ronny was a year older than me and he was the son of my mom's best friend. My mother and his mother used to go drinking at a bar nearby called "The Kopper Key." Each Sunday morning Ronny invited my sister and me to accompany him to the deserted parking lot. We would pick up change that had fallen out of the drunk's pockets on the previous Saturday night. I relished hanging out with my new crush and hearing his wild stories. Ronny had an older sister named Kathy. She occasionally babysat for us when our divorced mothers went out together.

One night, right before Christmas, there was a knock at our door. There stood Kathy on our porch, bloodied and bruised from her head to toe. Our mother tenderly took her in and cleaned her up. Mom said to us, "Kathy has run away from home and we aren't to tell anyone she is at our house."

Mom gave her a pair of her pajamas, and she climbed in bed between my sister and me.

"What happened?"

She very quietly said, with tears streaming down her face, "My mother hits me. I don't know why she hates me. I couldn't take it anymore. Maybe she will miss me if I'm not there and maybe, she'll stop hitting me."

While she spoke, she showed no animosity towards her abusive single mother. Kathy only wanted her mother to love her. A few days later her mom showed up to take her home. We watched her hug her daughter, "I am so sorry. I promise I will never hit you again."

She was overjoyed that her mother wanted her back. We would never know if Kathy's mother had kept her promise. My mom quit hanging out with her after that and I would never see my first crush again.

A few months later, my mom became friends with another lady who would soon become her new drinking partner. She had a daughter named Connie who was around my age. What I liked most about Connie was that she owned a brown and white pony named Judy and I was obsessed with horses. In Fontana, there were plenty of vacant lots to go riding. I can't count how many times Connie and I got together and rode Judy. Each time we spent the day together I felt as if I was experiencing a piece of heaven. My dream of riding a horse even if it lasted only a short time had come true.

Connie was a very sad girl and she too, craved her mother's love and attention. Our friendship was short lived, however, because for whatever reason our mothers stopped drinking together. Through the years, I often thought back to those blissful moments riding Judy, as I raced into the sunset and escaped the reality of my life. Alas, it wasn't Connie I would miss; it was my piece of heaven, her horse, Judy.

George was another friend who hung out with Mom. They were also drinking buddies and she would spend hours with him. She knew his family and sometimes we all got together and I hung out with his daughter Georgette who was a couple years older than me. Mostly George and Mom drank at the bars though.

One sad day Mom came home and sat us kids down and told us that George had committed suicide because he was an alcoholic. That was the first time I had ever heard those two words, alcoholic and suicide and it wouldn't be the last.

We were finally getting used to our new way of life with our dad gone and our mother constantly leaving to hang out with her new, pill-popping, alcoholic friends.

It was early summer when Mom woke us up one morning. "Now that you are all out of school it is finally time for us to move back to our old neighborhood."

Just as Mom had said, we moved into a house one door down from our old house on Ceres. In the fall of 1967 I would be entering the sixth grade and I was excited to attend school with my old community of friends.

During this time Dad didn't come around much. He and Glenda were living together and she was pregnant.

Even though we would miss our new house, back to our old neighborhood and to our roach-infested three-bedroom one bathroom house we went. It was a relief returning to our old friends. A few of our neighbors had gotten divorced since we had moved, and a couple of single moms had moved in so our situation didn't feel so weird anymore.

Since Mom didn't work, and Dad refused to pay child support, we had to go on welfare. A couple of months after we moved Mom began dating a man named Frank. She would leave us days at a time and play house with him. My brother and I took on even more responsibility taking care of our brothers and sister.

I would have done anything for my mother. Anything! I needed her love desperately and the more she was gone the more rejected and abandoned I felt. I continued to do my best to keep the house clean and take care of my siblings. I wished Mom would praise me and say well done. She rarely did. Compliments didn't come easy for her. Once she confessed, when I was an adult, "I didn't tell you that you were pretty because I didn't want you to get a big head." How I would have loved to hear those words from her.

I don't remember her saying very many nice things to us while we were growing up. She dwelled on the negative things, mistakes that were common to all children. The older I got the less I felt she was pleased with me. We often heard her moan, "Life is so hard." She was caught up in her own problems, she wasn't aware that her kids were suffering from their own emotional pain. Of course, she didn't realize what her frequent absences and mood changes did to us, she was only concerned with herself.

One of the things Mom did enjoy though was going to the vegetable and fruit stands that surrounded our town. She often took my sister and me with her. One summer afternoon it was just the two of us. After parking the car, Mom noticed several cases of vine-ripened, fire engine red, plump tomatoes sitting by our car. My mom loved her vegetables.

"Oh Deb, look at those tomatoes. Don't they look good? I wish I could afford a whole case of them. Won't you get me one?"

My mind started racing. She walked around with a few bags and plopped in green chilies, cucumbers, and onions while I was busy collecting my own stash. I caught up with her at the cash register, tapped her on the arm and whispered, "I got them Mom I got them for you."

"Shhh, I'm paying for our vegetables."

Hopping in the passenger side, we drove off. "Mom look." I pointed to the back seat. "You asked for the tomatoes and I got them for you."

She looked over her shoulder and there on the floor of the back seat was a whole case of luscious, mouth-watering red tomatoes. I was so proud of myself. I knew I had found a way to make my mother happy.

"Debra Ann, I did not really mean for you to get the tomatoes. I was only kidding."

After reprimanding me for stealing the vegetables, we had a good laugh over it. Luckily, I wasn't the sort of person to steal, and that was the last time I took something that didn't belong to me.

Once we were back in our old neighborhood, we made friends quickly with the family that had moved into our old house. Silvia was my sister's age. She would become Monica's best friend. I was also included in most of our social gatherings. Walking home from school we would head for the closest 7-11 to get mouth-watering Slurpies, afterwards, we'd walk to a nearby park or library. The three of us often hung out in her bedroom listening to 45's and dancing. It was one of our favorite things to do. Sylvia had a rare disease and when she turned twelve, she had to get all of her teeth pulled. For several weeks, before getting dentures, she had to attend school without any teeth. My sister and I made it our goal to protect her from any teasing from the kids at school.

Proudly we walked with her between us, prepared for any onslaughts. Fortunately, there were none; everyone was nice to her.

I met a new friend shortly after moving back to Ceres, her name was Pam, she lived across the street and she was my age. Pam's mother was an alcoholic and she left Pam and her two siblings alone without any food in the house most of the time. My new friend was a guest at our home for dinner fairly often. "I love your mom's fried potatoes," she'd often tell me. We walked to school together and hung out mostly at my house afterwards. But unfortunately, a couple years later Pam began taking drugs. She was quick to brag about the pills she popped every weekend. She called them yellow jackets, bennies, black beauties, whites, and reds. I didn't take drugs and I wasn't comfortable being with her when she took them. I didn't hang out with her very much after that. Through the years Pam's life escalated out of control although we stayed in touch for many years after we both moved away from each other.

Sixth grade proved to be a good year for me. My teacher, Mr. Covey taught us how to write short stories. I realized how much I enjoyed writing and I wasn't even afraid to read my theme aloud every Friday.

I was very shy around boys, but had many crushes on them from the time I was eleven. In the 6th grade two boys sat one on each side of me, but this time I didn't mind. Spencer was a lot cuter than Danny, but Danny's family raised boxers and I loved big dogs. For that reason, I had a crush on him. He had wavy black hair, and pimples, but that didn't deter me. Often the three of us would sit in the back of the classroom away from the watchful eyes of Mr. Covey and talk. I usually wore dresses or skirts and I would let those boys smack my naked legs with rulers. They would slap me so hard it left red marks on my legs. *Why did I allow them to hit me?* All I know is, I remember how good it felt to have a boy interested in me. I never did reveal the crush I had on Danny and soon he was replaced with a new crush.

Throughout the summer I had many anxious thoughts as I anticipated starting junior high school. I would not have my sister with me at school like the previous years. Mike still acted like the man of the house, but he also started running around with his friends more often. My little brothers had adjusted to life in our old neighborhood while Mom counted on me to take care of them, making lunches and dinners, cleaning the house and babysitting. It seemed she was gone more than ever and or she would hide in her room more often when she was home.

7

Our Pets

"The godly care for their animals." Proverbs 12:10

Our mother was an animal lover and throughout our childhood she allowed us to have many types of pets but all I ever wanted was my very own pony. I dreamed about them regularly, and at every opportunity and watched movies that included anything to do with horses. Riding on brooms, mops, or sticks pretending I was riding a horse was a much loved pastime.

Before my dad left we used to drive from Fontana to Anaheim to visit my father's family. Regularly, I'd pretend I was riding bare back on my mighty stallion running alongside the car. I always looked forward to the drive to my cousins.

Accompanying my mother to the local hardware store to buy chicken feed was a favorite thing for me to do. Right inside the door was a large barrel resting upon four pieces of wood with a saddle on top. Climbing on top of the makeshift horse, pretending to gallop, I'd wait for Mom while she bought her supplies.

"Let's go. It's time to get off that barrel."

"It's not a barrel, it's my very own pony with a white flowing mane. Isn't he magnificent?

I eagerly looked forward to the "Fontana Days" parade every year just to see the graceful horses prance through the streets.

Throughout my elementary school years and on into junior high we Griswold's were known around the neighborhood for our pets. The first dog Dad brought home was a huge German shepherd named Mark. We loved romping with him. My dad would often play a game with Mark. Sneaking outside he would quietly knock on the front door. Mark would instantly react, growling, barking, and lunging towards the door. My dad would sneak in the back door laughing and Mark's long tail would begin wagging swiftly. "See kids," he would explain, "Mark will always protect you."

We were broken-hearted when we had to find a new home for Mark because he killed the neighbor's chickens and a little Pekinese dog. For several years after that, my dad and mom would take us to visit the kind family who had given Mark a new home.

Even though we lived in a quiet residential neighborhood, we had numerous pets throughout our childhood. At any given time, our yard was filled with chickens, rabbits, guinea pigs, hamsters, various dogs, birds, a turtle, and an occasional cat. When we raised chickens, we couldn't wait to gather fresh eggs from our colorful Rhode Island Red hens.

Nosey was our first rabbit. He was a large albino bunny with red eyes, whose nose twitched incessantly, as all bunnies do. He lived outside of his cage most of the time and he had been paper trained by our mother where he would occasionally romp indoors. Hopping around in the front yard, Nosey chased small dogs that dared come onto our property. We all enjoyed feeding our pet rabbit carrots and bragging about him to the neighbors. Several years later I walked outside and found Nosey dead in the back yard we all figured he had died of old age. Thus began the Griswold funeral processions. Around the block from us there was an orange grove, this would become our pet burial grounds. We put Nosey in a cardboard box and loaded him in the red wagon while my older brother carried a shovel. Standing in a circle, Mike loudly said a goodbye prayer, "God, here lies Nosey, who we loved and we will miss. Amen!"

This went on numerous times when our little pets died. The neighborhood kids stood in their front yards watching us as we rounded the corner and they'd yell, "Which animal died this time?" They in turn would join in and parade with us around the block to bury our pets. Decades later, brand-new homes would be built on our sacred burial grounds.

We three older kids loved sleeping in our front yard, under the stars, wrapped in a blanket or a sleeping bag during hot summer nights. One night, Monica and I decided to bring out our longhaired guinea pigs, which we cherished. They had recently had a baby. We set the cage beside our heads and fell into a deep sleep.

Early the next morning Monica, shrieked. "Get up Deb. Where are Zelda and Thor and the baby? They're not in their cage!"

Suddenly, there was a flurry of excitement. The brothers came running out of the house.

"Where are they, where are they?"

Thus, we began our search on that early, July morning. It didn't take us long to find the half-eaten bodies of Zelda and Thor, but we never did find their tiny, unnamed baby. Later our funeral march was filled with all the neighborhood kids. It was a sad day in the Griswold household.

While in Junior high, Mike took up falconry. He taught us kids how to hunt for baby chicks so he could raise and teach his favorite bird. We spent hours in the front yard watching as Mike trained his young Red-Tailed hawk teaching him to retrieve food. He'd fly back and forth, then perch on Mike's tan leather glove. All of us got involved in my brother's hobby.

My brother, Dave, was the proud owner of a pet bird. He was a colorful parrot named Petie. Dave taught Petie how to say a few words and frequently allowed him to perch on his shoulder. He loved that bird! Also residing with us at that time was our coal-black cat, Midnight, who had given birth to kittens just weeks earlier. At this time someone fed Petie and accidentally left the cage door open. Unbeknownst to any of us, Midnight was watching the bird. She was weaning her little kittens and needed meat for them. Unfortunately, Petie became her victim. We found Petie dead in her claws and from that day on we never had another cat in our house. Dave still talks about his beloved pet parrot and to this day he despises cats.

Our favorite dog of all was Creole. He was a medium-sized mongrel, with long, black hair, short, stubby legs, and a curled up, wavy tail. He looked like a cross between a cocker spaniel and an oversized weenie dog. Several times Creole had been hit by cars and survived. He also suffered a near drowning, and even lived after being poisoned. So, we called him the king of the neighborhood. He was like a cat with nine lives. Our dearly loved pet chased every car that had the audacity to drive down our street. He'd yelp and bark loudly while trying to nip at the tires. He was definitely in need of "Cesar, the Dog Whisperer." But that was way before Cesar's time.

Through the years, Creole had also become a father to many puppies in the neighborhood. He would jump through tall windows, and crawl under gates. No fences or doors ever kept him out when a female dog was in heat. He was like Superman, able to leap tall buildings, and was faster than a speeding bullet. All the kids in the neighborhood joked about our dog's reputation. One time, the neighbor behind us called out to us kids while we were playing in our back yard.

"Come get your dog right now. He jumped through the bedroom window and broke it to get to my dog Queenie." I don't think my mother ever paid for the window Creole broke.

One hot, summer day, Creole suffered his demise. He had been missing for a while and we frantically searched for him till nightfall and throughout the next day. Early in the morning, on the third day, Creole came limping to the front door. His right shoulder had been severely injured. The skin was gone and pink flesh and blood oozed out. My mom quickly wrapped him up and drove him to the nearest veterinarian.

Within an hour she walked through the door, her eyes still red from crying. She sat us down. "It would have been thirty dollars to fix Creole's leg and we don't have that kind of money. I only had five dollars so I had to put Creole to sleep."

Big tears of grief rolled down our faces. We would have no funeral procession that day because the vet had disposed of our beloved pet. We didn't even get to say goodbye to Creole.

Shortly after that someone was giving away the cutest, golden brown puppies near the grocery store. My girlfriend, Pam, who lived across the street, came home one day with two puppies, one for her and one for me. We were so excited to have them. Mine was named Taffy. We crossed the street often and let our little puppy brother's romp together. Not long after that, the two dogs were chasing each other and were tragically hit by a car. Mine was killed while Pam's puppy lived. *I just knew my puppy died because of my secret. I'm such a bad girl.*

8

Holidays

"For everything there is a season, a time for every activity under heaven." Ecclesiastes 3:1

I remember the year I turned eleven. I wanted go-go boots and black stirrup pants and Dad and Glenda bought them for me. That was the last time I celebrated Christmas with my father. After the divorce, my mother always enjoyed making holidays special for us. Every Halloween she gathered extra wire clothes hangers, strung them together, spray painted them white and made a makeshift skeleton. Afterwards, she'd hang it on the huge oak tree in our front yard.

On Halloween, the year I turned twelve, I wanted to dress up like my favorite television character, Jeanie, from "I Dream of Jeanie." Mom pulled out her silky, black pajamas, put my hair up in a bun and wrapped a scarf around my face. That year I was I was the hit of the neighborhood Halloween party.

Thanksgiving was always a special event in our home. We had no family living close to us and never saw my dad's side of the family after the divorce. So, it was usually just my mom and the kids, although a few times whomever she was dating also joined us. The night before, Monica and I would peel and slice apples for homemade apple pie. Our mother also taught us how to make the flakiest homemade piecrust. Rubbing flour on our hands, we'd roll out the dough, plop it into a pie pan and pinch the edges. Afterwards, Mom would spruce up the house with bowls of apples, oranges, nuts, and even colorful turkeys made out of pinecones, felt, and construction paper.

Shouts could be heard throughout the house early at daybreak on Thanksgiving morning from Mom. "Come on kids, time to get up. The Macy's Parade is about to start."

It was an annual event. We loved sitting close to Mom on the couch, still dressed in our snuggly pajamas. When it was time to prepare the stuffing, and cook the turkey Monica and I were whisked away from the television to help out. My sister and I diced celery and onions while margarine slowly melted in a saucepan. After mixing it together and adding breadcrumbs we helped stuff the turkey, eagerly watching Mom sew it shut. It seemed like hours of chopping, mixing and baking. Mom always boiled the neck and innards to make the gravy. Monica and I would get a piece of the neck meat before the turkey was done since we helped prepare the meal. Nothing ever tasted so good.

I was always the one who was fortunate to mash the potatoes. We found the mixer but only succeeded in finding one of the beaters. So, year after year we had lumpy mashed potatoes but no one seemed to mind. Opening cans of black olives was amusing for my sister and me as we put olives on our fingertips and slipped them into our mouths while turning away from our mother's watchful eyes. We made candied yams, sprinkled with brown sugar and topped with fluffy, white marshmallows. Dinner was almost ready: the potatoes were peeled and cooking, cranberries prepared, and the table was set; all we had to do was wait for the bird to finish baking.

Our mother always preferred we dress up for dinner Thanksgiving dinner. My sister and I put on dresses and the boys wore their best button-down shirts, while mom teased and sprayed her hair and applied her makeup. The scent of our delicious turkey filled the air, our mouths watered as we impatiently waited for our feast. We sat together at our fatherless table, said our catholic prayers, *"Bless us oh Lord for these they gifts which we are about to receive,"* Dishes clattered, forks dropped, food scooped up we couldn't wait to cram our mouths full of our delicious meal. We always saved the tail for our mother it was her favorite part of the bird. 'Don't throw out the wishbone Mom would say.' Two of us kids would each grab a hold and break it, whoever got the slightly longer half believed our wishes would come true. Mom would cover the food with a clean, white sheet and hours later we ate leftover turkey sandwiches and sweet, creamy pumpkin pie.

My earliest Christmas memory was the year I turned five and my dad and mom were still together. I desperately wanted a horse. I could not wait to visit Santa Claus so I could ask him for a pony of my own. After ripping open my packages early Christmas morning, I pushed open the front door and ran outside. With tears streaming down my face, I ran back into the house screaming, "I can't find it."

"What's wrong? Why are you crying?" Mom asked. "What are you searching for?"

"Santa Claus didn't bring me my horse."

My mom tried to comfort me, "But honey you got lots of presents this year."

Somehow that didn't seem to make me feel any better. I will never forget the year I was angry with Santa Claus.

As a single mom, our mother tried hard to get us presents. When Christmas was several months away she would always put a few dollars down every week on layaway at Kmart for our gifts. The weeks leading up to the holiday was filled with excited anticipation. Mom wouldn't wait for Christmas Eve to get a tree like our dad used to. We all looked forward to accompanying her to the local tree lot. Afterwards, Mike helped Mom string the glittering lights. My brothers, sister and I hung up the ornaments and the paper red and green chains my mom had made earlier out of construction paper. We all took turns stringing popcorn to put upon our tree. Year after year, we'd impatiently watch Mom slowly put on the tinsel one strand at a time. We'd always lost interest and soon Mike would grab a handful from the box.

"Here Deb, watch this," Mike would say with a chuckle on his lips, as he threw the silvery, glittery mass on the unsuspecting tree.

Grabbing a piece of garland and throwing it around my shoulders, I'd strut around the Christmas tree and sing, "Whatever Lola wants, Lola gets." Mom couldn't help but join in on the laughter too.

My mother loved to sketch pictures of Santa Claus, Yule logs, Christmas trees and candles. She used markers and crayons to draw on cardboard and then put her drawings around the house for decorations. Gently, she would take the white angel hair she had saved every year and spread it on the end tables and coffee table to put under our holiday décor. She'd cut out a star-shaped piece of cardboard and wrap it in aluminum foil for the top of the tree. We loved her homemade ornaments. And we always put a miniature manger set under the tree on top of the smooth, soft angel hair. Mom taught us that Christmas was the time we celebrated the birth of Jesus. But it would be years before I would come to understand who Jesus really was.

Piling in the station wagon at night we'd drive around and look at twinkling Christmas lights that adorned other people's homes and sing holiday songs. *Rudolph the Red-Nosed Reindeer had a very shiny nose.* Year after year we had our favorite streets to drive down. It would become a tradition I would carry on with my own family.

When I was eleven, just weeks before Christmas, it was a particularly cold winter night and Mom called me to her room. "Come here, I bought you a furry, brown coat for Christmas, and I am going to let you wear it to the Christmas program at school. But as soon as you get home, we have to wrap it up and save it for Christmas morning."

I felt so special that year, that Mom and I had shared a secret from the other kids.

After the divorce, we always appreciated the small number of gifts we received on Christmas. Mom made our family time special as we all sat together, spending hours playing our new Monopoly game. Grabbing our presents, we'd run outside, knock on the neighbor's doors and ask, "What did you get for Christmas?"

Most Sunday evenings were movie nights. After a homemade meal of fried chicken, crispy on the outside and juicy on the inside and lumpy, mashed potatoes, gravy, and corn, Mom would put oil in a pan, pour popcorn kernels in and turn up the heat. We would all come running into the kitchen and listen to the "popping" sound of the kernels. Afterwards, she'd drizzle the crunchy popcorn with creamy melted butter and shake on lots of salt. We'd sit around the television set watching The Wonderful World of Disney.

"Look," nine-year old, Dave pointed, "There's my girlfriend, Tinker bell."

"I wish we could afford a color TV," Mom would repeat every Sunday. "The shows sure would look better in color."

My brothers and sister and I didn't care though. We spent holidays watching old favorites such as *Santa Claus is Coming to Town*, *The Wizard of Oz*, and at Easter, the unforgettable, *Ten Commandments*. Lots of happy times were spent around the tube!

Coloring eggs at Easter was a huge family event. Cups of all sizes and shapes lined our dining table, filled with a rainbow of colors waiting for seven sets of hands. We strung rubber bands around eggs, colored some with crayons, and then dropped them in the tinted water. Mom loved getting creative during holidays. Weeks before the celebration, she'd collect tree branches and make a homemade Easter tree. She would poke a pinhole at each end of a raw egg and blow through it until the raw egg came out of the shell. After dyeing the egg she'd glue a piece of ribbon on it and hang it up on the egg tree. It was quite unique.

My sister and I would pretend to be the Easter bunny to our little brothers with our mom's encouragement. After tucking them in for the night we would excitingly put together their baskets, filling them with delicious chocolate eggs, colorful jellybeans and sometimes, when we could afford it, a solid chocolate bunny.

Easter morning, while the ham was baking, Mom made us cover our eyes while she hid the Easter eggs outside. Some years, we would pack a lunch and head to Mom's favorite picnic spot, Lytle Creek, just twenty minutes east of Fontana. We'd spend the whole day hanging out, wading in the creek, hiking, re-hiding eggs, then eating them. We would only return home when the sun was setting behind the mountains.

Our mother like to be involved with the boys while they were young and several years in a row Mom held the proud position of Scout mother while Mike and Dave attended Scouts. Our mother made the coolest crafts and made up skits with the boys. One year she put on a play and all the boys wore Mexican sombreros and repeated, 'sitting on the cactus and trying to move.' Everybody laughed and laughed. Every year in February Mom put on the best Blue and Gold banquets. The purpose of the banquet was to celebrate the pack's anniversary. Mom would eagerly adorn the community center with decorations while Monica and I set the plates and utensils on the tables. Afterwards the rest of the family joined my mom and brothers for a wonderful dinner.

It was easy for my mom to be involved with her boys but when it came to Monica and me she did not encourage us to participate in any activities. But one year my sister and I were invited to join Brownies by a friend. We looked forward to going to the meetings and we eagerly consumed the tasty, homemade cakes and cookies set out by the other members. After we attended several times, the leader loudly exclaimed, "This is the third time in a row you have come to our meetings without paying your dues. Do you have any money?"

Monica and I looked at each other, our cheeks red from embarrassment. Sadly, we shook out heads.

"You need to leave, then." The leader escorted us to the door and we were promptly kicked out of the Brownies.

Fourth of July was always a big event in our neighborhood and Mom had saved up to buy fireworks. We would start the day by going on a picnic at a nearby park with our packed lunches. Later after grilling hot dogs at home and impatiently waiting for the sun to set we lit sparklers and waved them around towards each other before Mom lit the big guns. Most of the kids in the neighborhood joined us.

I'll never forget one birthday while I was in junior high. I wanted a pair of hot pink shoes and my mom ran all over town trying to find me that special gift. Monica's birthday followed mine by five days and all she got were promises, Mom would say, "On payday I'll get you a present," but unfortunately, she always ran out of money and my sister rarely got her gifts. This was a pattern repeated throughout Monica's childhood. It wasn't until years later that I would realize how cheated my sister felt on her birthdays.

Mom made holidays and birthdays fun and we rarely questioned where our father was. Once he was out of our lives we didn't speak of him or even think about him. Unfortunately, he didn't stay gone for long. Throughout the years he'd show up when you least expected him.

9

Times with Dad and Other Friends

"Wise people think before they act; fools don't and even brag about their foolishness." Proverbs 13:16

After the divorce, time spent with our dad was sporadic. Sometimes he would show up at the door after we had not heard from him for months or years. Dad had a good friend, named Bud, who lived in an apartment with a swimming pool. Sometimes Dad would pick us up and take us to Bud's apartment. Enthusiastically, we'd spend our day swimming, while, unbeknownst to us; my dad and his friends were cooking drugs in Bud's kitchen. A few years later we found out Bud blew his self-up making drugs in that very same apartment.

At this point my father was still involved with his young girl-friend, Glenda. They had a daughter named Jessica. My sister and I looked forward to holding and playing with our new half-sister. Dad always claimed Glenda was the love of his life. About three years after Jessica was born my dad and Glenda broke up. Several years later, Glenda was killed; it had something to do with drugs. Jessica was only six years old when her grandmother began raising her. Thankfully, she was spared from my dad's influence. We wouldn't see Jessica again until we were all adults.

Glenda's death hit my dad pretty hard. He talked of her often throughout his lifetime. Eventually Dad stopped coming around, unfortunately, we could never count on him leaving for good. Several years later he showed up again and introduced us to his new wife, Sandy, who was from Canada. She had two little girls and Monica and I enjoyed playing big sister to her daughters.

That Christmas, when Sandy's children were only two and three my mother gathered us kids together. "Your dad doesn't have money to buy Sandy's girls any presents. Let's go to the department store and buy them some toys and clothes."

We were excited to play Santa Claus to the two girls. It never seemed weird that my mom was concerned about my dad's new step-children. And the fact that she could barely afford gifts for her own kids didn't seem to daunt her generous spirit.

Sandy and my father lived on the edge, they talked of playing Russian roulette, a game that involved pistols and bullets. I would find out later that he and Sandy took lots of drugs. He also told tall tales about robbing the homes of celebrities. I don't know if he really did or not. He'd often boast about checking himself into the nearby mental hospital so he could get his drugs free. After a couple years, Sandy sent her two daughters back to Canada to live with their father. I always wondered if my dad ever touched them. Dad came around less and less and once again when he walked out of our lives no one seemed to care much.

Since Dad never paid child support, my mom continued to collect her monthly welfare checks. Standing in long lines once a month for our government food was something I looked forward to. I can still recall the cool breeze, bundled in our sweaters, in the early dawn waiting for the sun to come up while listening to the other welfare recipients talking. Maybe it was because Mom and I did it together that made venturing out in the wee hours of the morning and waiting in long lines seem like fun. Cans of shredded turkey, blocks of butter, bags of lentils and oatmeal, jars of peanut butter, and sacks of powdered milk were handed out. I don't know about the other kids, but I never felt ashamed because we received government food. Mom was very creative in the kitchen. We had family dinners mostly every night and when she wasn't there I always made sure our family had a home-cooked meal. We all sat at the table together with or without Mom being present.

Breakfast usually consisted of cold cereal, but often on weekends, Mom made flapjacks for the family. Her silver dollar pancakes were the best. Oftentimes we'd have a cold burrito for lunch or my personal favorite, a warm bologna sandwich smeared with mustard. That was until my sister and I hit Junior high, then we were too embarrassed to take a lunch. Having no lunch money, I was envious of my classmates as they waited in the food line for crispy French fries and hot cocoa.

One day, I came up with what I thought was a great plan. I would do anything I could to keep my sister from going hungry. Walking up to the minister's daughter, I tapped on her shoulder. "Katie, can I borrow a quarter? My sister and I are so hungry we can't afford to buy lunch."

"I'm so sorry, sure you can have some money, here is fifty-cents."

Grabbing the change, Monica and I feasted on delicious sidewalk-sundae ice cream bars. Other days we'd eat warm peanut butter cookies and drink steaming hot cups of cocoa. Throughout the year we gorged on our treats, all due to Katie and a few others I sought pity from week after week. As an adult, when I realized just how much I had conned my classmates, I was filled with guilt. But a girl has to do what a girl has to do and I had to take care of my sister.

During this time, Mom had friends named Howard and Gail. Mom knew Gail before she married Howard. Howard joined the army and I remember listening to the song "Solider Boy," with Gail while she was still a teenager. When he returned we attended their wedding.

Howard always made me nervous and he seemed to enjoy calling me names. Because I sucked my thumb until I was twelve my front teeth stuck out a little. Howard's favorite thing to call me was, "Bucky Beaver." I was very self-conscious about my looks and covered my mouth when I talked or laughed. Mom never seemed to notice that Howard had a penchant for referring to me as Bucky Beaver and if I complained she'd just shut me out, "Quit feeling sorry for yourself. He didn't mean anything by it."

It would be many years before I carried on a conversation or laughed without covering my mouth—not until I finally got my teeth fixed in my early thirties. I liked Gail, but tried to avoid Howard whenever Mom took us over to their house, although I looked forward to visiting them because they had a beautiful red Irish setter named Rusty. Willingly, I'd endure Howard's taunts just to have a chance to play with his dog. I'd spend hours outside watching Rusty chase butterflies. Tossing a ball to him and playing fetch seemed to go on for hours. A couple years later, that beautiful, magnificent looking dog was hit by a car and Gail and Howard had him put to sleep.

Aside from the name-calling, there were many happy times spent with Howard and Gail. They owned a boat and oftentimes they would take my mom and us kids to Salton Sea, the Pacific Ocean and lakes around our area. On Saturdays, we'd spend the day lounging at a nearby lake, while music played in the background. The adults drank beers, smoked cigarettes and laughed a lot while us kids found lots to do. Bob Dylan, the Beatles, and the Rolling Stones could be heard loudly over their conversations. Nowadays whenever I hear a favorite tune of my mother's I'm instantly transported back into that happy time of my childhood.

One cold, winter weekend, Gail and Howard invited all of us to accompany them up to the mountains to Big Bear. Pulling off the side of the road, we were amazed at the sight of steep slopes spilling over with snow.

"Come on kids," Howard called. "Help me make an igloo."

In no time, the igloo was complete and it was big enough for all of us to fit inside. Howard lit a Coleman stove while Mom fried ground beef, with slices of potatoes. Mom had prepared that meal many times before, but it never tasted so good as when we huddled together trying to stay warm in our homemade igloo. We spent many years hanging out with Mom's friends. I will always remember the fun times and their dog, but would never miss being referred to as "Bucky beaver."

Most of my friends lived in the neighborhood, so I rarely had to venture too far to hang out with kids my age. Roberta lived down the street and took care of her older father, who wore thick, horn-rimmed glasses. He was scary looking, and he reminded me of Mr. Magoo from the cartoon. Roberta always thought she knew everything, just because she was a year older than me. I was almost twelve. Although there was often animosity between Roberta and I, we still hung out together.

One afternoon Roberta adamantly stated, "Did you know babies drink from their mother's breast?"

I looked at my sister, and she looked back at me. Shaking my head, pointing my finger toward her face, I said, "You're such a liar. Everyone knows babies drink out of a bottle."

"No, they don't, they drink out of their mother's breasts."

"You're a liar!" I repeated.

Instantly, Roberta reached over and slapped me in the face. Walking away, crying and holding my stinging cheek, I felt hurt, but mostly anger at myself for being a coward and a crybaby just like my father. I ran all the way home and showed my sister the red mark on my cheek.

"I hate that Roberta," Monica said. "I'm going to get her back for you. No one is going to slap my sister and get away it."

Without my knowledge, my sister began formulating a plan of revenge.

All the neighborhood kids talked about Roberta stuffing her bra. Soon after we heard the rumor, we were on the school bus coming home from a field trip. My sister and I noticed toilet paper hanging out of Roberta's sleeveless blouse and we giggled. Later that day, on our way home from school, Monica and I walked home with Roberta.

"Roberta, do you stuff your bra?" Monica asked.

Roberta proudly stated, "Yeah, you want to see?"

Standing at a distance I watched as Monica peeked at Roberta's pulled down shirt. "First you fold the toilet paper like this, then you put it in your bra."

Suddenly, Monica grabbed ahold of the tissue and yanked it out. Clenching her fist, she punched Roberta right in the mouth. Blood started dripping down her chin. "That's for slapping my sister. Don't you ever touch her again!"

Roberta never hit me again and we remained friends throughout the next couple of years.

"Monica, you're the little sister and I should be protecting you," I said, feeling guilty as we strolled away.

"Deb, you're my only sister and I won't ever let anyone hurt you."

A few hours later, Gail and Howard and their new baby, Howie, stopped by our house. After dinner, the baby started crying and Mom motioned for my sister and me to follow her and Gail in the bedroom. "I want you and Monica to see how Gail feeds her baby."

Gail lifted her shirt and put the crying baby to her breast. My mom's words were a blur as she explained to us how milk comes out of the mother's breasts. I kept replaying Roberta's words in my head. Talk about having milk on my face. I guess she was right after all.

A few years later I found out the creepy, ugly little man who was Roberta's father had molested her. Roberta went on to marry an older man from our neighborhood and had a couple of little girls. She was later killed at the hands of a rapist. I always felt bad for the life that was handed to her.

Amelia and Mom renewed their friendship shortly after we moved back to the old neighborhood. She had a teenage daughter named Janie and a son Michael. Michael often played with my older brother my sister and me. The four of us spent the next couple of years hanging out at the nearby orange grove, sitting under the tree in our front yard or making crafts at Palmetto Park.

All of us neighbors borrowed from each other in those days: a roll of toilet paper, an egg, slices of bread, a cup of milk, or whatever else was needed. We didn't have much but we always shared what we had. Whenever my mom spent the day in bed or was gone, I usually answered the door when someone came borrowing. Some days, and for no apparent reason, Mom would bad mouth people and get angry and go on a yelling rampage, she was filled with a mean streak. It was at those times that us kids all tried to stay out of her way. One afternoon when I relayed to her what Janie had borrowed, she got that mean look on her face and yelled, "I'm tired of that girl sponging off us. Next time she comes over, don't let her have anything, no matter what it is. Do you understand?"

Nodding my head, I felt like the Gestapo. I would make my mother proud!

The doorbell sounded a few days later and Janie showed up while my mother was gone.

"I need something. It's really important," Janie frantically, explained. "It is called Kotex, go look in your bathroom and see if your mom has any…hurry please."

I ran into the bathroom, found the box of Kotex, and then the words of my mother came back to me, "*Don't let Janie borrow anything.*"

Carrying the box back into the living room and standing in the doorway, I glared at Janie, and held the sanitary napkins up. "My mother is sick of you borrowing things and she said I'm not allowed to give you anything, anymore." I promptly slammed the door in her face. I just knew when my mom came home and I told her the story she would be so happy with me!

"Oh no, Deb. You could have given her that," Mom said when I told her about the incident later that day.

I couldn't do anything right! After that I guess Mom figured out it was time she told my sister and me about menstrual cycles. Boy, was I ashamed of myself when I found out why Janie needed the Kotex so badly.

10

Mom's New Boyfriend and Life Goes On....

"O Lord you took up my case; you redeemed my life. You have seen, O Lord, the wrong done to me. Uphold my cause!" Lamentations 3:58

When I began Junior high I desperately wanted to tell my mom about the sexual abuse. I had never told anyone and it was getting harder to keep the secret even though my dad hadn't touched me for over two years. Many nights I woke up from horrible nightmares and often cried during the day, feeling anxious, ashamed, guilty and worthless.

Calling us into the room a year after I started seventh grade Mom said, "I need to tell you girls how babies are made."

I didn't have the courage to tell her I already knew what sex was. After all I had learned about it firsthand. That day I walked out of her room, hanging my head in shame and guilt, with my secret still intact, wishing desperately she knew.

After her first boyfriend, I was getting used to my mom going out, although I still didn't like it. She and Frank dated for nearly two years, so he had become a more permanent fixture in our lives. Mom rarely drank at home but sometimes she and Frank would have a cold beer while we barbecued, which we did often. They did the majority of their drinking at his house, unseen from our eyes. I wonder if she knew how hard it was for me to have her gone? Later she confided in us that Frank was an alcoholic. "His skin is yellow because he has a bad liver from drinking so much."

The thing I liked best about Frank was when he loaded up all six of us in the back of his black pickup truck and drive us down to Ace Liquor where he would purchase booze and buy us kids our favorite candy bars. My choice was always Rocky Road or Mr. Goodbar. All Frank wanted in exchange was to have his feet rubbed and his back scratched. I didn't mind, I loved those candy bars. Frank was a kind and decent man. He never abused us, he never called us names, and he never touched us inappropriately. I guess we all must have felt safe with him during the short time he was a part of our household.

Frank liked to hunt and fish, sometimes he would take Mom fishing with him. Other times he'd go off by himself and bring back his catch. He taught Mom how to cook wild rabbit, pigeons, deer, elk and fish. Frank didn't live with us, although he and Mom spent many nights sleeping over at one another's homes. As far as I could tell Mom had no morals but she drilled into my sister and me that we were to remain virgins until we were married. Later she told us she believed it didn't matter for her because she had been divorced and ex-communicated from the Catholic Church for getting a divorce, something that would always bother her.

One day Mom told us Frank couldn't be tied down with so many kids. "Inez, if you only had three kids I would probably marry you, but I can't handle six." It wasn't long after that statement, she and Frank broke up. I would miss our evening runs to the liquor store and I would miss having a father figure around.

My sister and I were starting to become young women. Our mother was often cold to us, ignoring us by retreating into her bedroom for hours and hours, and then demanding we bring her a glass of water, so she could take her many pills. I'm sure our mother, who was in her early thirties, often felt overwhelmed raising six children alone in the sixties, when most women were shunned for being divorced. Time and time again she'd go to the doctor complaining of lack of sleep or anxiety and he'd write her a prescription for sleeping pills or tranquilizers. "Take as many as you need. It's hard having six children and no husband."

During her dark days Mom never seemed to be pleased or happy. The house wasn't cleaned well enough, we made too many messes, and there was never enough money. All us kids grew up occasionally spanked by our mother but unfortunately Monica and Steve incurred the brunt of Mom's wrath and they were frequently beaten. My sister always threw terrible tantrums from the time she was a little girl. Monica was sometimes quiet and nice, sometimes mean and sullen. At times, for no apparent reason, she would shake her head, scream and act like she was out of control while running throughout the house. Mom's physical abuse to Monica started when she was very young and lasted until she became a teenager. We could hear my mom accuse my sister of having a demon inside of her when she threw her fits. Mom would catch her by her long, wavy, brown hair and swing her around, shake her, slap her face and sometimes beat her black and blue.

My poor brother Steve often got the same treatment. *Did he come at the wrong time in her life?* The rest of us would watch terrified, helpless to do anything for our siblings. Did my mom pick on my little brother because he was a product of her affair and she was constantly reminded of the man she couldn't have?

I was always trying to find ways to make my mother contended with herself and with me and I didn't want to be on the receiving end of her vicious attacks she inflicted on my siblings. Doing whatever I could to please her and take on all the responsibilities of a substitute mom I hoped to convince myself if only I said or did the right things in her eyes she would be happy with her life. I spent most of my waking hours when I wasn't busy trying to figure out how I could do things better.

Monica wasn't possessed by a demon, but she carried hidden scars that no one knew about. Mom disclosed years later that she hated herself and she was mean to my sister and brother because they reminded her of what she was like as a child. Our mother never felt loved and accepted by her own mother. On grandma's deathbed Mom asked her, "Mama did you ever love me?"

"Of course, I loved you Inez, I've always loved you. Where did you get such a silly notion?"

My mom was over fifty when she finally believed those words from her dying mother. She lived a half-century believing she was unloved and unlovable. *It is amazing how unspoken words throughout your childhood can affect your whole life!*

With six children, it wasn't often my mom and I spent time alone with one another and I longed for it. One of the memories that stand out, besides the welfare line, was accompanying Mom to the market to buy groceries. "Come on Debra, let's go shopping. I'll let you pick out your favorite cereal."

"Can I get Captain Crunch instead of Wheaties or Corn Flakes?"

"Whatever you want. It's your treat."

Ambling through the aisles, I'd help her toss meat, bread and milk in the cart. Driving home, we would both be starving "Find me that package of bologna and tortillas."

Rummaging through the grocery bags, I'd rip open the bologna, stick a piece in the middle of a flour tortilla and roll it up. We'd enjoy our "fast food" together while driving home.

My mom never had a checking account while we were young. And she would pay all her bills with money orders or cash. Pulling up in front of the local utility company, she'd hand me the invoice and cash. Jumping out of the car, I'd dash inside; pay the bill and race back to the car, ready to head out for the next errand. I felt important and grown up when Mom let me help her. My brothers and sister would be in the back seat of our big, blue Mercury station wagon. Oftentimes when we were all done, we'd take a drive to the vegetable stand, and then go to one of Mom's favorite picnic spots, such as Fairmount Park.

We never had the money to go out to eat, so we'd pack a lunch and head to the beach or Lytle Creek for picnics on the weekends. The only time we bought chips was for our weekend excursions. I loved the potato chips that came inside a large hatbox, to this day it is still one of my favorite snacks. Packing our cheap Styrofoam cooler with ice, hot dogs, hamburger, and buns, we could hardly contain our excitement, anticipating our fun outing.

Because of my love for horses, I looked forward to our weekend adventures. It always guaranteed me seeing horses grazing in the fields. As soon as I'd notice my favorite animal, you could hear me scream, "a horse, there's a horse, look at the horse! Oh, I wish I had a horse."

My siblings would just shake their heads, cover their ears and remark, "there she goes again."

When I got older I quit screaming but the ache and excitement in my heart continued every time I saw one of those magnificent creatures. I ached because I wanted one so badly. Just being close to a horse brought me unexplainable joy. Often times Mom would pull over to the side of the road and let me get out and pet the horse that was on the other side of the fence.

On warm, summer nights after barbecuing hot dogs and hamburgers our mom would make popcorn. She'd dump the warm, puffy white popcorn in a brown grocery bag and pour in creamy melted butter. After sprinkling it with salt and shaking the bag, she'd herd us kids into the family station wagon. "Grab some blankets, we're going to the drive-in."

We loved going to the movies. During intermission, my sister and I always took our brothers to the playground, near the concession stand. "Swing me again, Deb," Dave would yell. "Monica go down the slide with me," Rob said. "Will you take me to the bathroom," asked Steve?

On blistering, hot summer days, we'd make plans with the neighbors and pack our bologna or peanut butter and jelly sandwiches, take blankets and towels and head to Newport Beach where we would spend the whole day.

Our neighbor, Mrs. LaBree, was my favorite companion on those beach trips even though she was my mothers' friend. The first time I tasted cool, iced-coffee was when our neighbor pulled out her Tupperware pitcher, and poured the delicious-tasting beverage into a tall, Tupperware tumbler.

"Here, Debbie, would you like to try a glass?"

"No thank you, I'm not allowed to drink coffee. My mom says it will stunt your growth." Secretly, I wanted to taste the cool liquid and was more than willing to have it stunt my growth, I thought my legs were too long and skinny anyways.

Mom turned to me grinning, "Its okay, you can have one glass this time."

Mrs. LaBree handed me a glass of chilled iced coffee, I had never tasted anything so good. Our neighbor remained my mom's friend for a long time. She probably had the most normal family in our neighborhood and I often babysat for her. I always felt comfortable at her house. I can't remember hearing any drama about her, but who knows what she and my mom talked about when they would sit and drink coffee. On Saturday mornings, I'd help her clean her house and afterwards she'd teach me how to cook different dishes. She taught me how to follow recipes and how to make raisin bread, shepherd's pie, and other casseroles. I never forgot all she taught me, and to this day I really enjoy a frosty cup of iced coffee.

Although I was becoming interested in boys and the world outside of my neighborhood, I still did everything I could to please my mother. I continued to feel insecure and worthless and I would stuff my feelings and daydream instead. My mom's disapproval and verbal abuse no longer damaged me like it once did, or so I thought. There was a huge maple tree in our back yard and I loved climbing on it sitting atop the branches. I could see blocks and blocks away. I'd climb as high as I could and look out past the our street, pretending to be a newscaster, a dog trainer, a jockey or a famous writer. I'd get lost in my thoughts escaping real life. I could be anything I wanted to be. I dreamed about being a wolf, having a life that was simple and free—one that I could control. I fantasized about having my very own horse, which I could ride away in a moment's notice. At those times, gone was the constant nagging feeling that I was just never good enough, gone were the feelings of being bad, worthless shameful, and guilty.

One afternoon I climbed down from my favorite tree and continued to talk to myself as I walked around the back yard. I turned and noticed my mom staring at me.

"Debra Ann, what's wrong with you? Only crazy people talk to themselves. You're in Junior high now and you're too old to climb up that tree. I better not catch you talking to yourself again."

Was I crazy? With my head hung low, feeling ashamed, I vowed I would never again let her catch me go up the tree and from then on, I spoke softly, hoping she couldn't hear me talking to myself.

The grass near the edge of our house was high and I would lean against the house and feel the warm breeze blowing on my face, with the tall grass swaying all around me. The quietness, the sounds of the birds chirping, the wind rustling in the trees and the smell of a fresh summer rain made me feel calm. It was here I would sit when I knew my mom was gone and would make up different worlds in my head. I'd speak as loud as I wanted to and pretend that everything was good and perfect.

To get away from the constant noise and chaos at our house, I'd go in the bathroom and sit on the closed toilet lid, it was another place I could find solitude. Grabbing the plunger, I'd talk into it as if it were a microphone, pretending to be a famous actress or an author and I would make up a story and be all the characters.

Soon footsteps could be heard and a loud bang on the door. "Deb, what are you doing? You've been in there forever. Who are you talking to?"

Every Thursday the Bookmobile stopped at our school since we didn't have a library. I loved to read and would check out books about wolves, dogs, and horses. I would imagine I was Big Red, or Buck, the husky in my favorite stories. My fantasy life made it easier to get through 7th and 8th grade.

Strolling to the to the library on Saturdays, my sister and I chose our favorite books. Leaning against a nearby tree on the front lawn, I would read to Monica for hours before heading home. "Monica, are you listening? You're not looking at me while I'm talking!" I'd say while glancing up from the book.

"Yea, Deb, I heard what you said."

I was so bossy, but my sister was patient with me. Our favorite book was *A Wrinkle in Time*. It was a book I would go on to read to my own children.

Often on Saturday afternoons, you'd find the Griswold kids hanging out at the local indoor movie theater. We always seemed to come up with twenty-five cents for a movie and a five-cent candy bar, probably handed to us by one of Mom's many boyfriends. The smell of freshly popped popcorn permeated the lobby as we made our way to our seats. I loved movies, television, and books; anything that would help me to escape the awful memories that robbed me of a normal childhood.

We had been back in our old neighborhood for a little over two years. I still continued to go to confession on Saturday afternoons and Mass on Sundays, although not as often. Thoughts about what was done to me in secret were never far from my mind. When I wasn't daydreaming, I was still trying to be the perfect daughter, good in every way. I was always fearful when adults looked at me; I thought they knew the awful truth about me. How I longed to wake up one day and all the feelings of guilt and shame could be erased from my memory.

I enjoyed Junior high, I liked my classes and my teachers were nice to me. All the extra activities, such as dances and watching all the basketball and football games, were things I looked forward to. My best friend, Garrisann, and I went to all the school dances. We both had crushes on two basketball players, we would attend their games hoping to catch their eye. At nearly thirteen, I was still afraid of boys, but I sure liked looking at them and daydreaming about having a boyfriend.

In June of 1968, Bobby Kennedy was running for President. For some reason, he planned to visit our small town of Fontana. The neighborhood was ripe with excitement as we planned on leaving school early to head to City Hall. I especially liked Bobby because I had heard he had eleven children and he was the brother of John F. Kennedy. I made a handwritten sign on a piece of cardboard with a large stick attached. I had planned on holding it up so Bobby would see it. As a group of us started walking the three blocks to the mayor's office where Bobby was supposed to show up, one of the older neighbor kids pointed to my sign and said, "Look at the way you spelled Kenedy it's supposed to be spelled Kennedy."

Feeling embarrassed, I handed her the sign and said, "You can hold it if you want to."

My neighbor was glad to hold up my sign. I felt bad for my mistake but that didn't deter me from heading out to see the Presidential nominee. It proved to be an exciting afternoon. Sadly, within the week, Bobby was assassinated. I cried many tears that night when I found out.

During this time, our dad lived close by in a small apartment with Sandy. He rarely came over, although he started calling my sister and told her he'd pay her to clean up his apartment. Suspiciously, I wondered why he asked Monica to clean when he knew I was the tidy one. It just didn't make any sense.

I questioned her one day. "Why does Daddy want you to clean house? You don't even do your chores at home."

"I don't know Deb, he just does." Monica said with her long brown hair covering her face. She often walked around that way, with her face hidden.

Two days later on a Sunday afternoon Dad couldn't pick her up so I offered to walk her to his apartment a couple of miles away. A few hours later I walked to his house to walk home with her. Knocking on the door, I waited what seemed like an eternity, feeling anxious. *Why is it taking so long? I muttered under my breath. What are they doing in there?*

Monica opened the door slowly. Pushing it aside, I looked in and noticed the room was still dirty. "What were you doing? I can see the house it's still dirty. It looks the same as it did this morning, and where is Daddy?" I eyed her suspiciously.

Monica mumbled something as we walked home together. But crazy thoughts went through my head and a feeling of anger came over me

11

Truth Revealed

"There is nothing covered that will not be revealed, and hidden that will not be known." Matthew 10:26

Three days later on Ash Wednesday, which marks the beginning of the Season of Lent, I walked across the street from the Junior high school I attended to church. There was a morning service and all the Catholic kids were allowed to leave school. Of course, we were expected to return for the remainder of the day. Everybody knew who the Catholics were as we'd come back with ashes in the shape of a cross smudged on our foreheads.

As the service began, I don't remember what the priest was saying, but suddenly, I started sobbing. I swear I heard a gentle voice in my head saying, 'go home and tell your mother.'

Darting out of church, I ran home, sobbing all the way. Dashing in the house, my mom was surprised to see me home in the middle of the afternoon.

"What are you doing home? Why are you crying?"

"I was at church and I heard a voice telling me to come home and tell you something."

"Tell me what?" Mom motioned me to sit down and handed me some Kleenex.

"When I was a little girl, Daddy did ah, he did sex things to me and he made me do, do things to him," I stammered. "He kept doing it when we lived in the new, new house. Finally, when you guys got divorced it stopped."

"Exactly what did he do to you? Never mind. Don't tell me. I don't want to know."

"Mom, he did everything to me that a man and woman do when they are married." I sobbed in shame, my head hanging down. I couldn't look my mother in the eye, I felt so guilty.

"That Son-of-a_____. I'll have him thrown in jail," she screamed!

Crying uncontrollably, I begged her: "No, no, he said if I told, you'd put him in jail. Please don't, Mom, please don't, I couldn't live with myself if he went to jail. I feel so guilty, it's my fault he did those things to me. I'm such a bad girl. He told me if I didn't let him do it to me, he would do it to Monica. I had to protect my sister. But now I think he's doing it to her too."

"Why do you think that?"

"I went to pick her up at his apartment on Sunday. He said he wanted her to clean the house, and it was still dirty when I looked inside. Sandy wasn't there and he never came to the door. I think he was upstairs in the bedroom. I feel so bad." I could hardly talk as I laid my head in my hands and sobbed.

"Honey, it wasn't your fault. You had nothing to do with it," Mom said.

"But he told me it was."

"I hate that man!" Mom screamed. "He lied to you. He was a grown man and he knew better than to touch you and your sister."

Finally, Mom calmed down and I was relieved that I didn't have to give her the intimate details. She didn't blame me for anything. I knew that God had directed me to run home that Ash Wednesday and tell my mother 'the secret.'

A couple hours later, my little sister nonchalantly walked in the front door.

"Debbie told me that your father molested her. Did he ever touch you?"

Monica nodded her head and hid her face in her hands as tears rolled down her cheeks.

"When did it start?"

"I don't remember I was very young though, I didn't know he was touching Deb, too."

"Is it still going on?" Mom asked.

"Yes," Monica whispered through her tears, hanging her head in shame.

I was shocked and angry that my dad had touched my sister. I had believed him when he promised me he wouldn't. Mistakenly, I thought I had protected her all those years. My martyrdom had been for nothing. Despair poured over me and I could hardly contain the pain that intensified in my heart. I had failed to protect my sister. I felt even more worthless. "I'm so sorry, Monica. I thought you had been spared."

"It's not your fault, Deb," Monica reassured me.

"Your grandmother told me she thought Bob was messing with you girls. I just thought she was being a suspicious old lady. I feel so bad I didn't believe her. I never heard of a father touching his daughters. I am sorry, girls, I wasn't there for you." Mom tried her best to comfort us.

My little brothers had come home from school and probably over-heard bits and pieces of the conversation. Mom was still angry and continued to call my dad names and rant and rave.

My sister and I turned on the TV and avoided talking. It was just too painful.

Mom went to the catholic church early the next morning and talked to a priest. He encouraged her to reaffirm to us girls that we weren't to blame. We had done nothing wrong. He said we should not feel guilty or ashamed about what had happened to us. That evening Mom sat down with us and once again reminded us, "Your father is a grown man who did some very evil things to you and he knew better. You girls don't need to feel bad about it anymore. It wasn't your fault."

Because incest wasn't publicly talked about in the early sixties and no counseling easily available that Mom knew about, my mother thought we girls were okay. Even the priest didn't ask to talk to us, and by not talking about it we thought we were healed. It was then our mother realized why Monica had always thrown such horrible fits. Mom rarely hit Monica after that. We didn't speak of it again until after we were both married.

Even though I had told my secret and I was glad Mom knew, it didn't change how I viewed myself. I was still burdened with feelings of shame, worthlessness, guilt and self-hatred. Maybe in my childish expectations I thought I would somehow feel better when the secret came out, yet my perceptions about myself remained the same, even though Mom did her best to convince me that I had no part in the sexual molestation and I had nothing to feel responsible for. I still had a hard time believing her and I blamed myself. The self-hatred, blame, shame, and guilt would define my life for many years to come.

I still continued to take it upon myself to feel responsible for my mother's happiness and contentment. I felt compelled to be the good girl to ensure a place in my mom's heart and God's heart. I craved her love and affirmation. When she was good she was kind, comforting, and silly, but when she got into her moods, which seemed to be happening more often, she was depressed, angry, mean, and said hateful things to us. We never knew which mother we were going to get!

I don't know what happened between my mom and dad after the secret came out. He never did ask my sister to clean his apartment again and it would be sometime later before he'd show back up in our lives. He and his second wife Sandy would eventually move to Canada. My sister and I simply felt relief once again, when our dad left.

12

Wes and The Grand Canyon

"There is wonderful joy ahead, even though you have to endure many trials for a little while." 1 Peter 1:6

Not long after that, Mom introduced me to her new boyfriend. He was the most handsome man I ever met. He was a cross between Paul Newman and Robert Redford. Wes had a charming and boisterous personality. He roped the sun and made everything brighter with his laughter and his big plans. That is, until he got drunk, but I grew to love Wes and he became my new surrogate father. Wes was young and in the army and Mom lied to us kids about his age. She told us he was twenty-nine, but many years later she admitted the truth, he was only twenty-three when they began dating. I knew he was too young for me but I couldn't stop myself. I was almost ten years older than him, she later said.

After a few months, Wes left his quarters at the nearby army base and called our casa his own. I liked drawing and Wes encouraged me and he made us feel proud of who we were. "Your Griswolds, this is your street, this is your home don't ever forget how important you are." No one had ever made us feel like that before.

Wes often took us out to dinner; we had never done that before. Whether it was the local Pizza Hut, Kentucky Fried Chicken, or McDonalds, it was a treat for all six of us.

Early one winter morning, Wes got us all excited about a day trip he wanted to take us on. "Come on kids, get in the car, we're going up to the mountains for the day."

We could hardly wait to get there. It had been a misty-filled morning and had rained the night before. When we arrived at the mountain town of Big Bear, sixty minutes later, it was cool and cloudy. Marching up the street we noticed hundreds of little frogs jumping about. We were so excited. "Can we take them home?"

"Quick, let's find something to put these frogs in," Wes said, sounding as excited as us kids.

Hours later our car was filled with those little critters. It was my brother Mike's idea to sell the frogs to the neighborhood kids. So, over the next few days we sold them for a nickel apiece and collected lots of change. We were so proud of our resourcefulness and hid our small fortune in an empty peanut butter jar, somewhere inside the garage.

Coming home from a picnic a few days later, my brother noticed the side garage door was open. Back then we never locked our doors. Nobody did. Mike jumped out of the car, ran inside and came out with the empty jar in his hand. "Somebody stole our money! If I find out who did it I'm going to beat them up!"

We were angry and heartbroken. We never did find out who did it, but it was obviously one of the neighborhood kids.

The holidays that year were filled with excitement. Wes brought silliness and good times into our home. He suggested characters we could dress up as for Halloween. He helped my mom prepare the Thanksgiving turkey. We all picked out the Christmas tree and decorated it together. On Easter, Wes and Mom took us to Lytle Creek to hide Easter eggs, later we grilled hot dogs and hamburgers. We even hiked way up the hill to explore a large cross. On warm, summer days, we went on picnics and to the beach. Wes loved barbecuing on balmy, spring evenings. It was a good time in our lives and I was happy to see my mom laugh and smile once again. She spent less and less time hiding in her bedroom. It was even better to see her in love. Wes is the love of my life, she'd often express to us kids. She even tattooed a W on the inside of her right thigh. It hurt so much she never did finish spelling out the word WES.

Over the years we Griswold's were well known by our neighbors for many reasons, whether it was for our pets or our habit of collecting money. Traveling around our neighborhood with our beat up red, radio flyer wagon, we'd collect pop bottles to turn in for cash. Two of my brothers had already gone to camp by selling toffee-covered peanuts to our neighbors. The summer before I turned twelve Monica and I sold peanuts for the local YMCA. The rule was if we sold enough of them we could earn money to caravan to the Grand Canyon in a truck with several other girls. Nevada was the only place we had ever been thus far and we were thrilled with the challenge. We collected pop bottles and sold enough peanuts and the magical day finally arrived.

Mom dropped us off at the YMCA, took a few pictures, and waved as we headed out. We had our sleeping bags, pup tents, and clothes collected in a black garbage bag. We were loaded in the back of a pickup truck with wooden fences enclosed around us and covered by a large tarp. Ten of us girls were crammed into the truck along with the leader's ten-year-old son, Scotty. His sixteen-year-old sister, who traveled with us, was a chaperone. Riding in the back of the truck, proved to be an exciting journey for thirteen amazing days. Scotty's dad, mom and uncle rode up front they were our other chaperones.

We stopped in Flagstaff, Arizona and camped beside a stream in the national forest. Evergreen trees surrounded us and pops of yellow and purple wild flowers carpeted the ground. It was a spectacular sight! After dinner, we sat around the campfire and the leaders told us silly and scary stories. Later with the camp lights turned off and the fire burning out, I laid in my pup tent. My head stuck out of the opening, while my body was wrapped in the warmth of my wooly, sleeping bag. I looked up and noticed millions of twinkling stars overhead. It was incredible. I watched them until I fell asleep.

I loved wolves and hoped I would see a real one. Hearing high-pitched howls during the night and the hoots of great-horned owls brought me closer to nature than I had ever experienced before. Our mother was the one who taught us to love and appreciate nature. She showed us butterflies coming out of their cocoons. We watched her dig in the dirt planting her flowers and growing vegetables. She seemed to know the names of every plant, bush, tree and flower. She had an extraordinary green thumb and grew many plants she had placed around the outside and inside of our home. She encouraged us to notice brilliant sunsets and watch endless stars and planets on darkest of nights. She loved the mountains, oceans, waterfalls, rivers, streams, rainbows, thunderstorms and rainy days.

Early the next morning all the kids and leaders were up early and everyone was hungry. We stood in line for our breakfast. "Monica, look at these small, individual cereal boxes. We can even pour our milk right in the box."

"This is really good. I can pick out my favorite kind."

Plain old cereal never tasted so good. On Saturday morning one of the leaders made flapjacks; they were even better than my mom's special silver dollar pancakes. Roasting hotdogs over the open fire and later, making s'mores for the first time was a fun treat.

One afternoon, my sister and I spied the biggest toad we had ever seen. Sitting on a rock, sunning himself, he stared at us with one dark, sinister eye and the other eye was blood red.

"Let's call him Whiskey," Monica said. "He looks like he's had too much to drink with that red eye."

My sister and I carried that big, fat, ugly toad wherever we went for the next few days. We used Whiskey to scare the other girls who were afraid to touch him. Even Scotty got in the act, until his older sister caught him teasing someone with Whiskey. Regretfully, we had to say goodbye to our amphibian friend.

The sight of the Grand Canyon was heart stopping. Walking along the rim, we peered across the vast valley of peaks and plateaus. My sister and I had never seen anything more beautiful. We were so thankful to be able to visit one of the great natural wonders of the world.

Rising early one morning, we watched as orange, gold and crimson spotted the sky, until a blaze of red filled the canyon while the sun slowly rose. Sunsets were just as specular. Stopping along the way we explored unused roads, old graveyards, and small towns. We watched Native Indians put on a show and we talked to tourists as far away as Queens, New York. It was exciting for all of us. I had never been so far from home and had never talked to so many unfamiliar adults. Those were highlights of the trip my sister and I would never forget.

A band of five of us pre-teens separated from the rest of the clan and we became bosom buddies which included the leader's son, Scotty. He and I were developing a little crush on each other. One time our group decided to explore a nearby cemetery. People were buried there as early as the 1800's. As soon as we stepped through the enormous, wrought iron gates we were met with a looming, ominous-looking tombstone that stood over twelve-feet high. The sight of it sent chills up and down my spine. "This is scary. I don't like it here!" I shouted.

"Come on Deb, we'll play Hide and Seek, it will be fun."

"I don't want to I'm scared. You guys won't leave me, will you?"

"Don't worry we won't leave you," Monica reassured me.

We started the game and Mona was first. We blindfolded her then twirled her around till she was dizzy then stood her by a tree. She counted to thirty. We ran off. There were plenty of places to hide in the graveyard, but unfortunately Mona found me.

"Okay it's your turn to find us," all the kids yelled.

"It's going to be dark soon. You promise you won't leave? You know how scary this place is for me, especially that creepy headstone."

"We will be right here," Monica promised, with a twinkle in her eye.

They blindfolded me, spun me around over and over and stood me in front of a tree. "You have to count to one hundred."

"One, two… fifty-six… eighty-five…one hundred, ready or not here I come!" I screamed.

I could hear giggles and whispers, then eerie silence. Reaching behind my head, I untied the knot. Looking up, I realized I was standing in front of that sinister looking headstone.

"Ahhh, I hate you guys. You know this is scary. Where are you? You make me sick. You promised you wouldn't leave me!"

Shadows bounced around and played tricks on my eyes. The sun was beginning to set, making the place look even more eerie. With my arms flaring and my heart beating rapidly, I fearfully let out a blood-curling scream. "Where are you guys?"

Throwing open the huge iron gates I looked around for my friends and my devious sister.

Suddenly, I heard roars of laughter and I turned and saw them raising their heads. They had hidden behind an old brick fence on the other side of the immense iron gates.

"Ha, ha. You should have seen your face when you took off that blindfold," howled Monica with laugher.

"You scared me so much I begged you not to leave me and you said you wouldn't and then you stood me in front of that giant, creepy headstone. You guys make me sick."

"We were here all the time," Monica said still giggling. "You're so gullible!"

Later we had a good laugh over it—after my heart rate slowed down.

Not only were we fortunate to see the Grand Canyon, but we also traveled to Zion National Park in Utah. It was the first time I had ever seen incredible, breathtaking, rushing waterfalls and massive canyon walls ascending heavenward. The scenery was beautiful, with tall cottonwood trees over 100 years old. We saw mossy hanging gardens on the canyon walls and massive rock formations in the distance made us feel small amongst our surroundings.

Roaring, cascading waterfalls were heard as they crashed upon the rocks below. The cool, sparkling flow of the river showered us with a peaceful serenity, as we breathed in the fresh morning air. There were no worries or cares on the beautiful, green earth that God had created. For the first time, I understood what it was like to have peace in my life, if only for a few moments.

I loved opening my eyes first thing in the morning when the brilliance of the sun came streaming through my tent. Hearing the sounds of the cooing pigeons and the singing of the birds put a smile on my face. The sweet fragrance of the purple, orange, and yellow wildflowers permeated the forest as I breathed in the crisp, cool dawn air. Unforgettable sights and smells would always stay with me. I couldn't believe the freedom and joy I felt being out in the wild. Days turned into weeks and, regrettably, our time was over too soon. The trip back was bittersweet. To leave such extraordinary surroundings brought a note of sadness, but on the other hand it was the first time Monica and I had spent so much time away from home and we were anxious to head back and share our fun adventures with our family.

Sitting cross-legged in the back of the crowded truck, wrapped in blankets, our small group sat as far away as we could from the glaring eyes of our chaperone. All the girls urged me to kiss Scotty. "Kiss him, Debbie, kiss him, you know you want to."

I shyly shook my head and they tried a different approach. "Scotty, kiss her, kiss her."

He suddenly became nervous and shook his head. I would not get my first kiss until much later. On the rest of the ride home we all sang camp songs until we fell asleep.

The following weekend my sister and I met with our new group of friends at the orange grove.

"Try this cigarette," said Scotty.

I still had a crush on him and I wanted to please him so I took a puff and coughed like crazy. It left a terrible taste in my mouth. Immediately, guilt began to surround me like a dark cloud. Somehow Scotty's parents found out what we had been up to and I never saw him again after that.

Wes had been living with us for a while. He and my mother were smokers, but he always encouraged us kids not to start the nasty habit. When I arrived home, I marched to my front door, shaking but determined to be honest with Wes about my smoking. "I took a puff from a cigarette today and immediately felt bad. I am so sorry. I will never smoke again," I said with my head hanging down.

Immediately, he took me in his arms. "Thanks for being honest with me. It's okay. I hope you learned your lesson. It is such a bad, bad habit to start."

It felt good that he trusted me. After all I needed his love, affirmation, and approval. It was something I never got from my own father.

My need for Wes's love overruled what he did to my mom. Wes was charming when he wasn't drinking, but as soon as he got drunk he turned into an abusive, screaming maniac. Wes never verbally or physically mistreated my siblings or me. Unfortunately, his unwarranted anger was always directed towards our mother. I don't remember when it began but it lasted the whole time Mom and Wes were together for nearly two years. Often, they would go out drinking, and would come home drunk, then they would usually end up in the bedroom fighting. It wasn't just normal yelling, he would threaten her and call her names. Then we would hear a thud, then another thud, and then another. As we ran into the room we'd find my mom with her hand over her mouth, tears and blood spilling over her face, sitting on the edge of the bed while Wes stood over her with his large fists clenched yelling obscenities.

My older brother, who was small at fourteen, only standing about five feet tall, courageously stood up to Wes. "Stop hitting our mom?"

Mom turned on my brother when he was trying to protect her. "Get out, get out of here all of you. I deserved it, I made him do it, now get out. He wouldn't hit me if I would just keep my big mouth shut!"

"You're right, you B_____h!" Wes yelled, "it is all your fault."

Even after that, my brother still tried to intervene and my mom continued to blame herself for the abuse she suffered.

We had heard my mom and dad fighting and calling each other names, but this was something new to us. It was painful watching our own mother getting beat. Seeing Mom come home drunk was something we hadn't experienced either. Before she met Wes, we rarely saw our mother drunk. Some nights they'd come home, happy and lovey-dovey, holding hands like two teenagers in love. Everything seemed fine but ultimately the fighting would begin.

One day Wes took us all to see a rodeo and I invited my girlfriend, Garrisann to go. Afterwards, she was planning on spending the night. Mom and Wes had gone out drinking and they came home fighting. He began to hit her over and over while calling her filthy names.

I was so embarrassed! "Garrisann, I will walk you home," I said, grateful it was dark so she couldn't see my tears. We never talked about what was happening in my home. I only hoped my friend wouldn't tell other people. It wasn't long before I stopped inviting her over to spend the night, we usually ended up staying at her house. *Did these kinds of things happen in other people's homes too? I wondered but never asked.*

One time my mom came home with Wes staggering behind her, they were both covered in blood. Mom had a black eye and a swollen lip while Wes sported bruises and deep gashes on his arm.

"What happened?" We screamed in horror.

"Wes and I just beat up the Diablo gang," my Mother proudly slurred!

Do normal families go through this? What's normal anyway?

I was always trying to protect my mom but none of us could protect her from her boyfriend's rages and violence. Sometimes it felt like we lived in constant fear never knowing how long the calm would last. Mom swore in her drunken stupor that she loved Wes and he loved her. Even when she wasn't drunk we would overhear her say, I will never love anyone as much as I love Wes.

During this time, she also did illegal things. One time Mom encouraged my baby brother to take a tiny, black poodle out of the neighbor's yard. "Steve, go get me that dog. They keep him chained up all day and night, in the heat and in the rain. They don't deserve to have him."

Steve happily obliged. He was the cutest, squiggliest puppy we had ever seen. Mom named him Freemont. Eventually, Wes grew jealous of the dog, accusing Mom of spending more time with Freemont than with him. The little puppy became a source of their constant bickering when they were drunk and Mom was always trying to defend herself against his accusations.

We were so embarrassed because our mom had stolen someone else's pet, but we knew how much Mom loved Freemont. We tried to keep him hidden by concealing him in the house and backyard as often as we could. We were afraid for our mom. *Do normal moms ever steal their neighbor's pets?* Finally, the owner realized we had his dog and our mom ordered us to take Freemont back, while she hid inside. Luckily for Mom, the neighbor didn't file charges.

One gloomy, summer night, Mom and Wes went out. My three younger siblings were already in bed by the time they returned. Mike, Monica and me were up watching TV. In walked Wes and my mom, smiling from ear to ear. He carried a sewing machine, a record player, and an exquisite hand-knit lace tablecloth. My mom followed, bringing in a radio, a small black and white television set, and a few other odds and ends. They didn't tell us where they came from and we were happy with our new treasures. A few days later one of our neighbors returned from their vacation and realized someone had burglarized their home while they were gone. They were missing a sewing machine, a television set, a radio, and other knick-knacks.

We were mortified when we realized what Mom and Wes had done. Once again, we had to keep silent to protect our mother. A few days later they went out on their usual weekend jaunt. Within a few hours Wes staggered into the house, alone!

Looking up from my television program I casually called out, "Where's Mom?"

Gazing at me with a glassy look, Wes announced, "She's dead!"

13

Fears

"For God has not given us a spirit of fear and timidity, but of power, love, and a sound mind." 1 Timothy 1:7

"What, what, she's dead, what do you mean, what are you saying," I yelled hysterically, tears streaming down my face. Running out to the driveway, I found my mom stumbling out of the car.

She reached out to me slurring her words, "What's throng, honey?"

"Wes said you were dead, he said you were dead!"

Wes, in a drunken rage came running out the front door holding the sewing machine. He threw it in the middle of the street. Dashing back into the house he grabbed the black and white television set and did the same thing. Then it was the radio and knick-knacks. By this time my little brothers were out of bed standing in the doorway rubbing their eyes. They stood there, tears falling down their faces, crying hysterically while watching this madman destroying the very items he my mom proudly carried in the week before. We were all so confused.

The next-door neighbor flipped on his porch light. "What's going on here, buddy? What's all the noise about?" he said, walking out to his lawn, standing near the chain link fence that separated our yards.

Wes reached over, grabbed the guy by the shirt and hit him right in the mouth. After cussing the guy out, he rubbed his hands together and calmly walked back in the house.

"I'm so sorry Mom, it's all my fault. I should never have overreacted about the comment Wes made." *Why was I so stupid?*

Mom, still drunk, tried to reassure me. "Honey its snot your fault."

But I was sure I was to blame and I spent the night feeling bad about myself. Afterwards, we could hear Mom and Wes screaming at each other in the bedroom.

Even after this, I loved Wes and forgave him. When Wes wasn't drinking, he was a different person and I could overlook his abuse to my mother. He warned me about boys and spent time listening to me. He encouraged me to draw. He told me he was proud of me when I cooked a good meal, cleaned the house, or brought home a good report card. Wes laughed and made jokes, made fun of people and made all of us laugh. When he couldn't afford to take us out to eat, he helped Mom in the kitchen and taught her how to prepare ground beef several different ways to stretch the budget.

I thought I had finally found a daddy who loved me. When Wes and Mom weren't drinking we had happy family times. He took us on our first real vacation. Our adventure started with a fun-filled day spent at Disneyland—something we had never done while Mom and Dad were married. My sister and I looked adorable in our matching orange and white flower print, frilly tops, and bell-bottoms. The boys all wore matching blue, button-down shirts, light-brown pants, and brand-new tennis shoes. Afterwards, we made plans to drive to Henderson,

Nevada to visit our grandmother. We stopped at Hoover Dam, billed as a National Historic Landmark. After taking a tour, we stood on top and looked all the way down. The sound of the roaring water was deafening, but I loved it. I appreciated learning about the history of the dam. We took lots of pictures and there were lots of smiles that weekend. When we returned home, the inevitable drinking and fighting started and Mom ended up with a black eye and several bruises.

Often on Sunday afternoons, Wes and Mom would load us into the family car and take us to their favorite bar. Their preferred bar was The Schooner. It was shaped like a large ship and inside was the biggest aquarium we kids had ever seen. Country music played in the background.

Mom would motion to us. "Look girls, see that blue and yellow fish, it's so pretty. Come over here boys, look at that funny-looking seahorse in there."

At first it was exciting. But then I began to notice the dark, dank, atmosphere, the smell of stale beer, and the sound of pool balls clinking together. Besides, I hated hearing the sound of Hank Williams and Willie Nelson. *To this day I have an aversion to country music and bars.*

Wes and I shared something in common: we both loved horseback riding. Wes took Mom, Monica, and me to a nearby horse stable several times a year. My favorite horse was Big Red. He was by far the largest horse I had ever seen and I felt like a queen sitting high atop his burly, auburn back. Cool, overcast days in southern California still remind me of those times at Jurupa Hills horse stables.

After they had been dating for nearly two years, Wes got orders to go to Turkey for a few months. My mom was broken-hearted. I knew I would miss him and our horseback riding adventures. I would also miss the way Wes encouraged me and the way he had made the family laugh.

But none of us would miss his screaming and yelling. Most importantly we would not miss Wes hitting our mom.

I saved all the letters Wes wrote to me. Once he sent me a newspaper article about entering a drawing contest. I never did submit my pirate picture but I worked on it until I discovered something much better--boys!

After Wes came home it wasn't long before he lost interest in my mom. He had met a much-younger, Hawaiian lady. He couldn't decide if he wanted to go back to his ex-wife and his young son, stay with his new girlfriend, who my mom angrily referred to as "Pineapple," or resume things again with my mom. Eventually, he moved in with his new Hawaiian girlfriend.

Our mother was filled with sadness and depression. She entered a downward spiral in her life and made a major decision that would ultimately change our lives forever.

Seven years later I heard from Wes, after my mom had tracked him down. I don't know if she ever got over him. He sent me a nice letter and inquired about my life. I wrote him back but I never heard from him again.

14

Changes! What Now?

"Seek good, not evil, that you may live. Then the Lord God Almighty will be with you." Amos 5:14

Mom started spending more time in her room demanding her pills. When she did come out, she was usually withdrawn or angry. Being the good girl, I continued to take care of the family. I wanted everything peaceful so she wouldn't have any reason to get mad, but it didn't matter what I did because she was still unhappy and she still continued to take out her frustration on us. Although I tried to do what I could to make her happy, I realized it was sometimes better to stay away from home as much as possible. I hung out with the kids in the neighborhood and with my best friend Garrison who lived a few blocks away as often as I could.

I was never tempted to do things like drink or take drugs like my friend, Pam did.

One time when I was bored, I dropped in on Pam. She and several of her friends were practicing a new trick.

"Hey Deb have you ever made yourself pass out?" Pam asked.

"No, why would I do that?"

"It's fun. Try it, you'll like it."

I watched as she held her breath and fell to the floor. After she came to she acted as if she didn't know where she was. It seemed like a silly thing to do, so I walked out and vowed for the last time to cut ties with my mixed-up friend.

A girl named Celia lived down the street from us. She was a bully and a couple years older than me. I always tried to avoid her. She occasionally teased me, made fun of me and told lies about me. I was afraid of getting beat up by her. One time she came up behind me when I was stopped on my bicycle. Viciously, she slugged me in the back.

"That's for wearing a dress while you're riding a bike. You're so stupid!"

After she punched me, I took off before she could hit me again. Berating myself I thought, I'm a coward, just like my dad. I hate myself, I'm turning out just like him.

Celia was too old and too big for my sister to intervene this time.

One night I prepared a unique dish for Celia. I had just poured some urine in a rectangle cake pan and placed it in the oven to bake. A timer went off. Immediately, I woke up from my crazy dream and I could smell a disgusting odor. In my dream, I remembered the urine was burning.

"What's that smell?" I yelled to my sister who was sleeping next to me and then I bolted out of bed. Suddenly, I realized it was a fire I smelled. Flinging open Mom's bedroom door, I looked towards her bed, I could barely see her as thick, black smoke billowed in front of me. Flames were shooting out of her pillow with her head still upon it. Mike was in her room trying to put out the fire.

"Mom, Mom, wake up. Your pillow is on fire," we screamed!

My brother and I continued pounding the fire with towels. Mom finally sat up and Mike grabbed a towel and wrapped the smoldering pillow around it, he then threw it in the bathtub.

Thankfully, after much coughing our mom was okay. We figured Mom had fallen asleep smoking. We found out later she also had consumed too many sleeping pills. She was remorseful and swore she'd never smoke in her room again. Our mother was lucky, this time. The incident could have turned out so different.

Gino and Virginia Picarillo were friends of our parents and we grew up playing with their five kids. Lynn was a year older than me, her little sister Tammy was Monica's age and we always looked forward to excursions with their family. They had a large above ground Doughboy pool we'd go swimming in, while the parents' grilled hamburgers and hot dogs. There were many late-night games of Hide and Seek, Mother May I, and Red Light, Green Light.

We continued to see the Picarillos sporadically after Mom's divorce. The summer after I turned thirteen I got a phone call from Lynn. "Debbie, it's been awhile since I've seen you. Do you want to come over and stay the night with me?"

"I would love to."

Spending the afternoon swimming in the pool was lots of fun but I immediately began to feel uncomfortable when her older brother made a weird comment to me.

"I'd sure like to cut the grass with you." Sixteen-year-old Steve said with a grin and a wink.

I giggled, although I felt embarrassed, and walked away confused. Later I asked Lynn about it. "What does cut the grass mean?"

"Oh, you're so lucky. That means my brother wants to have sex with you," Lynn laughed.

I wanted to go home after that but instead I tried to avoid Steve for the rest of the evening. Lynn and I got up early the next day on Saturday morning and we walked a few blocks to her friend's house. When we arrived, she informed me of her plans. "We always play Strip poker on the weekends. Are you going to play with us?"

My mouth must have fallen to my knees. "I don't want to play Strip poker. Can I just go back to your house?"

"No, then my mom will wonder why we're not together," she said, motioning to the bedroom. "You hang out in there and read those comic books and wait for us to get done playing. Whatever you do, don't walk back to my house!"

I wasn't happy with her plans for me and was shocked that my old friend was playing disgusting games. I sat and stewed about my predicament while listening to hysterical laughter from the other room.

"Debbie, come here, Joey is taking off his underwear. Come and see him. Hurry, open the door, he's coming into the bedroom."

I had never seen a boy naked and I wasn't interested. My heart began beating wildly. Slamming the door shut I turned the lock and I stood against it. "No, no don't come in, please don't come in."

I could hear loud roars of laughter outside the bedroom door. What seemed like hours later, they were finally done with the game and Lynn came to retrieve me. As we walked to another friend's house, she and her friend, Wendy who also played, discussed the game. "It was so fun watching Joey undress."

Lynn said, "Yea, the first time I had to take my clothes off, I was so embarrassed but now I sometimes lose on purpose just so I can strip."

"I think that's disgusting. How can you take your clothes off in front of boys?" I said.

They tried to convince me what I had been missing out on. "We felt the same way as you. We finally let our friends talk us into trying it and we love it. You will, too. Maybe next time you stay over you'll change your mind," Lynn giggled.

I silently vowed that would be the last time I slept over at my old friend's house.

A few weeks later, my mom told me the sad news, "Lynn and three other girls were walking down the street and a drunk driver hit them. Lynn went into a coma and never came out and died."

"I can't believe it," was all I could say.

The funeral came and went and I could not bring myself to go. The thought of coffins, and graveyards frightened me. We had never known anyone close to us who had died. Sure, my grandmother and my grandfather had died on my dad's side, but I hardly saw them and they lived in a different state. I didn't go to either one of their funerals. This was different; this was something I had never experienced before. I felt sad for Lynn's family.

After Wes and Mom broke up, she began staying out late with her girlfriends. They would travel to Cucamonga. It was only about thirty minutes away. I thought it was just a made-up name. Years later I realized there really was a town called Cucamonga nearby. Mom was often gone for days at a time. She made sure to let us know it was none of our business what she did, so we never questioned her. I did overhear her talk about how much she loved going dancing, though.

Mike and I took care of the family. I made dinners, cleaned, got the little ones' ready for school, making sure they had clean clothes and a sandwich for lunch. If Mom didn't come home we'd lock up, turn out the lights, and wonder when we would hear from our mother. I always hated her being gone. Even though I was older, I still worried that something awful would happen to her. I never forgot her prophecy and was still afraid that it would come true.

One weekend Mom ran off to Tijuana. Two days later she returned and with her was handsome, young Mexican man. "This is my new husband," she proudly announced. "We just got married in Mexico!"

Mike stared at me with a look of horror on his face. *What had our mother done this time?*

A few hours later there was a loud pounding at our front door. There stood an angry, dark skinned woman. "Get out here right now, Jose." She ordered her husband in broken English. "Get out of that house and come home with me this instant."

Our mother had married someone else's husband. Thankfully, he left with his wife. That was the first and last time we ever saw him. Were we ever relieved!

15

My Boyfriends

"And what does the Lord require of you? To act justly and to love mercy and to walk humbly with your God." Micah 6:8

I had just started Junior high and many of my friends had boyfriends. When a boy asked a girl to go steady in 1967 he usually sealed the deal by giving her a St. Christopher medal to wear around her neck. Doug caught my eye we were both twelve and in several classes together. Although he was short, freckled faced and had stringy blond hair, I thought he was cute. We had a crush on each other and I eagerly awaited my medal.

Pam, my neighbor was the go-between. She caught up with me after school and presented me with a handmade necklace of shiny, colorful beads that were popular during that era.

"These are from Doug, he wants you to go steady with him."

"What! Where's my St. Christopher?" I was so disappointed.

The next day Doug wanted to carry my books home from school. We walked together the few blocks to my house.

Later that night Pam said, "Doug sure wants to kiss you and he wants to take you to the movies and make out with you. First he is going to French kiss you and teach you all different ways to kiss."

Feeling scared, I realized I didn't want him to kiss me. I just wanted to wear a St. Christopher medal like all the other girls that were going steady, and I didn't even get one.

The next afternoon, sure enough, after school Doug again walked me home from school and carried my books. Stopping at the corner from my house he handed me my books back, reached over and planted a wet, juicy kiss on my lips. I was shaken up and I didn't like it at all.

The thought of him kissing me made me feel anxious and afraid, luckily that night my necklace broke. Salvaging a few colored beads, I put them in a white Styrofoam cup. Taking it to school with me the next morning, I handed my cup to Pam, "Tell Doug, I broke up with him. Will you give him his beads back?"

It would be another two years before I would experience my first French kiss, which much to my surprise, I would thoroughly enjoy.

By this time, I was enjoying life at school. My best friend, Garrisann, and I spent our days dreaming about the boys we had crushes on. We spent the night at each other's houses on the weekends. Every month we went to the school dances and hoped the boys we liked would ask us to dance, but they never did. We attended every basketball game that our crushes played in. Al and Bill became our obsessions. Her older sister kindly drove us to the away games. Garrisann's mom even planned a Halloween party and we were excited that the two boys would be coming. However, nothing ever came of it, and we were severely disappointed. They began and ended just as crushes.

When I turned fourteen and was in the 9th grade, I met an older boy and I was immediately infatuated. My old babysitter, Debbie, was nearly 20 and married to Bill. Bill had an eighteen-year-old brother named Jerry. He started coming to our house when Bill and Debbie came over. From the moment, I laid eyes on him I thought he looked like the actor, Robert Mitchum.

While babysitting one night for some friends, Jerry showed up at the house. "How did you know I was here?"

"I have my ways," Jerry said smugly.

I stood at the front door, blocking him from coming inside the house.

"I've only been babysitting for Linda for a few weeks and she really likes me. She and her husband even took me to the horse races. I don't think you should be here."

I was thinking back on my conversation I had the first time Linda asked me to watch the kids. "Do you like moon pies and cupcakes? We also have chips and Coke. Help yourself to anything, and eat as much as you want."

I thought I had died and gone to heaven. I had never had so many tasty treats at my disposal. I loved everything about my new babysitting job.

Jerry stuck his foot in the door. "Come on, you know you want me here."

Fortunately, the kids were sound asleep and I finally relented. My heart did a flip-flop when he entered the house and looked at me in a way that took my breath away.

"Have you ever been French kissed?"

"No, I'm afraid, and I don't want you to kiss me."

He persisted. "Come on, I'll stop anytime you want me to. There is nothing to be afraid of. I promise you will like it."

He followed me into the kitchen and pinned me against the refrigerator. The next thing I knew he had his tongue in my mouth and he was right: I liked it.

Now I knew what all the excitement was about when the girls at school talked about it.

I told you, you would like it," he said as he headed out the door. "Do you want to go out next Friday night?"

"Yes, but I have to ask my mom first."

I convinced my mother it would be a good idea. On our first date, we went to the drive-in movies. Jerry bought a six-pack of beer and drank it all, while we both watched the movie.

Afterwards we went parking and did a little kissing.

Jerry had had numerous girlfriends before me and he was very experienced. Since I had never dated before I was very innocent and naïve, insecure and gullible and my maturity level was closer to a twelve-year-old, while Jerry's maturity level and experience with girls was closer to a twenty-year-old. Of course, I didn't realize it at the time. I had high morals and wanted to remain a good girl. I knew I was expected to be a virgin; after all I was a good Catholic girl. And I also wanted to make my mother proud. It was my desire to remain pure.

Jerry and I went to the drive-in almost every weekend after that. Each time he would borrow his grandmother's car and he always had a six-pack of beer with him. I never drank, I wasn't even interested and he never offered me even a sip. Each week we would make-out and he would drive me home after the movies were over. My mom was usually up when I got home. Jerry always walked me inside. I said goodnight and went to bed. He stayed and drank with my mother.

Jerry drove a motorcycle and he enjoyed taking me for rides. He taught me how to hold on tight and lean to the right or to the left when he turned a corner. I felt honored that this older boy showed such interest in me. I wore his favorite, fringed buckskin jacket (that was popular in 1970) and looked forward to our next date.

One day he bragged to me. "I collect Chiquita banana stickers and stick them on my wallet every time I've been with a girl."

I honestly did not know what he meant.

Each weekend, Jerry did more things to me and each weekend, I felt guilty for letting him. I tried to tell him no, but he kept persuading me, until I gave in. I never told my mother or my sister or anybody else about our intimate dates.

Unfortunately, my Mom was still depressed about her break up with Wes. I thought it was weird that she and Jerry hung out with each other and drank after I went to bed. I suspected things later when I was older but I never knew if anything happened between them.

One day, Jerry and I were sitting in the back seat of Mom's car listening to the radio. Mom and Monica got in the front.

"I'm going to the liquor store do you two want to drive along?" Mom asked.

"Sure, we aren't doing anything anyways."

Mom bought some beer, and before she got home, she started drinking. After guzzling a few cans, Mom's mood suddenly changed. Gunning the engine, she sped home. Pulling up to the house, Mom slammed on the brakes and screamed, "Get out! Get out now of the car now!"

My sister obediently opened the passenger side door and stepped out.

I reached for the door handle but Jerry grabbed my hand. "She's not going to do anything. Don't get out." He pulled me back down.

Abruptly, Mom hit the gas petal and sped away from the curb.

The next thing I remember was a loud smashing sound. It was our car hitting something. As I shielded my eyes from the bright lights of red flares, I noticed a fire truck, police car and an ambulance, I felt like I was floating and everything was happening in slow motion. Blood was dripping down my face and more blood flowed down my leg. Someone helped me out of the backseat and led me into the front of the ambulance. At the same time my mother was put on the stretcher and wheeled into the back of the ambulance. Sirens blared as we were driven to the hospital.

Panic took over, *what happened to my mom? Where was Jerry?* It didn't take long to arrive at the hospital. A cut above my left eye bled profusely. It was soon stitched up. My leg was bandaged with a butterfly Band-Aid. Thankfully, those were my only wounds.

Fortunately, my mom suffered no broken bones, or internal injuries, but she was bruised, swollen, and sore from her head to her toes. We were both released from the hospital that night. Jerry was uninjured and I was mad at him for forcing me to stay in the car. Years later Mom would admit she had deliberately driven into a tree and was trying to commit suicide.

Jerry hung around the next several weeks, taking care of my mom as she spent most of her time in bed or lying on the couch. Soon we resumed our Friday night dates, he with his six-pack and me trying to remain pure. It was getting harder and harder for me to fight him off. Lately he had been getting extremely angry with me when I said no, and he'd speed out of the movie while screaming at me. "Are you scared yet, are you scared?"

I promised myself I would quit going out with him. I was afraid I would eventually give in to his demands. I had no one to talk to about him and the way he coaxed me to go further every weekend. I suffered alone in silence and felt guilty every week. Jerry began to control me in other ways too, asking me why I wore a certain style of clothes, or why my nose was always shiny and why couldn't I fix it. He'd say, "You can't even be yourself around me." *What did he mean by that statement?*

Towards the end of the school year, the ninth graders went to Disneyland. I was thrilled. It had been almost three years since I had been to "The Happiest Place on Earth." Jerry was going to follow the bus and meet me at the parking lot. We would spend the whole day together.

A couple hours later I asked, "Are you having fun?"

He seemed unusually quiet. "Yea, sure."

I didn't realize it at the time, but we had never done anything together except go to the movies, go parking, and go on motorcycle rides. Although he seemed distant I still tried to enjoy the amusement park and bought an ice cream from the snack bar. It was so good I wanted another one.

"Do you think you need another one?" Jerry asked, sarcastically.

"No, I guess not."

At 5'5" tall, I probably weighed 90 pounds and I couldn't understand why he discouraged me from eating another treat. I began to feel self-conscious. Soon I realized I always felt that way around Jerry. Thankfully, our trip to Disneyland was almost over.

On a Sunday, a few months after our mother hit the tree she made a surprising announcement. "We are moving to Colorado to live with my sister and her six kids. Uncle Ray and Aunt Lena will be here on Friday. We will drive back with them and we can only take what will fit in their small trailer."

"What are you talking about? Are you saying were moving in five days?" my oldest brother asked.

"Yes, we are."

"Why are we moving?" I asked.

"I can't live in this place anymore. If I don't get out of this state I'll end up dying here."

I quickly calculated: Since Mom was still only thirty-four she had one more year before her self-fulfilling prophecy could perhaps come to pass. Somehow, I believed if we didn't move she would end up dying too. Although we were disappointed at our mother's announcement we knew no amount of persuasion on our part would make Mom change her mind. She had already decided we were moving without talking about it to us first. We only had five days to tell our friends goodbye and pack up a few of our meager belongings.

I was scheduled for a date with Jerry on Friday, the day we were leaving. I was so relieved that I wouldn't be going out with him. I clearly remember our last time together: The movie was boring. He had gulped all six of his beers. He wanted to go parking. I didn't, but I gave in. After too much touching, too many liberties taken, I tried saying no, over and over. He finally listened, but not before getting very angry. He put the key in the ignition, and we adjusted our rumpled clothing. Zooming towards the highway, Jerry began driving faster and more erratically. "Are you scared yet, Deb?" He shouted over the blaring music.

I was angry but not scared, but I didn't tell him that. "Yea, slow down please."

"When are you going to let me go all the way? I'm tired of you stopping me week after week. I can't take it anymore," he said, pushing his foot even harder on the gas pedal.

"Please slow down. Next week, I promise."

Five days passed quickly while we were getting ready to leave our home. One of my girlfriends said, "You're so lucky, at least you'll be breathing fresh air. Not like the smog we have here." Was that supposed to make me feel better about leaving? *Lucky! Right! Are you kidding? Leaving everything we knew, including our friends. What was my mom thinking?*

I don't even remember my dad coming around to say goodbye. The last person I saw as we piled into my aunt's car was Jerry. Nonchalantly, he sauntered over to the automobile. Handing me a half-smoked cigarette he had snubbed out, he leaned in to kiss me goodbye.

"Here Deb, take this to remember me by."

As we drove away I was sad but relieved. I mouthed the words, *thank you God.* Now I wouldn't have to go through with the promise I had made to him. My virginity was still intact!

16

Colorado

"The Lord Himself will go before you. He will be with you; he will not leave you or forget you. Don't be afraid and don't worry." Deuteronomy 31:8

Our move out of California to Colorado would change our lives forever. That summer of 1970, the war in Vietnam was still going strong, although over 40,000 troops had been pulled out. *The Brady Bunch, Little House on the Prairie,* and *The Walton's* were popular television shows. The Beatles broke up that year. "Aquarius/Let the Sun Shine In" was on its way to becoming the song of the year. Richard Nixon was president of the United States. *Midnight Cowboy,* starring Jon Voight, would win best picture. Eighteen year olds were given the right to vote in federal elections, and floppy disks were invented.

And in the summer of 1970, the only world I had ever known was unraveling, changing too fast, and falling apart. I was driving away from the only state I remembered ever having lived in. Most of my childhood friends I would never see again. My father's relatives, who we had not seen for several years, might never know we had left. I was leaving my school, my neighborhood, the Catholic Church where I had made my first communion. We were all leaving the only world we had ever known because my mom wanted a fresh start. Thus, we began our thousand-mile journey to our new life.

"But Mom," cried the little ones. "What are we going to do on the Fourth of July? It's tomorrow. Can't we leave afterwards?"

"Your Uncle and Aunt need to get back home. They left their children and they were nice enough to come all the way to California to move us in with them."

"But why do we have to leave? We won't even be able to blow off fireworks!"

"Quiet down kids. That's enough whining," Mom said.

We were all angry with our mother. We were going to miss Independence Day, and live in some stupid state called Colorado.

As we got closer to our destination I began to notice the majestic mountains that Colorado is known for. Soon we came upon the Continental divide. There were winding roads and hairpin curves. The scenery was breathtaking, huge evergreens growing everywhere. Blue spruce, Aspen trees, and Ponderosa pines bordered the mountain highways. We stopped the car at a scenic overlook and looked down towards the valley at a place called Wolf Creek Pass. First of all, I loved it because of the name and the scenery was exhilarating. The mountains rose over 10,000 feet they were unlike the ones I had seen in California, they had a sheer beauty all their own. Pine trees were everywhere and a plush carpet of green grass covered the meadow. And my friend was right; the air was cool, fresh, and free of smog. I was intoxicated by its beauty and fresh scent. My mom loved nature and she taught us to appreciate colorful wildflowers, brilliant sunsets, the abundant beauty of the mountains, and the scent of fresh, cool rains.

"Wow, it's so beautiful here," I said.

My aunt said, "That's why we refer to it as colorful Colorado."

"Would you like to take a drive through the city where I was born?" Mom asked.

"Where were you born?"

"Right here, after we get out of Wolf Creek Pass, we'll come to a little mountain town called Pagosa Springs."

Turning off the main highway, my uncle drove us through the narrow, winding streets and Mom pointed to the house that used to be hers. "Right there. That's the street I lived on and there is where Aunt Betty lives, this is where we will stay tonight."

"What's that awful smell?" the boys asked. "It smells like rotten eggs!"

"It's from the natural hot springs that surround the town and you're smelling sulfur." Mom explained.

"Phew, it's yucky, it stinks," eight-year-old Steve reached up and plugged his nose.

My mom grew up the youngest of three siblings. Her father was German, Dutch Scottish, English and a Heinz 57 mix of other nationalities, while grandma's relatives were mostly Spanish and American Indian. Dave Lister, my grandfather, was a logger in the early forties. He moved his family around Colorado, Arizona, New Mexico and Nevada while he followed the logging industry. Once they even lived on an Indian reservation in Arizona my mother had fond memories of those times. Grandpa Dave worked hard and other than working in the sawmills he became a gardener and landscaper when the family finally settled in Nevada a few years before my mom met my father.

My grandmother, Rita, was in her late-thirties when Mom was born. That was considered old back in 1936. Mom remembers her combing her long hair and telling her stories about the olden days and the religious ceremonies she attended. She was a Catechism instructor for a long time. Mom said she remembers being beaten by her mother with a willow stick until she was black and blue and sometimes bled. Our mother said they didn't consider it child abuse in those days. That's just what everybody did. They believed children were to be seen and not heard. Grandma spent some time in the hospital when Mom was younger and it took a long time for her to recover, Lena, the oldest sibling took care of the family while her father worked. When she was younger, they often lived off the land, her daddy hunting for their supper. At that time, she regularly saw wildlife such as: deer, squirrel and mountain lions. They had rabbits, chickens and ducks as pets and sometimes they had to eat them. They were so poor but she never realized it. My grandmother and grandfather loved each other very much and Mom grew up with a lot of love from her father but she remembers her mother never said she loved her.

Our mother always felt like the black sheep of the family when she got older. Being rebellious and strong-willed she did not like to be told what to do. For many years she resented her sister for trying to act like her mother. She always felt as if she were a mistake because her mother was older and sick when she was born. Mom was also insecure about her looks. She thought she was scrawny with her long, skinny legs. She hated wearing her over-sized, horn-rimmed glasses, which she had worn since the early age of three and with her long, jet-black braids, Mom looked like an Indian.

I'll never forget the joy our mom finally felt when she was in her late forties and was able to get Lasik surgery. She was thrilled she wouldn't have to wear glasses ever again. Unfortunately, our mother never realized she was a real beauty. Regrettably, she always dwelled on her perceived negative features and Mom would continue to feel insecure about herself throughout her lifetime. Her bad habit of smoking began at the age of eleven just like all the girls she hung out with. She'd often boast, "I like smoking. I'll never quit."

Mom loved to tell us tall tales about living on the Indian reservation, and her childhood experiences. My grandpa died in his early fifties, but he lived long enough to see mom's three older children, although he never met my little brother, Dave, who was named after him.

My dad was born in Boston, Massachusetts. He was thin and handsome, with baby blue eyes, and he was Irish Catholic. His mother, whom we affectionately referred to as Honey, was born in Great Britain. Punkie, my grandfather always made me feel uncomfortable. He seemed gruff and impatient, I don't think he liked small children around, but Honey was kind and sweet and she cared about us kids. We loved to sit on her lap as she snuggled us. My dad had four siblings. He was third of five kids. He had lots of energy and was friendly and liked people. When Mom was sixteen her family moved to Henderson, Nevada. She used to babysit for my dad's older sister, Phyllis.

My dad was in the Air Force and he was on leave from Maine. One day he visited Phyllis and Mom happened to be there, he liked her immediately. They wrote letters to each other every day for a year. When Dad returned home to Nevada it wasn't long before they were married, she was only seventeen. Immediately she got pregnant with my older brother and he was born ten months later. Within eight years they added six children to their union. Mom spent her young adulthood sleeping very little. She spent approximately ten years changing and hand washing dirty diapers, squishing carrots and peas and warming baby formula for her babies. It eventually took its toll on the marriage.

She felt my dad never wanted the responsibility of taking care of his large family.

17

Chaos and Kenny

"Let him who walks in dark who has no light, trust in the name of the Lord and rely on his God." Isaiah 50:10b

We moved in with my aunt, uncle, and their six kids and lived there for four months. There was constant commotion between our two families. I thought my mom was mean, but her sister, Lena was even meaner. I did everything I could to stay out of her way, to obey the rules, and keep peace in the household. My cousins' ages ranged from six to eighteen-years-old.

My sister and I met a couple girls our age that lived on my aunt's street. As we walked to the bus stop together they clued us in on the local gossip. Since my aunt and uncle brought seven more people into their home, money was tight. My mother couldn't contribute until she received her welfare checks. One day my uncle and aunt brought home a truckload of gaunt white hens. "Kids come out back, your uncle is going to kill the chickens and you have to help pluck them. They will be our dinner for the next few months," Mom said.

"Oh, how gross," the California cousins, screamed. "We're not going to watch Uncle Ray kill those chickens."

"Yes, you are," screamed my aunt even louder. "If you want to eat you are going to help pluck them too!"

My aunt and uncle gathered us out in the back yard where we watched in horror as my uncle chopped off the chickens' heads. It's true, chickens do run around after their heads are lopped off. It was disgusting, dirty work, pulling the thin feathers off. It was even worse when we knew our aunt would fry the chicken and we would have to eat that tough meat or go to bed hungry.

None of our friends in civilized California would have ever believed we had killed, plucked, and eaten those scrawny chickens.

A few months after moving to Colorado, school started. I arrived at the school bus stop and noticed an attractive, clean-cut, blue-eyed guy.

"Kathy who is that good-looking guy standing over there?" I asked my new friend.

"That's Kenny. I've known him since elementary school. Do you think he's cute? I'll introduce you to him, if you want."

"No, no that's okay," I said shyly.

A couple of weeks later, as my friend and I were walking to the bus stop, a car drove up behind us and screeched to a stop.

"Hey, you want a ride?" Kenny motioned to us.

"Yea, let's go, Debbie. I know this guy, its Kenny the one you thought was a hunk, remember?"

Climbing in, I locked eyes with Kenny and my heart melted.

"Is this your car?" I asked.

"No, I'm not old enough to drive yet. It belongs to my friend and he lets me cruise around whenever I want to. Do you live around here?"

"We bought a house on Kiva road although we haven't moved in yet. Since the house is old and broken down, and overrun with weeds, we work on it every weekend. We should be able to move in sometime in October."

"Oh, I know the house, I live right around the corner," Kenny looked in the rear-view mirror with a great big grin on his face.

He made me giggle as I saw him watching me.

"Where are you from?"

"I came with my mom and five siblings from California."

"What grade are you in?"

"I'm a sophomore."

"Me too, I wonder if we will have some of the same classes."

"I hope so," I whispered to my friend, sitting next to me.

I was enjoying my new school. My sister and I walked to the bus stop every day. Some days Kenny was there, too, and I looked forward to the way he teased me. Everyone was aware I was the new girl in town and I had heard rumors that a lot of boys were interested in me. But I was always insecure about my looks and personality, so I rarely spoke to the boys, although I liked them looking at me. Oftentimes, when Kenny's older friend let him use his car, he'd drive my friend and I to school. At other times, we sat together on the bus.

One day, several weeks after sitting with him on one of our bus rides home, Kenny started mocking a mutual friend. The teasing turned to anger and Kenny and Bob got into a fistfight right in front of everyone. The driver stopped the bus and ordered both boys to get off. Bob and Kenny continued to hit each other as the rest of us watched from the windows. The next day Kenny and Bob came to school joking around as if nothing had happened. I realized that Kenny had a bad reputation for fighting and starting trouble, but obviously there was something about his tough-guy image I liked.

It wasn't long before Kenny asked me to go steady. He started coming over to visit me and he charmed my mother immediately. He'd offer to help out with chores. He'd run errands for my mom and he always brought back her favorite sunflower seeds. Kenny even made up poems to convince me of his genuine love for me. Needless to say, he didn't have to try too hard because I thought about him day and night. It didn't take me long to get over my old boyfriend in California. Even when Jerry came to visit me a few months after we moved, I knew then it was Kenny who stole my heart.

Mom already had several boyfriends after moving to Colorado. We lived near the Army base, so it was easy for her to meet men at the local bars. My brothers where still young, instead of looking for a job, Mom collected food stamps and welfare. Her late-night drinking binges increased. Less than a year after we moved into our new home Mom began drinking heavily. I came home from school one day and found her and her boyfriend drunk. She was sprawled face down, on the living room floor. I was so embarrassed!

When my mother wasn't drinking and our friends came to visit she was usually fun to be around. My sister and I both had boyfriends and we enjoyed having them over. Mom always clowned around with them. She made tacos or spaghetti, and whoever happened to be there at dinner was invited to eat with us.

Our first Christmas in Colorado, we couldn't afford a Christmas tree. A few days before Christmas, Mom was trying to figure out how to get a tree for us kids. All of a sudden there was a knock on the door.

Standing on the porch was my boyfriend proudly holding on to a white, flocked Douglas fir tree. It was the prettiest tree we had ever seen.

It was evident from the trail behind him that he had dragged it all the way to our house. My mom was overjoyed. Kenny had certainly made brownie points with her.

Later he bragged to me when we were alone. "I stole the tree from 7-ll. There is a ditch right beside the store. I just pushed the tree down and dragged it all the way through the drainage ditch till I came to your street."

I was happy we now had a tree to decorate, but it bothered me that Kenny had stolen it. He said it as if he had no conscious. But even that didn't stop me from falling head over heels in love with him.

When my mom went out drinking in the evenings, I continued my habit of staring out the living room window, trying to keep myself awake so I could make sure she came home safely. I had not forgotten her words about her dying at age thirty-five. I'd fall into a deep sleep then wake up suddenly. Walking into her bedroom my heart pounding swiftly, hoping she was home always filled me with anxiety. Sometimes she was safely in her bed other times she wasn't. *Oh God please protect her, please don't let her die!* I counted down to her birthday a few months later, and then I was finally able to relax a little bit when she went out. Although I still waited up for her as long as I could and still worried about her safety.

Mom met and married her second husband, Smitty, shortly after I turned sixteen. He was in the Army, and she let him live at our house for several weeks before they married. The next thing we knew. She left town, drove to Las Vegas and married the guy. We hardly knew him she had only dated him a few months. We kids were livid!

Smitty was big and rotund and he was always drinking beer. After they were married, we saw Mom drunk at home more often, and she still continued to take her prescription drugs.

Mom let my brothers do just about whatever they wanted, but she held a tight rein on my sister and me. My new stepdad was extremely controlling, he and Mom didn't allow my sister and I to go out with our friends.

I spent many days and nights staring out the bedroom window, peering at Kenny's house, hoping he'd come over and visit me. I did this even during our frequent breakups, throughout our high school years. I could see the front of his house from my bedroom window and could see when another girl was there. Lots of rumors were flying around about Kenny being with other girls. After wrestling with my thoughts for a long time I would finally get up the nerve to question him. "Who was that girl who came to your house last night? Her car was there for quite a while."

"Come on babe, she and I were doing homework together. You know I'd never two-time you."

Other times he'd notice me at school looking dejected. "Deb, what did you hear this time?"

"So, and so said they saw you out with Tina, last night. Is that true?"

"No, I was out with the guys. Don't listen to those rumors. You know you're my woman."

Kenny would grab me and hold me tight then he'd kiss me passionately. I always melted in his arms, and I always believed him while blaming and hating the other girls for flirting with him. I'd beg his forgiveness for my suspicions and swear I'd never believe the gossip again. Of course, I believed him. I only felt truly happy when I was with Kenny or spent my time thinking about him. When he came around and professed his love for me, I felt as if my life mattered, like I was finally worthwhile and I was worthy of his love. He became my god and I vowed I would do whatever I could to keep him in my life. Pleasing him and being with him became the most important thing to me. I never wanted to lose his love.

Much later, I'd find out most of the stories of his infidelities were true. Unfortunately, I was so gullible and desperately wanted to be loved, I believed everything he told me. In fact, during most of our dating days, Kenny went to parties while I cried alone in my bedroom, all the while trying to be the perfect, understanding girlfriend.

"I love it that you're not like the other girls. You'll stay home and wait for me." He'd often say.

During one of our many breakups my mom brought home a scrawny German Shepard. I named Bummer. Bummer had a peace sign between his ears and he became my buddy. He'd sleep at the foot of my bed and wait at the bathroom door for me to come out. After Kenny and I got back together, unfortunately, Bummer took second place in my heart. He would often chase Kenny and nip at him. He did not like my boyfriend. I should have trusted my dog's instinct. It would have saved me years of heartache.

18

My First Job

"Lazy people want much but get little, but those who work hard will prosper." Proverbs 13:4

After about a year, we began to really enjoy the state that had become our new home. For the first time in our lives we experienced the four seasons. Raking the newly fallen red and gold autumn leaves and jumping in the piles we made became a fun chore. As winter approached we eagerly waited for the first snow. We'd watch the white flakes drifting downwards tasting the coolness on our tongues when we ventured outside, wrapped in heavy coats, with bread bags covering our tennis shoes and gloves warming our hands. After the long winter, we would enthusiastically watch for tiny, pink crocuses to peek through the frosty ground in the early spring, with their promise of warm months ahead. Summers were filled with late nights, drive-in movies, popcorn, pizzas, and lots of kissing with my boyfriend. All these things confirmed our love for this place we called home.

Mom and her new husband seemed to get along right after they were married, but it wasn't long before they began to argue mostly about who would get the last beer in the refrigerator, or who would make dinner that night. Once they brought home a dog and named him after the beer Olympia (we called him Ollie for short), and they fought about him, too. It seemed like drinking was involved in every part of their lives; even the name of their dog.

Smitty was a cook in the Army, and he helped my brother Mike and me get our first jobs. Mike worked in the mess hall and I worked at the Accounts Receiving office. As a junior, I got out of school at 12:30 p.m. and had to be at work forty-five minutes later. Sometimes my mom would let me drive the station wagon, but usually, if we weren't broken up, my boyfriend took me and picked me up. I worked a three-hour shift, but during Christmas and summer vacations I worked 8 hours. I was so proud to be making $1.60 an hour—much more than I had ever made babysitting.

Time went on and I began to form friendships with some of the army men who worked in the office. We all had pet names for one another, such as Del Monte, or Shaggy, and I was called Dobie. I enjoyed laughing and being silly with the guys. During the course of my shift I had to walk from one building to another and, inevitably, someone would notice me and say hi. After all, I was a nice looking, trim teenager, and a fresh new face on the base. After Kenny and I got back together, I always felt guilty talking to the soldiers in my office and I knew I would get the third degree when Kenny picked me up. As soon as I sat down in the passenger side Kenny would began to drill me. "Did any of those doggies talk to you? Did anyone look at you today?" He kept badgering me: "I bet you're always talking to those doggies, aren't you?"

"You shouldn't call them doggies, that is really derogatory."

"What do you care? Everybody calls them that. I mean it, I better not find out you're talking to them. Promise me you won't ever talk to those guys."

"I won't."

"You better make sure you don't, because I'll kick their ass if anyone tries to talk to you. You got me?"

"Yea!" *Please don't ask me any more questions.*

I soon realized it was just better to keep my mouth shut and quit talking to the soldiers. I also realized if I walked with my head down while I delivered packages to other offices, nobody would say hi to me then I wouldn't have to lie to Kenny about somebody talking to me or looking at me. I don't know why I looked forward to him picking me up. I probably thought his jealousy and controlling ways proved how much he loved me.

Eleventh grade was a great time because Kenny and I dated almost the entire school year. We went to all the dances, football games and drive-in movies. Never had my life felt better. I was working part-time after school and I spent every spare moment with Kenny. But still we fought. I continued to hear rumors about his infidelities and I always blamed myself and begged for his forgiveness. He always forgave me. He never took responsibility for what went wrong in our relationship and I never expected him to. After all, I reasoned if things went wrong, it must have been something I did to cause it.

That year my mom's drinking continued to slide out of control. I still cooked and cleaned and took care of my little brothers and I argued constantly with my new stepdad, about his stupid rules.

Weeks turned into months and I experienced many firsts with Kenny. Skipping school was one first, but I was so worried about getting caught I never did it again. Another first for me was skipping work; a little white lie to my boss took care of that.

"Don't go to work today. Come spend the afternoon at my house. My mom and dad are at work and we will have the place to ourselves."

"No, I'd better not do that. My mom can see your house from our front yard and I can't miss work. I don't want to lie to my boss again."

"You know you want to stay with me instead of working. I will park my car in the alley behind my house. Your mom will never even see my car."

After a little bit of prodding, he would talk me into it. I felt guilty, but it still didn't stop me. It was so much easier to skip work instead of school. I found myself doing it a lot.

The first time I ever got drunk was with Kenny and a group of his friends. I was barely sixteen and my mom didn't allow me to go out to parties. I didn't really want to go to parties. I just didn't want to be left out when Kenny went. One night, when my mom's husband was out of town, she agreed to let me hang out with my older brother and his friends.

"Deb, we are planning on picking up Kenny and his friends." Mike said after I hopped in his buddy's car.

"Oh, thank you," I said to Mike.

We rounded the corner and picked up my boyfriend.

"Hey Mike did you get the booze?" Kenny asked.

"Yea, my friend got it for me. There's Boones Farm, Mad Dog, Ripple wine, and Jack Daniel's. Here, help yourself."

I was so glad to be included and I know it was because of my brother. Kenny rarely took me when he went out with his friends. I wanted to be like the others, so I mixed the alcohol, threw back my head and guzzled whatever I could get my hands on. It was a bitter cold night and ice had formed on the nearby streets.

"Have you ever gone skitching?" One of the guys asked.

"What's skitching?" I asked, naively.

"Stop the car Greg. Let's show Debbie how to skitch," Pete laughed.

A few of us stepped out onto the street and crouched down behind the back of the car.

"Now hold on to the bumper. And whatever you do don't let go." Pete said.

"Go, Greg, take it slow," shouted Kenny to the driver.

"Wow, thus is sooo much fun!" I said, slurring my words, holding on to the bumper as we slid behind the car. We all took turns that night watching each other through the opened windows. We were having a blast.

My next memory was tripping into my house. Apparently, I ran in, missed the bathroom, and threw up all over the hallway while my seventy-five-year-old grandma slept soundly in one of the bedrooms and Mom was out doing some drinking of her own.

Coming into my room the next morning, Mike said, "Deb, after you puked, I cleaned you up, pulled your hair back in a rubber band and put you to bed. Mom is really mad at you. You'd better go talk to her."

"Did you tell her?"

"No, I think Grandma heard everything. She must have told her," Mike explained.

She was waiting in the kitchen. Nervously, I sat down at the table. "I can't believe I got drunk. I'm so sorry it was the first time I ever drank. I know you're disappointed in me and I feel so sick."

"I wish your grandmother hadn't heard anything that went on last night. But I believe you, I know you feel bad. You usually don't do anything wrong. Having a hangover is punishment enough this time. I trust you to make better choices and I am glad your brother was with you."

"I will make better choices. I promise you I won't ever drink again." I reassured her. I couldn't believe she had been so nice to me.

And true to my word, I didn't ever get drunk again as a teenager.

One week later, my boyfriend invited me to go to a party with him, I was so thrilled.

"Mom can I go, please? I won't drink." I wanted my mother to trust me.

"I know you learned your lesson, so I'll let you go. Don't let me down." *Luckily Smitty was still out of town.*

"I won't, you can trust me. Thanks, Mom." I hollered as I ran out to Kenny's car.

19

A Night Gone Bad

"An honest witness tells the truth; a blasé witness tells lies."
Proverbs 12:17

A couple of hours later, I was wondering what all the excitement was about attending a party. It seemed kind of boring to me. The guys and girls were hanging out, talking and drinking. I stood next to Kenny and listened to him boast, brag, and laugh. Kenny and his friends were the only ones I even knew at the party. I felt very uncomfortable being there, but I clasped onto my boyfriend's hand, happy that he had invited me. And true to my word, I had not even sipped a drink.

Walking into the hallway, I followed Kenny as he headed for the bathroom, much like a loyal puppy would. As I stood near the door, waiting for him to finish, two guys walked past me. I noticed one playing with a switchblade pretending to stab at the other guy. I turned to step out of their way. Just then I felt a searing pain above my knee on the outside of my right leg.

"Oh, man, I'm sorry, didn't mean to stab you." Turning to the crowd, Frank yelled.

"Hey, we need some help in here."

The next few minutes flew by as Kenny grabbed a towel and held it on my bleeding leg. Carrying me to his car, he turned on the engine and sped towards the nearest hospital. Suddenly, sirens blared and a flashing red light was behind us.

"Officer my girlfriend has been stabbed. I'm rushing her to the hospital." Kenny explained with a little slur in his voice.

"Hold on, let me pull in front of you and give you a police escort."

My mother was called and came to the emergency room just after my deep gash was stitched up.

"Mom, I swear I didn't have anything to drink, I promise!"

"I'm so sorry for what happened. I know because the doctor told me he didn't smell any alcohol on your breath. And I am very proud of you.

That would be the last house party I went to.

I missed a whole week of school and then had to go back and walk with crutches. I was embarrassed as I walked amidst all the stares, and felt so angry with Frank for cutting me. He never did get in any trouble for it!

Shortly before the stabbing incident Kenny's parents bought him a super-fast, super-cool car for his birthday, it was a 1965 blue Mustang with white racing stripes on each side. All the kids at school ogled over it. Gone were my days of riding the school bus at least while Kenny and I were still dating.

Kenny loved screeching out of the parking lot, revving up his oversized engine. There was always a collection of girls hanging out at his car. I was so jealous and afraid of losing him.

"Kenny, give me a ride in your new car," they'd say.

Eventually, he grew tired of me and decided to take them up on their request. Brokenhearted, I resumed my old habit of spending most of my time in my bedroom, watching out the window as girls drove up to his house. Other times I'd notice him driving up the street with someone else sitting next to him, *in my place!*

A couple of weeks later I found out Kenny was planning to go to Pueblo, a town thirty minutes away, with his new girlfriend and another couple. I watched as he pulled out of his driveway and roared down the street. Sitting alone, in the dark I felt unloved and depressed. *It should be me in that car with him.*

The next day at school while walking to my locker, my friend called out. "Did you hear the news? Kenny got in a wreck last night. Another car hit him. Lorraine was sitting in the front seat next to him and her face was all cut up from the windshield. She has to get plastic surgery."

"Did Kenny get hurt?" I asked, my heart pounding.

"No, no, he and Bob were fine, but Bob's date got a concussion."

Later I told my mom what had happened.

"I'm so glad you and Kenny broke up, otherwise that would have been you in the front seat."

On Sunday, I was sitting in the living room when I heard a knock on my door. There stood my ex-boyfriend. My heart throbbed and a rush of excitement swept over me.

He pulled me outside and looked into my eyes. "What was I thinking? I should have never broken up with you. Lorraine is so ugly! I went over there yesterday to see how she was and she had her hair pulled back. She had pimples all over her forehead. It was so gross. I want you back."

I had secretly hoped Kenny would come back to me. Reaching out to me he kissed me and I melted in his arms. I felt loved once again, but it would prove to be a tumultuous, summer.

Just weeks after we got back together he broke my heart again, he had met someone new. I fell into a deep sadness. After all, I only felt alive and worthwhile when I was with him. He was my world. If he didn't profess his undying love for me, then I felt as if I didn't matter. Part of the summer of 1972 I walked around in a daze, feeling worthless and unloved. I'd hear rumors and gossip about my ex-boyfriend from my friends throughout the summer. Staring out my window I'd often see him speed up and down the street with some girl sitting beside him. All I wanted to do was crawl in my bed and never wake up. Although a new boy got my attention and I went out with him, I continued to focus on Kenny even comparing him to everybody else. No one could fill up that empty hole in my heart caused by his absence.

My senior year began. Walking into first period, I realized Kenny and I were in the same class. My heart did a little pitter patter once again when I looked into those sky-blue eyes, as I watched him shake his shoulder length, chestnut hair. He stood outside the door waiting for me as my new friend Ginger and I stepped into the hallway.

Grabbing me roughly, he pulled me towards him and looked deep into my eyes.

"You want to go out with me again, don't you? I've missed you."

He touched that soft spot in my heart once more and I clung to him. After kissing me passionately he turned and walked with my friend Ginger. They were both in 2nd period together. A few weeks later, I found out he was saying the same things to my new friend. She kept it a secret for a while but I heard a rumor and finally confronted her. "I can't believe you've been hanging out with Kenny. You know I'm in love with him. I've even shown you pictures of us together."

"That's not true! I have not gone out with him. You know how unhappy I've been since my boyfriend was killed in that accident a few weeks ago."

"I'm sorry about Russ, but my friends have seen you with Kenny and they wouldn't lie to me."

After a few days Ginger finally admitted she had been going out with him and promised to stop. It was easy for me to confront the girls, but I would never confront the person who was really responsible, Kenny, of course. Regretfully, at the time I lived in a state of denial. When I did question him, he would just blame the other girl for coming on to him. Like the fool I was, I believed him. In the end though he ended up with Ginger for a while and once again bid me farewell.

They broke up a few weeks later and Kenny reached out to me again. He promised to never break my heart. *Would I ever learn?*

Handing me a poem, he said, "I wrote this myself."

Did you know that god above,
created you for me to love?
He picked you out from all the rest,
Because he knew I'd love you best.
And if I go to heaven, and find you are not there,
I'll write your name on the Golden Stairs.
And if on your judgment day
I find you went the other way,
I'll give the angels back their wings,
Golden harp and other things.

And just to prove my love is true,
I'll even go to hell for you.

Immediately after I read the poem, I vowed my undying love to him. Tears of joy fell down my face. (I found out much later that he didn't really write the poem, but by then I didn't care.) For the next several weeks I did his homework for him, wrote fake excuses so he could skip school and cried every time he went out without me. I promised myself I would not be jealous and insecure when Kenny was out of my sight believing in his eternal love for me.

It was not long after we got back together he began to constantly beg me to give in to his sexual demands. "Ah, come on, we've been going out for over two years and everybody is doing it. You know I love you and we will get married someday."

"No, no I can't. I want to be a virgin when I get married."

I had been fighting similar sexual demands since I dated my first boyfriend when I was fourteen. Kenny finally wore me down. I was tired of fighting. Maybe I really wanted to do it. Who can remember the exact reason, but I finally gave in to Kenny's request. Each month would be a scare until my period came. Relieved, I would pledge to him and myself, "this is the last time, and I mean it!" It never was. I truly believed his promise of a future marriage with him.

And each month when I gave into his demands, I felt used, dirty, shameful, and guilty, but I just couldn't say no. It was necessary for me to feel loved and I mistakenly believed that if I gave him my body he would love me and never leave me again. I thought he would stay with me and never want anyone else.

20

No! Please God, No!

"Not a word from their mouth can be trusted; their heart is filled with malice." Psalm 5:9

A few months after we started going all the way I was convinced I had the flu because I had begun throwing up every morning. I always felt better after my trip to the bathroom and I'd head for school. Sometimes I'd even puke before it was time for work. My period was late, Must have been the flu, I thought, I had heard that threw your whole cycle off. Two weeks later, still feeling nauseous, I was filled with fear.

"Kenny, I haven't started my period yet. I'm afraid I might be pregnant."

"No, you're not, I'm sure you will start."

Later that day I remembered the doctor who had given a health talk at our school a few weeks earlier. With trembling hands, I took his card from my purse and dialed his number.

"Hello, Dr. Watson's office. Can I help you?" The receptionist asked.

"I think I'm pregnant. How do I take a test?" Saying the words made me feel even sicker.

"It's called the rabbit test. Just bring in a urine sample and we can give you the results in a few days. If the rabbit dies that means you're pregnant."

"What was your name?"

Slamming down the receiver, I felt like I was going to throw up again.

"No, no, no please God, I can't have a baby!"

Hours later I reached out to my sister. "Monica, I need your help. I need to take a pregnancy test. Promise you won't tell Mom."

"I won't tell her. What can I do to help?"

"Will you and your boyfriend, pick me up from work and take me to the doctors?"

"Of course," Monica said.

I knew I could trust her. After all, we often shared secrets. Early the next morning, I took a plastic cup in the bathroom with me and peed in it almost to the top, put a piece of foil over it, took it with me in Don's car then he and my sister drove me to my job.

After work we dropped my sample off at the doctor's office. I wouldn't have had the courage to do it without her.

"Oh Miss, we don't need the whole cup, just a few drops," said the nurse.

My face was red. "Oh sorry."

Three days later, I called the office again. "I'm sorry Miss Griswold but your sample was inconclusive. You'll have to bring us another small sample."

The next day, Monica and I drove to the doctor's office and dropped it off. Days seemed to pass in slow motion. Different thoughts raced through my head a hundred times. *If I'm not pregnant I will definitely say "No" to my boyfriend and mean it. That is, it! I will be strong and start over fresh. If I'm pregnant, maybe I could go to a home for unwed mothers, have the baby, adopt it out and come back and resume my life as if nothing happened. There is no way at seventeen, a senior in high school, that I can raise a baby. But on the other hand, I've been taking care of my little brothers for years so maybe I should keep the baby and name him Rusty. And please God, if I am pregnant let it be a boy and look just like Kenny so he'll love me forever. And please let him marry me! But don't let me be pregnant!*

I was dreading calling the doctor but I finally made the call from work. I couldn't risk doing it at home where too many people could overhear.

"This is Debbie Griswold. I turned in a urine sample three days ago. Can you tell me if the rabbit died?" I whispered into the phone.

"Hold, on let me get your file."

My heart felt like it would beat out of my chest. Seconds later the receptionist was back on the phone. "Yes, it's positive."

No, no, please God no; it can't be true! Fleeing out to the parking lot, I saw Kenny waiting to take me home. Feeling depressed and sullen, I hardly spoke a word on the drive home.

"What's your problem?" Kenny said sarcastically, "Did some doggies talk to you today?"

"No, no, I got the results back today from my test and I'm pregnant."

"What? You told me it was negative."

"They wanted me to retake the test and it came back positive."

"Are you sure?" He asked, the blood draining from his face.

Nodding my head, I kept my eyes towards the floor. Neither of us said a word. He stopped in front of my house and before I opened the door, he reassured me. "Don't worry, I will marry you."

The weeks dragged by and several times I found myself in the bathroom feeling like I was going to vomit. Kenny hardly said anything to me as we passed one another in the hallway at school. I borrowed my mom's car and drove to work after school. Each day I found myself more and more depressed, wondering about my future and the status of my relationship with Kenny. I continued to write long letters to him explaining my love for him.

"Did you get my letter?" I asked later when he'd glance my way at school.

"Yeah, but I didn't read it. It's in the drawer with all the others you've written through the years." He said flippantly, as he walked away.

Rumors began to surface about a sophomore named Nancy who was going out with Kenny. But I once again refused to believe them. Shortly afterwards I saw Nancy drive up to his house in her sporty, black, brand-new Camaro. I had my suspicions that this time the rumors were true and I was desperately afraid that he wouldn't marry me.

Days later I was standing in my room, head leaned against the windowsill staring at Kenny's house when my mom came up behind me.

"Debra Ann, are you pregnant?"

"What!" I spun around. "No, no I'm not pregnant. Why would you ask me that?"

"I noticed you have been sick lately."

"Oh, I've had the flu." I tried to convince her.

She shook her head, muttered something under her breath and walked out. I made sure my bedroom door was shut, collapsed on the bed and stuffed the pillow over my face and cried. *I wish I could die right now.* I refused to tell my mom the truth. I was pretty angry with her these days and I couldn't stand her husband. He was controlling, mean and was always saying bad things about Kenny. I hated the way he and my mom sat in front of the television set, eating dinner and drinking their beers, while my brothers, my sister, and I had to sit silently at the dinner table. I didn't mind that my mom and Smitty weren't eating dinner with us, but if we so much as giggled at the table they screamed at us from the other room.

"Shut up in there you know there is no talking or laughing allowed at the dinner table."

It had never been that way before she married that man. I hated him!

Mom had rarely been nice to me since she had married that disgusting man a year earlier. None of us kids liked him. His huge beer belly just kept growing and he enforced his rules with an iron fist, while my mom stood mutely by and watched or took his side. I hated his new rule that I had to be in the house at 9:00 p.m. sharp on a Friday night. One night Kenny and I had gone on a date and we were walking up the sidewalk at 9:05. My mom's jerk of a husband met us outside, with my mom close on his heels, carrying a can of Olympia beer. "You're late!" He yelled.

"It's five after nine, I'm not late."

"You're grounded," he fired back.

I gave him the dirtiest look I could muster and screamed, "I hate you," as I ran into the house.

"I hate you, too," he screamed back.

My mom started yelling at me, too. I was furious! I couldn't believe she took his side. I quit listening. I just wanted to run into the safety of my bedroom. There was no way I was going to tell my mom the truth about being pregnant. Not after what she'd put us kids through.

A few weeks later my mom walked into my room again and kindly said, "I know you're pregnant!"

I burst into tears this time. "How did you know?"

"I had six of my own. Now let's make an appointment and get you to the doctor.

Not only was I was shocked by her reaction but I felt relieved the secret was finally out!

After the doctor checked me he said, "You're pretty young and you're not too far along. Have you thought about an abortion?"

Although abortion had just become legal that year in 1973, I couldn't bring myself to even say the word. I didn't want God to be disappointed in me. Even though I didn't know exactly what abortion meant, I hesitated, but finally said, "No."

I was too scared to get an abortion and too scared to have a baby. I was a senior and I only had a few months before graduating. I needed to finish school. Still I had no idea what I was going to do.

When my pants got too tight, I wore a long shirt with my zipper and snap undone.

I began to tell my friends that Kenny didn't care about me and that I was pregnant believing that they would keep my secret, and hoping for their sympathy. Many felt sorry for me but nobody reached out to me and nobody kept my secret. Before long, I suspected everyone at school knew and whispered about me as I walked through the hallways. Once I overheard one girl say, "Why didn't she just take the pill?"

My self-denial was so strong, I didn't realize until much later I didn't take the pill because then I would have had to admit to myself that I was committing a mortal sin and I was having premarital sex.

Unhappy at home and unhappy at school, my refuge became my job. But even there I stopped joking around with my co-workers. I only talked to my boss, a sweet, older lady who took me under her wing although I still didn't trust her enough to share my problems with her.

Kenny actually started hanging out with me more, but then one minute he was promising to marry me, and the next weekend he would forget about a date we had made. To make matters worse I heard that he was still interested in Nancy. In my ignorance, I still trusted him. I believed he loved me. At the time, I didn't realize he was just coming back and forth to have sex with me, I felt like such a fool.

One day my mom came into my room as I was looking out the window at Kenny's front door. "Has Kenny told his parents yet?"

"No, he said he would soon."

"Well it's been four months. You're going to graduate in less than six weeks. Don't you think they should know?"

"He says he'll tell them, and I'm sure he will!"

Kenny and my mother's husband never got along. In fact, he hated Kenny. He and his best friend Mark wanted to beat him up, but Kenny was underage. Mark was angry with Kenny for calling his wife filthy names. So, he was just waiting for a way to get revenge on Kenny.

A few weeks later, on the night my boyfriend turned eighteen, Smitty and Mark waited outside a club called, "Outer Limits." It was a bar that served 3.2 beers to eighteen-year-olds. It was the legal drinking age back then. As Kenny walked out of the bar, they attacked him and gave him a black eye and bruised his ribs.

The next day Kenny knocked on my door to tell me what had happened. My mom and her husband answered the door.

"Your mom's worthless husband and Mark attacked me last night," he yelled, through the closed screen.

Standing behind them, I noticed my boyfriend's black eye, and began screaming , "I hate you! Let me out, let me out of here!"

"You're not going with him, young lady. You're never going with him again," Mom and her husband hollered as they tried to barricade my way.

Suddenly, Kenny clenched his fist and punched the window in the living room; blood started pouring from his hand. Running out the back door I jumped into his car, which was parked in the middle of the street.

As Kenny and I drove away, I swore I would never go back home again. During the drive to the emergency room we felt like lovers in a romantic, Hollywood movie. This had to be true love, I reasoned. After the doctor stitched up Kenny's hand he eventually took me home. *Where else was I going to go?*

Mom and her husband were in the living room drinking their beers. I walked into my room and angrily slammed the door. I put my head on the pillows and sobbed. Nothing else was mentioned at home after that. I saw Kenny at school and snuck away with him when my parents went out drinking.

A few days later Kenny and I were sitting in front of his television set watching, *The Wizard of Oz*. I overheard his mom answer the phone.

"Yes, this is Evelyn. Are you sure? She is. Oh my!"

"Kenny come here," his Mom called and whispered something to him.

Kenny came back into the room and ushered me outside. "That was your stepdad he told my mom that you are pregnant. I'm so mad. I hate that guy. Come on, I will walk you to your house."

"What did you tell her?"

"I told her it wasn't true."

"What!" Now I was not only angry with my mom and her husband, I was angry with Kenny as well.

"Please tell your parents the truth." I angrily turned and walked into my house.

My mom was waiting for me inside the door. "Why did you tell? Kenny was going to tell his parents."

"He would've never told them and they need to know."

I ran to my room, buried my head in the pillow and cried. Seems like I was doing a lot of crying these days.

21

Too Young to Marry

"Do not gaze at wine when it is red, when it sparkles in the cup, when it goes down smoothly! In the end it bites like a snake and poisons like a viper. When will I wake up so I can find another drink?" Proverbs 23:31-32

"Let your wife be a fountain of blessing for you. Rejoice in the wife of your youth" Proverbs 5:18

My stepfather kept calling Kenny threatening to press charges for the broken window. Since Kenny had had several run-ins with the law for unpaid parking tickets and illegal shocks on his car he was scared of going back to jail where he had previously spent a few hours. Finally, promises of marriage came immediately after my mom's husband reassured Kenny he would not press charges for trespassing and breaking the window if he married me right away. We set the date two weeks after our high school graduation, June 16. 1973.

We went to Kmart and bought our wedding bands. My mother bought me a long, colorful wedding dress. Of course, white was out of the question. I hoped the dress would hide my bulging belly. Although I was self-conscious, I still felt ecstatic that I was getting married. My neighbor fixed my hair, and added a large, white lace bow. Monica was my maid of honor, while Kenny's best friend, Rick stood up with him. We were married in the judge's chamber at the Colorado Springs courthouse.

Our parents stood quietly by the door as our vows were exchanged. Kenny's ring would not fit over his knuckle so my sister pulled out a pat of butter from her purse. We had joked about bringing butter hours earlier.

Taking a smidgen between my fingers, I rubbed the butter on Kenny's ring finger and slipped on the wedding band and happily said, "I do."

As soon as the short ceremony was over, both sets of parents left to throw together the reception in Kenny's back yard. The four of us took our time getting home. We passed the batting cages and the guys got out of the car and hit a few balls. Monica and I watched and cheered them on. Nothing could change the unspoken joy I felt at that moment.

Arriving to see our guests, I was thrilled to see a wedding cake, balloons and party favors strewn on the tables. We cut the cake, fed one another, and his friends laughed when he smashed the cake in my face. He pulled the cork out of the champagne bottle took a swig and poured two glasses of the sparkling wine. I watched my handsome, young husband with his shoulder length hair blowing in the wind thinking how happy I was that my dreams had come true that day.

We spent our wedding night in his bedroom, where we would live for the next two months. He went to work the next day with his dad. I didn't care that we didn't have a honeymoon; I was just thrilled to be married.

Although my mom and siblings lived around the corner, I rarely went to visit them. Sometimes one of my brothers or my sister would come over during the day when Kenny was at work. I spent my days cleaning the bedroom, or laying out in the backyard, pulling up my maternity shirt trying to soak up the sun. There were many afternoons I spent feeling sorry for myself because I thought things would change after we were married, and Kenny continued to go out without me no matter how often I begged him not to.

One day I opened up the bottom drawer of his dresser and found every letter I had ever written him. Several were still unopened. When Kenny returned home from work that day I cried, "You didn't even read some of my letters."

"My dad went through my drawers one day and read them so big deal."

"I can't believe your dad read all the personal stuff I wrote to you." I buried my head in my hands. "Doesn't that bother you?"

"He said you probably got pregnant on purpose just so I'd have to marry you. Now I know he was right."

Burying my head in my hands I cried uncontrollably.

"I'm sick of your crying. I'm going out."

"Please take me with you," I begged as I reached out and grabbed his shirt. "Please!"

Shoving me aside, "get out of my way," he screamed.

I watched him walk past me, helpless to stop him from leaving. "I'm sorry I shouldn't have said anything. I'm so stupid. Please don't leave me."

Sobbing, I fell asleep and didn't wake up when Kenny got home. The next morning, I tiptoed out to the kitchen hoping not to wake his folks up; feeling embarrassed about the events from the night before.

I was sure they had heard Kenny yelling at me, after all it was a small house. I was relieved to find out they were gone.

"Where are your parents?" I asked hours later when Kenny finally got up.

"My mom probably went to get her hair done and I don't know where my dad is."

"Were you drunk last night when you got home? Where did you go?"

"Don't start with me or I'll leave again as soon as I take a shower and you can go over to your mom's house."

I hid my feelings and pretended everything was okay. I made him breakfast and put a smile on my face. I didn't want to spend the day without him.

Every day, I walked on eggshells afraid of saying anything that would prompt him to leave. I had gotten pretty good at burying my feelings. Two months later we had saved enough money to rent our own place. It was a one-bedroom apartment on the other side of town. He picked it out one day after work. Apparently, it was close to his job, but forty-five minutes away from our folks.

There was usually very little money left after payday and we still had not started shopping for baby things even though I was over seven months' pregnant. We had one car. It was a stick shift and Kenny wouldn't teach me how to drive it, so I was stuck home every day. Feeling lonely day after day I decided to decorate our furnished living room with knick-knacks Kenny had taken from his job. He was a furniture mover and he packed up people's personal belongings and moved them from one place to another. I surrounded our small television set with stuffed animals that Kenny had won for me over the last two years.

Since we had no phone and I had no one to talk to anyways, I spent my mornings watching hours of soap operas. Feeling isolated I was almost afraid to leave the safety of my apartment. But at least once a day I forced myself to go outside to the dumpster and throw away our trash. Every night I cooked dinner, never knowing what time Kenny would come home from work. I had no visitors. My sister didn't have her driver's license. My little brothers were all too young to drive and my older brother had joined the Air Force. My mother had a job and kept herself busy. I had no friends.

Kenny started smoking cigarettes, which really upset me.

"You never even smoked in high school. Why are you smoking now?"

"Everybody takes a smoke break at my job and I don't have anything to do. I feel stupid standing around doing nothing."

Kenny would drive me down to our hometown of Security where our folks lived for my doctor's appointments each month. He never went in with me. He waited in the car. After the appointment, he'd drop me off at my mom's house and leave me there all day and pick me up to return home. On the weekends we'd gather up all our dirty laundry, take it to his parent's house and his mom would wash and fold our clothes. Sometimes he would take me driving around with him and meet up with some of his old high school buddies. Most of the time I sat by myself at my mom's feeling left out while he went driving around. Never had I felt so lonely. On Sunday nights, my mother-in-law made a big dinner and I was surrounded with his family. It gave me a chance to get to know my new sister-in-law who was due two months after me with her first child.

I was so unprepared for having a baby. We didn't go to any classes about childbirth. I didn't read any books or even talk to anyone about what to expect. My mom just told me not to scream, it didn't hurt that bad. Most of the time I wasn't even thinking about a baby. I just wanted my new husband to love me and spend time with me. It was easy to forget I was pregnant, until I looked down and noticed my growing belly.

22

Jeremy

"My frame was not hidden from you when I was made in the secret place." Psalm 139:15

On September 11, 1973, I had just turned eighteen. Three days later I woke up with mild cramps. My baby wasn't due for 2 1/2 weeks. I felt uneasy but I had a doctor's appointment that afternoon. Luckily, Kenny would be home from work to take me.

"You're probably in false labor," the doctor explained. "If you keep getting pains you can go to the hospital."

We decided to stay with our parents and not to return to our apartment. At 7:00 pm, the pains were getting stronger and we headed to the hospital. After the doctor checked me, he assured me I was in false labor. "If nothing happens by 10:00 you can go home," he said.

Feeling angry and scared because Kenny had refused to go to a birthing class and not knowing what to expect, I remembered what my mom had told me. "Don't be a sissy girl and scream. Everyone has babies. It doesn't hurt that bad."

I thought, she should know, she had six of them. Later I found out she had a spinal anesthetic, which caused her to feel nothing below her waist, for every one of them. Of course, it hadn't hurt!

It was 9:30 p.m. and my mom decided I should get up and walk around the hospital to hurry the labor process. Thirty minutes later we all found ourselves standing in front of the nursery window, that is when I heard a pop and saw the words POP, in my head. Looking down I noticed water dripping down my leg. "What's happening to me?"

My mom was excited, "Your water just broke."

As I walked back to my room, unbearable cramps began to tighten around my abdomen.

Kenny stood around feeling uncomfortable and the nurse finally told him to leave and wait with everyone else in the waiting room. Mom walked in and out of the delivery room, but she wasn't much help.

The nurse kindly held my hand, "Honey, pant like a puppy dog."

I did and within two and a half hours our son was born. I don't remember it being too painful and I was determined not to scream. I wanted to make my mom proud. She was!

My little bundle was finally placed in my arms, Kenny was called in to welcome our new son. I looked down at my baby, he was tiny; weighing only 5 pounds 10 1/2 ounces. Smiling at the little stranger making sucking noises, I instantly felt a surge of love and fear. *I wasn't ready to be a mother!* The next day Kenny told me he was taking my sister to see *American Graffiti*.

I wish I wasn't in the hospital so I could go, too, I whispered to myself as I watched the two of them walk out of the room. If I had been older maybe my thoughts would have been on my newborn baby. Instead I was consumed with Kenny's attention or lack of it for me and

I was jealous that my sister got to spend time with my husband and I didn't.

Luckily, my mom and Smitty bought us a crib, diapers and some baby clothes, which they set up for us in our one-bedroom apartment. Jeremy was small and had wisps of black hair and bright blue eyes. I fed him his bottle and counted the hours until I could go home. Back to our small apartment with my baby beside me Jeremy and I became a team, while Kenny continued to go out after work and I never knew what time he would come home. Unfortunately, he didn't take the loneliness away I felt and I desperately craved my husband's attention.

Every morning I'd make sure I cooked a hearty breakfast for him no matter how tired I was. After preparing scrambled eggs, bacon and toast I'd ask, "What time will you be home?"

"I don't know, just make sure you have dinner ready."

"Okay, I love you."

Sometimes he would repeat the words, other times he'd walk out of the house with only a wave. My mood for the entire day was determined by Kenny's actions towards me. I would be depressed for hours if he had not said the words I longed to hear, "I love you, too."

After Kenny left for work, I would sit the baby close to me while I watched soap operas and munch on salty potato chips and moist chocolate chip cookies. Early in my marriage I learned to console myself with food. With no phone and only one car (that I couldn't drive), I spent long, lonely days at my apartment, cleaning up after the baby, watching television, and preparing dinner. I'd pop a bottle in my son's mouth and share my fears, anxious thoughts and unhappiness with him, remembering my mom's words, *it doesn't matter what you say, he just needs to hear your voice.* I tried hard to do the right thing. Even though he only looked up and cooed or fell asleep, I loved having his company.

Jeremy was a content baby and seldom cried. The tasks of bathing, changing, and feeding him became routine. I rarely had a visitor and felt like nobody cared about me. Kenny hardly changed the baby's diaper or even held his newborn son. Sometimes Kenny went out drinking right after work. I never knew when he would come home, regardless of the time, I always had a nice warm dinner prepared. As soon as he got in the door, I'd warm it up and wait on him until it was time to go to bed. Other times he'd come home from work start a fight with me, take a shower, slather on his cologne and leave.

"Where are you going?"

"I'm going out with my friends tonight."

"Please don't leave we have a baby now. Can't we go with you?"

"You can stay home and watch the kid. You're the one who got pregnant." He'd say, slamming the door on his way out.

Quite often I'd cry myself to sleep until the baby woke up. Kenny always slept through Jeremy's cries at night. Sleepy-eyed, I'd get him out of his crib, walk into the living room, warm his bottle, feed and burp him. Jeremy was easy and he would go right back to sleep without a fuss. I found myself becoming resentful towards my baby because Kenny rarely took me anywhere. *If only I didn't have him then Kenny would want to spend time with me.* Then I'd feel guilty for thinking those horrible thoughts. It seemed Kenny tried to avoid me as often as he could. Marriage hadn't brought us closer, and having a baby drew us further apart.

Most weekends, Kenny would drop me and Jeremy off at my mother's and show back up late at night or early in the morning after the bars closed. This was not how I had pictured my life. Our fighting consisted of me begging him not to leave as I stood against the door pleading. "Please don't leave me. Don't go out again. Why don't you ever take me with you?"

He'd call me names, make accusations threaten me while shoving me aside. "Get out of my way."

Sometimes he'd hit me in the mouth or slap my face or slug me in the shoulder then walk out with a smug look on his face.

Devastated, I'd throw myself on the bed and cry until the baby woke up. As I went through the motions, changing diapers, warming bottles, talking to him, my thoughts were always on Kenny. *Why doesn't he love me anymore? Why doesn't he want to spend time with me? Why is he mean to me? I must be a terrible person.* Most nights I tried staying awake waiting for him to come home, hoping he'd come home or worried that he'd be involved in some terrible accident and finally exhaustion would get the better of me and I'd end up crying myself to sleep.

The next day Kenny would act like nothing had happened. Sometimes he'd even apologize. One time when he hit me in the face and my eye was black and blue, he convinced me to lie to our folks. "Kenny threw a can of corn at me to put away after grocery shopping a couple days ago and I missed. I feel so silly." I never told anyone he hit me.

When Jeremy was about six weeks old, I ran into a mutual friend of ours from high school. "Hey Deb, my birthday's coming up. You want to go to that new nightclub Superstar with me? They serve beer to eighteen-year-olds." Rhonda asked.

"Kenny would never let me go."

Rhonda bravely approached Kenny a week later. "Can Deb and I go out to the Superstar with me tonight?"

He turned to me, "Promise you won't dance with other guys? In fact, promise you won't even look at another guy."

"You mean I can go?" I looked dumbfounded.

"Ya, I guess, I was going to meet one of my friends anyways. Maybe I'll drive down to the city of Fountain and steal some tires for my car."

I didn't know if he was kidding or serious, I just couldn't believe he was actually letting me go. Rhonda and I spent a few hours getting ready, afterwards, I dropped Jeremy off at my mom's house, and headed for the club.

"I'm so excited, I can't believe Kenny gave me permission to go out. Do you think he's planning something?"

"Like what? I can't remember the last time you went anywhere, without him," Rhonda smiled.

"You don't think he'd go out with Nancy, do you?"

"What made you think of her? I think you are just feeling suspicious. Let's just go and have a good time.

True to my word I did not dance with anyone. Although several guys did approach me, "Hey beautiful, want to dance?"

"No, I promised my husband I wouldn't dance with anyone."

"Your married! Is he crazy letting someone as gorgeous as you come here without him?"

I felt myself blushing. Even though I had just had a baby my thin, small waist had returned back to the way it looked before. I had a nice shape. I was embarrassed he had flirted with me, but I secretly liked the attention I was getting. I knew I would have to keep it to myself. It would only make Kenny mad if he found out. Superstar closed its doors at midnight. As Rhonda and I drove back towards my mom's house, we passed our high school, Rhonda pointed. "Is that Kenny's car?"

"Yes, it is. Why do you think it's here?"

"Let's park and see what happens," she suggested.

Parking up the hill we had a clear view of his car parked downhill. We slouched in the seat and waited. We weren't worried that Kenny would recognize Rhonda's car because he hadn't seen us leave in it. Time passed, but Kenny was nowhere in sight. Eventually, we noticed a black Camaro pull up and park behind his car

"Looks like my suspicions turned out to be true," I shouted angrily.

23

Betrayal

"Give honor to marriage, and remain faithful to one another in marriage." Hebrews 13:4

"He's driving Nancy's Camaro. I'm so pissed right now. You remember that is the tramp he was fooling around with after I told him I was pregnant."

"What are you going to do?"

"I don't know yet."

Quietly, I got out of Ronda's car and tiptoed towards Nancy's car I peered in and noticed my husband sitting in the driver's seat and he was making out with her.

I normally was not a violent person, but I began pounding on the passenger car window. "Get out you b___h! That's my husband you're kissing."

Kenny opened his eyes and began yelling at me. "Get the f___ out of here. I'm going to divorce you b____."

He started the car and pressed the gas pedal while I desperately clung to the passenger side door handle as he turned the corner. I hung on determined to win back my husband.

Banging on the window, I cursed Nancy as she scooted closer to Kenny.

Finally, he jerked to a stop, got out of the driver's seat and yanked me away from the car. Pushing me up the hill towards his parked car, he shoved me inside. He started the engine and sped away hurling accusations at me as he drove. "It's all your fault. You're the one who had to go out so badly. You were probably doing the same thing."

"I wouldn't even dance with another guy. I didn't even look at another guy."

"How do I really know? I wasn't there to watch you."

"You know you can trust me. Why were you kissing her? Did you do anything else?"

"No, we just kissed."

"But you're married to me. We have a baby."

"I didn't even want to marry you, Smitty forced me, I want a divorce!"

Pressing my hands against my ears, I refused to listen to him, his words became a blur. I just wanted him to believe I was a good wife. I hadn't done anything wrong; even though he was trying to convince me everything was my fault.

We stopped to get the baby. He waited in the car, I quickly grabbed Jeremy and couldn't look my mom in the face. I didn't want her to know about our fight and hoped she hadn't noticed my red, swollen eyes.

Screeching around the corner, Kenny continued to scream at me. "I swear first thing Monday morning I'm going down to the courthouse and divorce you. He swung his first at me while calling me names.

I ducked holding Jeremy tightly in my arms, crying loudly. "No, no please don't divorce me. I love you."

"If you don't shut up I will turn this car around and take you and the baby back to your mom's house."

"I forgive you for being with Nancy, please don't leave me!"

He staggered up the stairs to our apartment screaming at me the whole time. I noticed people peeking out of their doors. I was so embarrassed!

"If only you hadn't begged to go to the dance club tonight I would have never gone out with Nancy."

I didn't blame Kenny because I told myself Nancy threw herself at him. "I'm sorry I wanted to go out to a dance club tonight. I'll never go again, I promise." Later after he calmed down he swore he didn't touch her, only kissed her and I believed him.

A few days later I opened up the front door of our apartment and overheard Kenny in the lobby talking on the payphone at the bottom of the stairs. With the door cracked, I listened, still feeling distrustful. He was making plans for another rendezvous with Nancy. Furiously, I stormed down the stairs while he was still talking. He quickly hung up the pay phone.

"Who were you talking to?" I screamed.

Kenny grabbed me, shoved me up the stairs and threw me into the apartment. Then he punched me.

Another punch was coming towards me, covering my head with my arms, I pleaded with him. "Please don't hit me anymore."

"How dare you listen in on my phone calls! I'm leaving you. I never wanted to marry you in the first place. Get your stuff. I'm taking you to your moms!"

Why does he hate me? Why doesn't he love me? What's wrong with me?

Crying loudly, begging him to change his mind, I threw a few things into a bag as he pushed me out of the door with Jeremy in my arms.

Several people stood outside their apartment doors and cheered as we walked by.

"Good, you're leaving. We're so sick of your fighting. Hope you never come back."

Nobody noticed the bruises on my face and nobody reached out to help me. I believed it was my fault. *I should have just kept my mouth shut. I made him hit me.*

Kenny dropped Jeremy and me off and left.

Noticing my black eye, Mom took Jeremy out of my arms and tried to console me. "Did he do this to you, honey?"

"Yeah, but it's my own fault. I couldn't keep my mouth shut."

I told her about our fight and the recent events involving Nancy. "What am I going to do now? Kenny left me!"

My mom just recently divorced my step-dad and had begun attending Alcoholics Anonymous. She had some good advice for me. "It's not your fault and you don't deserve to be hit. You did nothing wrong. He is the one who is wrong. He should not be seeing other women. And you're better off without him."

I didn't want to believe that.

The next day Mom made arrangements for Jeremy and me to stay with one of her new AA friends. "Take some time and think about your life. It would be better if Kenny does not know where you are."

I was lonelier than ever and I missed hearing Kenny's voice and his apologies. I felt so hopeless and alone. Still, I believed the reason he was jealous and possessive was because he loved me so much. I thought if I were a better person he wouldn't get angry and say mean things to me and hit me. If only I was as pretty as Nancy, maybe he wouldn't want to be with her. I was convinced that my husband would love me more if I was thinner and had bigger breasts. I knew that's what he preferred because he made sure to let me know. I thought if I weren't a mother or if I went out drinking with him (although he never invited me) he would want me and only me. I loved my baby but he wasn't enough to help me feel good about myself. I believed only Kenny could make me feel worthwhile. I was ready for him to come back to me. I just wanted to go back and resume my life with him even though I never knew what would set him off. Somehow it felt normal! After all, I had grown up hearing my dad verbally abuse my mother and had watched her boyfriend beat her up.

Kenny too, was going crazy. He called my mom every few hours for days at a time. "Inez, please tell me how I can get ahold of my wife. I'm sorry for how I treated her."

After a few days, my mom gave in and told him how to get in touch with me.

He called me. "I'm so sorry, please come home. I promise it will never happen again."

That's all I needed to hear. My mom picked me up and dropped me off at our apartment. We clung to each other and swore things would be different this time.

And things were different for a couple of weeks. He came home right after work, we ate dinner as a family, sometimes we drove to Security and he actually took me riding around with him as he looked up old school buddies. Then one day he didn't come home till midnight and I knew things with him hadn't really changed. Thus, began the same old pattern, waiting hours for him to come home, hoping he'd walk in the door before the sun set. I'd put the cold food away, tuck the baby in for the night and cry myself to sleep. Sometimes he'd actually come home right after work and I'd sit on the bed while he'd shower and watch him slather on cologne. As he changed into fresh clothes, I'd timidly ask, "Are you leaving again?"

"Ya, I'm going out. Work was tough, the boss yelled at me all day."

"Please don't go, you said you changed." I'd stand against the door, believing I could keep him from going out.

"Get out of my way. This place is filthy. What did you do all day while I was working? You have it made. You don't have to go to work. I go out and work my butt off every day. I work hard and deserve to go out. Now move!"

As he'd raise his fist towards me, I'd duck, move out of the way and hope he'd change his mind at the last minute, but he never did. Just like before, I would run into the bedroom, throw myself on the bed and cry until my eyes hurt, hoping the baby wouldn't wake up. Things hadn't changed at all.

One night after dinner, when Kenny started a fight and went out yet again, I decided to try something different when he got home. I actually got the idea from my favorite soap opera. With the baby tucked in his crib, I put on some sexy new lingerie I had secretly bought a few days earlier, and waited for him to come home. He never took the key to the door of the lobby when he went out, instead he would throw a small rock at our bedroom window, and I would run down to the lobby and let him in. Fortunately, I didn't have to go far, the entrance was right down the stairs from our apartment.

I felt like we were Romeo and Juliet, it seemed so romantic. That night I covered myself with my bathrobe, ran downstairs and opened the lobby door. Kissing him passionately, I took his hand and he followed me to the bedroom. I slipped off my bathrobe.

"What are you wearing? You look so sexy." He threw me on the bed and we made love.

After a few weeks of this Kenny came home from work and gazed at me suspiciously. "My friends at work think you're having an affair."

Shocked, I said, "Why would they think that?"

"Well, every time I come home you have a good dinner on the table. You're so nice, you have your makeup on, your hair curled and you don't try to stop me when I go out."

"I'm just trying to be a good wife. What am I doing wrong?"

"Then you wear your sexy little nightie and when I get home you always want to seduce me. What's that about?"

"I can't believe you are accusing me of having an affair because I want to make love. I'm just trying to make you happy and I want you to stay home. Why are you telling your friends about our private lives anyways?"

Our talk soon escalated into raised voices and cries as I hid my face in my hands, trying to guard myself against the slaps that I knew would come my way.

"My friends are probably right and you never had it so good. You had nothing until I came along. I gave you everything, without me you'd be nothing. You'd still be living in the poor house with your mom."

After a few more shoves, he'd shower, changed his clothes and leave.

Sobbing, uncontrollably I allowed my dark thoughts to overtake me. *I hate myself! I'm such a bad girl even God hates me. I deserve to be treated this way.* I felt guilty and embarrassed for seducing my own husband. After that night, I never again reached for him first.

The next day Kenny came home early and threw his lunch pail across the room. "Well, I've been laid off. We need to move out. We're moving back in with my parents. Pack up the apartment."

And that was that! I did what I was told with no questions asked. We left and moved back into his tiny bedroom. Later that weekend we went back to clean our apartment and get the rest of our things. Once again, the neighbors stood at the stairway clapping as we carried our belongings out.

Somehow, I thought things would be better after we moved in with his folks. Within a few days he began working with his dad at a local warehouse loading and unloading furniture. Most nights the men wouldn't come home for dinner, even though Evelyn, my mother-in-law, always had something hot and delicious waiting for them.

Although she was extremely nice to me it was hard to make conversation when all I wanted to do was feel sorry for myself. Just like before when Kenny did come home right after work, he'd, start a fight with me and go out.

Leaning against the bedroom door, I'd plead with him. "Please don't leave me."

"Move out of my way." He'd shove me or hit me and walk out.

I felt to embarrassed to leave the safety of the bedroom. Holding my son in my arms, I'd sob piteously. For the first few weeks Evelyn left me alone, but then she began coming to the door to our room and tap lightly. "Debbie, will you be coming out for dinner?"

"No, not tonight," I'd say through my tears.

"Would you like me to take Jeremy?"

"No, it's okay! Thank you, though."

"I will take him for you."

"Okay, if you're sure it's no trouble."

"No trouble at all. Can I leave you a tray of food at the door?"

"No, that's okay. I'm not really hungry."

Opening the door, she'd take Jeremy from me and then come back and leave a tray of food for me. I was always ravenous. She knew me better than I knew myself. We never talked about our routine I think we both knew it would happen night after night.

On the weekends when Kenny didn't work he would spend hours cleaning his car. Sometimes afterward he'd take Jeremy and I with him as we drove around looking up his old high school friends.

We had been living with his folks for several months when we ran into some mutual acquaintances from school. Kenny and I made plans to go to Superstar with them. Evelyn agreed to baby-sit. I had just turned 19 and I was excited about finally going out with Kenny.

After a night of dancing and watching Kenny drink, it was time to leave. We all knew that Kenny had too much to drink, but he insisted on driving and none of us tried to stop him. As we drove around laughing and making jokes, Kenny decided it would be funny to drive on the wrong side of the road. Suddenly, a car came toward us; we jumped the curb and landed just fifteen feet away from somebody's front door.

When he slammed into their light posts, near their front door, Kenny sobered up quickly. He jammed the gear into reverse and we drove around the corner, where he parked the car.

We all got out and noticed the driver's side was dented, and the front tire was flat.

"Don't tell anyone what happened," Kenny demanded. "If anyone asks, say you were driving. I've already had too many traffic tickets and I don't want to lose my license again."

"But I never renewed my license when I turned eighteen, I'll get in trouble and besides I can't drive a stick shift."

"Nobody knows that. Just say you were driving. Don't argue with me. It's agreed then. We all have to tell the same story. That is, if we get caught."

I was only too happy to take the blame if we got caught. I wanted my husband to love me and this was one way to prove my love to him. Our friends quickly nodded their heads, we walked to his parent's house, they quickly l left.

The next morning Kenny's dad went outside. "Hey Kenny, where's your car?"

"It's parked around the corner. Last night I turned too sharply and accidentally ran into a high curb and got a flat tire. Come on I'll take you there. We were able to drive the car most of the way home before the tire popped."

Kenny drove with his dad and pointed to a curb near the high school. "See that's where I slammed into the curb." Then he and his dad drove to where the car was parked.

His father eyed him suspiciously. "What happened here? It's all dented in. Looks more like you've been in an accident."

After changing the tire, they drove the car home and parked it in the driveway. Kenny thought we were home free.

Later that evening a policeman knocked on the door.

"Kenny, what are we going to do? I'm scared," I whispered to him.

"Just stick to the story." He gave me a stern look

The policeman walked in and noticed Jeremy sitting in his high chair. He looked kindly at Kenny, then at me, then back towards the baby. Casually, he asked, "Is that your baby?"

"Yes, his name is Jeremy." Kenny said.

"Why is your car dented?"

We told him about hanging out with our friends and then Kenny mentioned the story about running over the curb.

The police officer said, "Would you mind going over to pick up the other couple? I would like to talk to all of you."

Kenny borrowed his mom's car and we went to pick up our friends. We were all a little shaken but we decided to go along with the story Kenny had suggested.

"There was a hit and run last night and the man whose light pole you ran into was at the front door after he heard the crash. He wrote down your license plate number. I checked your car while you were gone and the dents matched up with his damages. You want to tell me what really happened? And who was driving the car?" The policeman asked.

Feeling nervous, I stammered, "I, I was, sir."

He looked from me to Kenny to the other couple. "Is that true?"

We all nodded our heads in agreement.

"You know this is going to cost you your license. Are you sure you were driving?"

Trembling, I was determined to prove my love to Kenny. "Yes sir, I was."

"Were you drinking?"

"No, I wasn't." *That part wasn't a lie.*

"Well I really like your son here and I realize it was an accident so I will only give you a ticket for driving with a suspended license and leaving the scene of an accident. But make sure you never drive like that again. Is that clear?"

"Yes, yes sir. Thanks."

He wrote me the ticket and left. "Take care of that baby. He sure is cute," he said on the way out.

"He knew we were lying." Kenny whispered. "It was because of Jeremy. My mom said he was playing with him the whole time we were gone. The funny thing is you don't even drive a stick shift," he laughed.

I hating lying to the police and I didn't think it was funny. I just felt guilty.

My license was only suspended for a few months but it would be years before I would drive again. I figured out later Kenny liked having me stuck at home.

I didn't spend much time with my mom that year I lived at Kenny's childhood home. Since my mother and father-in-law both worked full time, I spent the days alone with Jeremy at my side. My mom worked and spent her spare time going to Alcoholic Anonymous meetings. Occasionally my sister and brothers came over but I rarely went anywhere. I was too embarrassed to put Jeremy in the old-fashioned pram my mom had purchased at a garage sale.

I spent most of my time cleaning our bedroom, doing our laundry, watching television and hanging out with my son. I counted down the minutes until my husband would come home hoping he would actually come home right after work.

I never cooked a meal. Evelyn never asked me to help and I never thought to offer. We ate together in silence when the men didn't show up. I had no friends to talk to. When I occasionally walked across the street to visit my family I felt lonely still wanting desperately to feel loved and accepted by my husband. Sometimes on the weekend Kenny's brother and his wife would come over with their baby who was only six weeks younger than Jeremy. I looked forward to the times we spent together.

We never completely stopped fighting and Kenny continued to stay out late and drink usually with his dad.

"Don't leave me," I continued leaning against the bedroom door hoping he'd change his mind and stay home.

He always shoved me out of the way. "Get away from the door. You know it doesn't do any good. I'm still going out."

He tried not to yell too loudly as his parents were in the next room but sometimes he'd raise a fist and blacken my eye instead. Afterwards I'd stuff my face in the pillow so no one could hear my sobs and I'd berate myself for causing him to hit me, yet again.

The next morning, I would be ashamed to see his parents, but Kenny always made up a fake reason. "I accidentally slugged her in my sleep, didn't I, Deb?"

"Yes, you did," I'd say.

Sometimes after coming home late from nights of binge drinking, Kenny was too lazy or too drunk to walk to the bathroom and he'd open the window and puke outside.

"Kenny," his mom would yell the next morning, "what's this out your bedroom window."

One of us would get up, run outside, (usually it was me) turn on the hose and squirt the side of the house till all the vomit was cleaned up. "Sorry mom, I'll never let it happen again."

Then there were the days when Kenny couldn't go to work because he was still drunk from the night before. "Hurry call my boss tell him I'm sick and I can't go to work today."

"Of course," I'd say. I would go to any lengths to protect him, and we couldn't afford for him to lose his job.

We never paid his parents any money. We could come and go, as we liked. We never bought groceries or even took them out for a meal. I never even thought about paying them back for their extreme kindness in letting us live there rent-free. Finally, after a year we moved into our very own apartment once again.

24

Sober?

Don't be drunk with wine, because that will ruin your life. Instead, be filled with the Holy Spirit." Ephesians 5:18

We still had no phone, but there was a payphone downstairs in the lobby right below our apartment. On paydays Kenny and I would go shopping together, pick out a sliced honey-baked ham, buy some French bread and go home to our very own place and eat sandwiches together. I never shopped alone. I didn't drive and I never carried any cash. I fixed Kenny breakfast each morning, packed his lunch, kissed him on the cheek, and waited for him to come home. In the meantime, I cleaned up the place, played with the baby, bathed and dressed him, and sometimes took him for a walk around the inside of the apartment complex. I was too fearful to walk around outside the building. Continuing to watch soap operas and getting caught up in the world of make-believe when Jeremy took his long naps was my way of escape.

One time I did venture outside with my son pushing him in the oversized pram. Fear gripped me while I stood at the crosswalk near a busy intersection. As I crossed the street I imagined I could hear people saying, "*What's she doing walking down the street? She's ugly and worthless. She's no good. She got pregnant before she was married. Her father molested her and it was all her fault.*" I quickly ran back to the safety of my apartment.

One day I went to do the laundry inside the apartment building. I noticed a little girl about Jeremy's age and her mom standing near the washer. "Hi my name is Sue and this is Charlene. What's your name?"

"I'm Debbie and this is Jeremy."

Sue said, "We just moved in and I don't know anybody."

I was thrilled to meet a friend. Sue was a nice Mormon gal about my age. We would sit in our apartments together and talk while we watched the kids play. Sometimes we even went downstairs and took our children to the indoor pool. It was nice to finally have company during the day.

Nights were still the hardest, especially after payday. I would cook a nice meal, and then eat with my son while I'd wait for my husband to come home. After waiting several hours, with Jeremy on my hip, I'd go down to the payphone at the bottom of the apartment stairs in the lobby and call the local bars. "Is Kenny there?"

"No, he just left."

Sometimes the bartenders would ask, "What does he look like? No, sorry, haven't seen him."

Night after night it was the same scenario. Sometimes he'd hear about my calling and come home angry and scream at me. There were the usual fights, he calling me names, and shoving me. Sometimes he'd repeat, "You were nothing till I met you, and you'll be nothing when I leave you."

Shortly after I met Sue, she invited me to go with her to the woman's group on Tuesday mornings at her church. It was fun. We learned how to cook sourdough bread. We sewed and made crafts. I heard talk about God, which I liked. I even joined the woman's basketball team. Kenny wasn't very supportive. He went to my first game and promptly made me quit, yelling at me all the way home, "Other guys might be looking at you. I don't want you out there with your short shorts and tank top."

I cried and begged him to change his mind, but he wouldn't. Soon afterwards I stopped going with Sue to her woman's group too. Kenny didn't approve.

After payday Kenny would lay the money out on the table and count what we had left for the week. "This is all we have, you need to get a job. I'm sick of you sitting around this house all day doing nothing. It must be nice to sit around and watch TV while I go out every day and work my butt off. I'm tired of being the only who works in this house."

I didn't want to leave Jeremy but my desire to please Kenny became more important. After sharing the news with my sister, she told me about her friend who worked at a restaurant and they needed people to bus tables. I was so excited and my sister and I both got the job. I talked to Sue about the possibility of watching Jeremy while I worked. At first Kenny seemed happy with the news so Monica and I started training for three days. I hadn't work since I got married and I enjoyed being away from the house for a few hours. I learned how to set up the coffee machine, and clear the tables. My first day on the job would be on Saturday.

Saturday morning, I woke up early and started getting dressed.

"How you getting to work today?" Kenny asked.

"Aren't you taking me?"

"No, and I'm not watching Jeremy either."

"What am I going to do they are expecting me to come in. I have to show up."

"You need to quit after today, I don't want you working anymore."

"Please keep Jeremy today. I promise I'll quit after I finish my shift."

"Well you better not talk to any guys. You hear me," Kenny screamed.

"I won't. I promise."

Reluctantly, I called Sue and she drove me to work. I told the boss it was my last day. He paid me in cash. After my shift was over Kenny pulled, up kissed me and took my ten dollars. So much for working!

A couple weeks later I would be turning twenty. Kenny invited Sue and her husband, Brett over to help me celebrate my 20th birthday. He bought me a low-cut long, sexy, black dress and a dozen roses. Kenny always liked to make a big deal of things when there were people to impress, of course I didn't realize it at the time. Sue baked me a cake and the four of us, and our kids, sat around eating and talking. It was so much fun. After they left Kenny looked at me suspiciously, "I saw you flirting with Brett."

"What are you talking about?"

"Don't play innocent. I saw the way he was watching you in your sexy dress. I could tell he was thinking about having sex with you. Don't act like you didn't notice." He raised a fist at me.

I ran into the bedroom as he pulled at my dress and tried to rip it off of me. Grabbing Jeremy out of his room because he was crying hysterically, I tried to reason with my husband, but he just stood over me calling me names and make allegations against me. Finally, he slammed the door and left. After consoling Jeremy, I buried my head in the pillow and sobbed and cried myself to sleep.

After that, I tried to avoid Sue, making excuses about why I couldn't hang out. I couldn't tell her what Kenny suspected. Eventually she stopped coming over and they finally moved away. I was so lonely with only a small child to spend my time with.

One day there was a knock on our apartment door. It was an acquaintance from high school. Myrna had been popular in high school and I couldn't believe she was standing at my door. "I found out you lived here and I want to take you to lunch."

Going out to lunch was so foreign to me. Who did that anyways? And Kenny would never allow it even if I wanted to!

"I will have to call and ask Kenny's permission first, but I'm sure he won't let me go anyways"

She gave me a hug. "Get your coat, let's go. We will just walk next door to the fast food place. I'm sure Kenny won't mind." She said as she grabbed Jeremy's hand.

"I don't have any money."

"Silly, I'm going to pay for it, I invited you."

"Oh no, I can't let you do that. I'd better run down to the pay phone and call Kenny's work and ask him if it's okay."

"Debbie, It's fine. We won't be gone long. I will have you home long before Kenny gets home from work."

"I don't want him to get mad at me."

"You're not doing anything wrong. It will be okay, trust me."

After much cajoling, she talked me into it and the three of us walked across the street and sat down for a lunch of hamburgers and French fries. Once I relaxed, I started enjoying myself.

"It's so nice to be out of the apartment."

It was even better to have someone to talk to. I was so grateful to Myrna. Over the next few months she'd pick me up take me down to the city of Security where she still lived. It was only a few miles from my mom's house and Kenny's folk's house. She would make lunch for Jeremy and me. I was always back home in time to make Kenny dinner. Sometimes he even met me at Myrna and Frank's house for dinner. I was so grateful to have a friend.

During this time, my mom had been attending AA for over a year. She showed up at my door unexpectedly one day, "Debbie, you need to go to Alanon."

"What's that?"

"I believe your husband is probably an alcoholic and Alanon is a support group for friends and families of people with drinking problems. It's based on the twelve steps of AA but it's for people who don't drink. They learn how to live and be happy in spite of the fact that they're married to alcoholics."

"But Kenny's not an alcoholic. He doesn't get drunk every day." I was angry with her for even suggesting it.

"Listen to me, he doesn't have to drink every day and get drunk all the time. It's what happens when he drinks. It changes his personality. He tells himself he's going to stop and he can't. An alcoholic will deny he has a problem while he's falling down drunk, even after he's lost his job and his family. He will blame everything and everybody else but his drinking. It's a disease of denial. He denies he has a problem and his family and boss keep protecting him and they deny he has a problem. But the family gets sicker and sicker right along with the alcoholic."

I did not know what she meant when she said the family gets sicker and sicker.

She said a higher power could restore me to sanity, *was she saying I was insane?* She explained how she had found a higher power that gave her courage to stop drinking one day at a time. She admitted her thoughts were twisted in her drinking days. "I am an alcoholic and I didn't get drunk every day, but I still had a drinking problem and an addiction to my pills. That's why I acted the way I did."

I was still confused. "But Kenny works hard every day and he pays the bills. How is he an alcoholic?"

"Does his drinking ever cause a problem for you guys? Do you call in sick for him? Do you take the blame for him? Does he act like a different person when he's been drinking?"

She knew I had to answer yes to all those questions. She got me thinking. Weeks went by and she kept prompting me to get help. She found a group that met close to my house on Wednesday mornings.

"The meeting only lasts an hour and there is childcare available. I even talked to someone and a woman name Rosa will stop by and pick you up."

"But Mom, I can't go. Kenny would never allow it."

"Kenny won't even know you left the apartment. He will be away at work on Wednesday mornings and without a phone he can't check up on you. Don't be afraid."

"But I'm scared of what he'd do if he found out."

"Please, just try it, I will do whatever I can to help you out," my mom reassured me.

The next day was Wednesday, I somehow found the courage to get Jeremy dressed and wait outside for the women my mother had spoken to. Rosa was eight years older than me and she agreed to pick me up and drop me off every Wednesday morning after that. Each Wednesday I was sure Kenny would know I was attending my meeting but every week I began to feel stronger and vowed that I would continue. Jeremy even liked having other kids to play with at the nursery.

The first thing I learned was to quit arguing with Kenny. At the meetings, I heard things such as: Just keep your mouth shut, especially when he's been drinking. You can't reason with a drunk, and he can't argue with himself. Quit calling the bars. Don't pour his alcohol down the drain, he'll just get more. You didn't make him drink and you can't make him stop. It's not your fault he drinks. He had a problem long before you married him. There were phrases such as "live one day at a time," "keep it simple," and "let go and let God." It was a different way of looking at life. I was beginning to understand what the words "sick" and "insanity" meant. Alanon defined insanity as doing the same thing over and over and expecting different results. I had never heard that definition before. The more I kept an open mind and examined my motives, and beliefs, the more I realized how irrational and unreasonable I had become by believing I was powerful enough to make Kenny behave in a certain way. If I just treated him well and cared more about him he would want to change. I had been living in denial and Alanon was giving me the tools to reach for sanity, one day at a time.

I realized that insanity in my relationship meant I focused more on Kenny than on myself and my child. I let Kenny dictate my self-esteem, blamed myself for his addictive behavior and his meanness. I tried to hide the fact that my husband had a drinking problem, tried to control his behavior and made excuses for him. I originally attended Alanon because I wanted some pointers on how to get him to stop drinking, soon I began to realize the program was about changing me for the better.

Kenny never drank at home and we didn't keep liquor in the house. He simply stayed away from home and drank after work or he'd come home, initiate a fight, take a shower, put on his cologne and stay out till all hours of the night, all the while blaming me for the fight.

It gave him a good excuse to get drunk. I also learned alcoholics need a reason to make excuses for their drinking. I was beginning to quit blaming myself for his drinking.

I was slowly learning what serenity meant. God became my higher power but it was not easy to trust him with my fears and emotions. For instance, every time Kenny went out I would ask God to help me to think positive and to not blame myself for him leaving. I tried not to take it personal every time he left to go drink. I also asked God to help me sleep at night instead of lying awake wondering if Kenny would come home safe. I could actually fall asleep feeling peaceful. Although at times, I felt like I was taking one step forward and two backwards, but at least I was working the program and trying to grow and change.

Kenny began to get suspicious. "You're too nice. How come you're not begging me to stay home? Are you messing around on me?"

I refused to argue with him. It was hard to hold my tongue when he started accusing me. I desperately wanted to defend myself and I was sure all my good actions would someday lead to his sobriety. I finally got honest with him and told him I was going to my meetings.

Not long after I started going to my 12-step program we went on our first vacation. It had been six long years since I had moved to Colorado and we decided to go back to my childhood town. Driving to my old neighborhood in Fontana, California, I was excited to introduce Kenny to my old friends who I still kept in touch with. The two weeks we spent there was amazing. Kenny even spent time playing with Jeremy, who was nearly three. We seemed to grow closer and we didn't argue about anything. There was even talk about adding a second child to our family.

As soon as we returned to Colorado we were fortunate enough to buy a house. It was a three-bedroom ranch-style home on a corner lot.

It was about five miles from where our parents lived. We were thrilled to be back in Security. Kenny's mom and dad lent us the money for the down payment and we moved in with hardly any furniture. But we didn't care. It had a big fenced-in backyard, and we got our first dog and named him Toby. Kenny enjoyed doing yard work and he expected me to help every weekend. He was overjoyed to finally have a place to wash and maintain his Chevy Nova. Kenny hadn't taught me how to drive a stick shift. I was twenty-one and I hadn't driven for nearly three years.

Life seemed peaceful in our new home for a while. Kenny even stopped going out drinking. We acquired furniture, Jeremy and Toby played outside every day, and we made friends with the neighbors. I was getting used to Kenny working overtime nearly every Saturday. At first it was hard, but the extra money sure was nice.

One day the neighbor across the street noticed I never drove the car.

"Debbie, do you know how to drive?"

"Yes, but I never got my license renewed after I turned eighteen and I can only drive an automatic, which we don't have." I didn't think it was important to tell her about me taking the blame for the car accident when I was nineteen.

Betty kindly let me practice driving her car and a few weeks later she took me down to the DMV to get my license. Of course, I had no car to drive but at least I had my license.

I was still attending my weekly 12-step meetings. Since things were still going so well between us, Kenny didn't try to stop me. Rosa still picked me up. Our house in Security was even closer to her. Rosa and I became good friends on our drive to and from the meetings.

25

Kristy

Behold, children are a heritage from the Lord. The fruit of the womb is a reward." Psalm 127:3

Kenny and I were almost twenty-two. Kenny had gotten rid of the Chevy and bought a used Dodge Dart and this car was an automatic. Occasionally, he'd let me drive him to work then I was able to use the car to run errands or go to my job. I had just started working at a nearby elementary school as a part-time, on-call teacher's aide. I was so grateful that my neighbor, Betty had offered to watch Jeremy whenever I was called into work. She had four girls and one was Jeremy's age. I think she liked having a little boy around.

I loved hanging out with the school children and felt more comfortable on the playground with them instead of sitting in a stuffy break room filled with women eight to twenty years older than me. Even when I didn't have playground duty I'd still go outside and the little kids would come up to me. "Teacher, can I hold your hand."

Actually, I loved them all vying for my attention and we'd walk around the play yard laughing and talking. It wasn't long that I began to get an uneasy feeling as I watched the little girls play. I was a little child their age when my dad molested me. I noticed how tiny they were and felt physically sick thinking about what he had done to me. Sometimes on the way home I'd cry for the little girl I once was. Other times I felt comfort as I held the children's tiny hands throughout recess. I never wanted the bell to ring. I wanted to keep all those little ones safe, so they wouldn't have to ever experience what I had gone through.

In the summer of 1977 we prepared for the birth of our second child. My baby was almost due and I begged God for a girl this time. Sure enough, Kristy Debra was born twenty-four hours after my water broke. Even though labor was a lot harder and more painful than with Jeremy I still opted for a natural childbirth with no medications. This time I read books and Kenny had even gone a few times with me to my Lamaze class. I proudly held my tiny five-pound baby in my arms and thanked God for his precious gift.

Months earlier Myrna, my old high school friend and her husband bought a house behind ours. She had just had her first child whom she was breastfeeding and she talked me into trying it with Kristy. At first, I thought it was gross, a baby sucking at your nipple but Myrna began to convince me it was normal. After all, that's why women have breasts, she'd say to me.

She lent me a book about nursing, I read it and was eager to do the best job I could feeding my baby.

Kristy was born two weeks early and had a condition called jaundice. Jaundice refers to the yellow color of the skin and whites of the eyes caused by excess bilirubin in the blood. I tried to nurse her right away but my doctor asked me to stop, he believed that breast milk made the jaundice worse. Kristy was put under special lights at the hospital to help rid her body of the excess bilirubin. It was not a serious condition but it was heartbreaking knowing I couldn't bring my baby home from the hospital for almost a week after she was born.

Myrna encouraged me to pump my breasts and freeze the milk. "There's still a chance you can nurse her."

I went to the hospital every day and spent time with my baby giving her a bottle. Finally, it was time for Kristy to come home.

"Are you still going to nurse her?" Kenny asked.

"Yes, I want to try. I have been looking forward to it, since I didn't with Jeremy."

"I think you should just give her a bottle. She is used to having one now."

"Please, can I just try?"

"All right but if she doesn't eat today, you just better put her back on the bottle."

Reluctantly, I agreed, I was still afraid to do anything without Kenny's permission.

All through the morning I tried to put Kristy to my nipple but she refused. I called Myrna, feeling discouraged. "What should I do? Should I keep trying?"

"Don't give up. Even though she's used to having the bottle I know she'll come around. I'll come over and get Jeremy. After he's gone and the house is quiet, relax on the bed and take off your shirt let her feel your skin. Try not to tense up. Please don't give up. It will all be worth it, I promise you."

This was something I really wanted to do. But I could hear Kenny's words echoing in my head. *If she doesn't eat today you better put her back on the bottle. Just forget about trying to breastfeed her.*

All day I refused to give her the bottle and I continued to try and coax my newborn into nursing. I still had to clean the house and start dinner. It was six o'clock and Jeremy had been home for a couple of hours. He was playing in his room. Dinner was warming on the stove. Sitting down with Kristy, I unbuttoned my shirt, but she still refused to drink and I was getting worried, Kenny would be getting off of work soon.

Just then, his car pulled in the driveway. I knew he'd question me. *Did she eat?* And then he would order me to bottle feed her, even though I didn't want to. I knew I would not be able to fight his control. *Please God, let her eat,* I said under my breath. Instantly, I felt her latch onto my breast and heard her gulp. She was nursing. She was nursing!

As Kenny walked in the door, he glared at me. "Did she eat?"

"Yes," I said with a satisfied look on my face.

From that day on Kristy nursed until the tender age of twelve months.

The reprieve we had in our relationship was only temporary. Kristy was just a few weeks old when Kenny started drinking again. Since having the baby, I hadn't gone to any of my meetings.

Kenny got impatient when the baby cried. He got angry cause his dinner wasn't on time. After late night drinking bouts, I started arguing with him again. He didn't like me hanging out with my only friend, Myrna. He'd show up more often during the day, unannounced, hoping to catch me in compromising circumstances; such as the time I had a water fight with the neighbor kids in our back yard wearing a two-piece bathing suit. I should have been inside scrubbing the floor. "You just want those teenagers to see you in a bathing suit," he had accused. Other times he'd say, "Why are you watching TV? The dishes have not been washed. Dirty clothes are on the floor and you're sitting here wasting time while I am out working my butt off for you and the kids. This place better be clean when I get home." *Of course, it always was.*

One morning after I had cleaned up Kenny's vomit, fed the kids, changed the baby's diaper and put dinner in the crock-pot, I started feeling overwhelmed again. I thought things had really changed and I was disheartened. Kenny had not really changed his bad habits and it was too easy for me to fall back into mine. I was tired of being afraid of my husband and his violence. I was sick of his accusations and the things he did to control me. I was worn out from walking on eggshells all the time and trying to defend myself. It was just too exhausting now that I had two kids to care for. I felt like a child asking for permission to do the simplest things. "Can I drive the car or go to my meeting? Can I take my neighbor who doesn't have a car to the grocery store? Can I have a few dollars?"

Even though I had gone to meetings for over two years I felt like I had no right to my own opinions. My life still revolved around how Kenny would act, react or feel about something. I wondered, was it really supposed to be like this?

One morning after a fight with Kenny the night before, I was standing in the kitchen doorway talking to my friend on the phone. "Myrna, I'm so unhappy. Kenny never helps with the baby. He always comes home late. I never know where he's going after work. He tells me he got drunk and fell asleep in the car. Come on, almost every night till four in the morning! He constantly yells at me and accuses me of wanting to be with other guys. Even the smallest things make him angry. Either I made the wrong thing for dinner or the house wasn't clean enough. I'm still so afraid of him."

"Debbie, does he ever hit you?"

Hesitating, I finally blurted out, "Yea, sometimes he does hit me."

Just then I heard footsteps behind me, the phone went dead immediately, I felt a sharp pain between my shoulder blades. I turned and Kenny had his fist raised towards my face, ready to hit me again. I ducked!

"I heard what you said. Next time I'll hit you in the face. You've never had it so good. If you don't like the way I treat you, get out. Go back and live with your mom. You were in the poor house till you met me. You're lucky I married you."

Raising a fist, he taunted me; I cowered in the corner of the laundry room.

"Why don't you ever stand up for yourself?" Dropping his hands to his side, he gave me a dirty look and walked out. "You are pathetic! You're lucky I have to go to work now or I'd hit you again."

This time I watched him drive away, still sobbing, I called Myrna back.

"What happened? Why did the phone go dead?"

"Kenny overheard me! I thought he had already left for work then he hung up the phone and slugged me in the back. He told me to leave if I didn't like the way he treated me."

"Debbie, you need to get out of there now."

"I can't leave! I have a six-week-old and a four-year-old. Where am I supposed to go? I'm so scared of him. I don't know what he'd do to me if I left."

"Call your mom. You can't stay there. Don't you realize you are an abused wife?"

"What do you mean?" I wailed into the phone. "Kenny doesn't hit me every day, just once in a while. I probably deserve it, anyways. Sometimes I have a hard time keeping my mouth shut. If only I didn't talk back to him. I should not have been talking about him. And I really should try harder to keep the house clean. It's all my fault."

"Don't you realize you are never to blame when someone hits you. He's making you believe it's your fault. Remember what you told me about your mom's boyfriend he used to hit her and she blamed herself. You sound just like her. You're repeating your mom's past. What's your mom's phone number? I will call her while you get the kids up and ready to go someplace. We need to get you out of there right away."

Halfhearted, I gave her my mom's number although I really didn't want to involve my mother. I still did not understand anything Myrna had said. *What did she mean I was an abused woman?*

Thankfully, my mom made arrangements for me to stay at a place called the County Poor Farm. One of her AA friends had just purchased it. Myrna came over and we packed the kids and a few belongings into the car. We did it as fast as we could in case Kenny showed up unannounced for lunch, which he often did. Myrna drove me to the County Farm. I had never been so scared in all my life. I was leaving my husband. I had no money and no possessions, only my two children at my side. Myrna stayed long enough to help me settle into my room.

The County Farm was a huge house on several acres. I was told it might have been an orphanage at one time. There were several dormitories, a kitchen, several bathrooms and offices. Families who were homeless could live there for a few days or weeks until they got on their feet.

We stayed in one of the dorms. There were over fifty beds in one long room. Jeremy thought we were on an adventure. We chose a bed toward the back of the room. I scooted our twin beds together and placed the bassinet near us. Kristy was easy, all she did was eat and sleep. Jeremy was good-natured, he took my hand while I carried the baby and we explored our surroundings. I felt brave and scared all at the same time. But I felt guilty because Kenny had no idea where we were.

There was a pay phone outside the cafeteria. I had enough change to phone my mom after dinner.

"Kenny called again looking for you. I told him I didn't know where you were."

"But Mom, he's going to be so mad at me. I don't like this."

"Debbie, your husband needs to go to Alcoholics Anonymous and stop drinking. He needs to realize he can't mistreat you anymore and you are the only one who can convince him of that. Please don't call him. He needs to think about the way he treats you."

"Okay, I won't call him but what if he finds out where I am?"

"He won't and don't worry you're safe there. Everything's going to be fine. Just take some time to think about your life. I want you to get to a place where you never allow your husband to hit you again."

"But Wes hit you and you always said it was your fault. Sometimes I think when Kenny hits me and I deserve it and I'm too blame."

"I was wrong for putting up with it, when a man hits a woman it's never the woman's fault."

"But Mom, he doesn't hit me all the time. He's only hit me a few times since we have been married."

"Once is too many times. I was wrong to put up with it. I didn't know any better and I was drunk most of the time Wes hit me. Hopefully you can learn from my mistakes. You're still young, don't wait as long as I did to believe you deserve to be treated better."

The first night was lonely. It was frightening to be in that great big room with all the empty beds surrounding me. When we arrived, we were the only ones at the County Farm except for the employees.

After tucking the kids into bed and waiting for them to fall asleep, I laid awake with a bright lamp overhead and thought about my life. What was going to happen? I loved Kenny and believed if only he stopped drinking all our problems would be solved. When I got tired of thinking I pulled out a book I had found in the library earlier that day and began reading until I fell asleep.

To my surprise, a couple days later another family arrived, a man, his wife, and their two toddlers. Finally, I had company. The woman, Leslie, and I enjoyed each other's company right away. She and her husband were homeless. They invited me to go to the drive-in that night. We all climbed inside their old station wagon and watched as the movie began. Her husband pulled out a bottle of wine and a few cans of beer and began to drink. During intermission, Leslie and I took the kids to the playground and laughed and played with them. I had done something without asking Kenny's permission. It felt good.

Leslie's husband drove us back to the farm, clearly drunk, and it didn't occur to either Leslie or me to drive. Obviously, we both shared the same kind of life. The next few days Leslie and I spent a lot of time talking, but I didn't talk about my husband's drinking problem or his violent temper. I had learned to keep secrets. She didn't talk about her husband's drinking either.

Some nights I'd cry myself to sleep after the kids went to bed. I missed my husband. I wanted things to work out. I didn't want to get a divorce. I would change and do whatever it took to save my marriage. Fortunately, my mom continued to talk to me, insisting that I persuade Kenny to go to AA before I made a decision to return home.

Kenny constantly called my mother demanding she tell him where I was. She refused to tell him. Instead Mom tried to talk some sense into him and encouraged him to stop drinking. She felt like she understood Kenny since they were both alcoholics.

After almost two weeks, my mom stopped by to see me. "Kenny said he promised to go to AA if you come home. This time I think he's serious. You need to call him and tell him you'll come home."

Feeling a little anxious, I dialed my phone number.

"Where are you? I've been talking to your mom and I promise if you come home, I'll go to AA. I'm sorry I hit you."

Those were the words I needed to hear. My heart softened. I had made up my mind. I believed things would change. I was going home.

The first few weeks after I returned home Kenny faithfully went to AA. Shortly afterwards, my father and his wife, Sandy had moved into town and we let them park their dilapidated trailer in front of our house and plug into our electricity. Even after all he had done, I still needed my father's love and approval. I wanted to convince him that he was forgiven for the past. I still believed that everything that happened to me as a little girl was my fault and I had no ill feelings towards him, but it was me I couldn't forgive. Dad cooked dinner for us whenever Kenny went to his AA meetings, two or three times a week.

My dad and Sandy finally left and rented a house and life went back to normal for us once again. Things seemed to be going along just fine and then Kenny came home drunk and it started all over again. Apparently, Kenny's first binge started when he stopped by to visit my dad and he offered him a drink. *Thanks, Dad!*

The little bit of hope I had held on to left me and I retreated further into my sorrow and self-pity, wondering what I had done wrong this time. I felt like a failure. I forgot about my threats to leave if he started drinking again. I was too scared to do anything. *Why are you punishing me God?*

It was easy to feel like everything was okay during the day. I was home with my children while my husband was at work. Although I still had my part-time job at the elementary school, I usually only worked a few times a month. By now Kristy was nearly six months old and Jeremy was a very helpful preschooler. Kenny and I had not been getting along very well. I had my Alanon on Wednesday mornings and I was working on the fourth step, which was to make a fearless and moral inventory about myself. Since I enjoyed writing, I picked up a notebook and every chance I got I wrote down all my angry and resentful thoughts and other things I needed to work on. I wrote about my unkind thoughts towards others. And how I had harmed others with my expectations or judgmental attitudes. I thought about my fears and worries, and listed all that I was grateful for. After finishing I slipped the notebook in my bedroom drawer. My next step was to share that inventory with another member and then to make amends to everyone I had harmed. Afterwards, I would throw the notebook away.

One day I came home from grocery shopping and realized Kenny had come home early from work. As I walked into the bedroom I saw him reading everything I had written down. I stood in the doorway filled with fear and gasped.

"What's this? I can't believe you wrote all those awful things down. Who am I married to? What a b___h you are!" Throwing the notebook at me, he screamed, "I don't even want to look at you. You disgust me." Kenny immediately slammed the door and left.

It was hard to follow the regular routine and get supper started. Later, after getting the kids to bed for the night, I collapsed on my bed and cried out to God asking him to forgive me for being such an awful person, and felt angry with myself for having written everything down. After calling my sponsor she helped me to understand how important it was to journal my thoughts. I decided I would just have to be smarter and hide my notebook. She assured me I had done nothing wrong.

For several weeks after that, every time we argued, Kenny would bring up all the things I had written. When that finally ended, he resumed his old habits, staying out drinking till all hours of the night.

Even though I never knew when Kenny would be coming home it was still my habit to stop whatever I was doing at four o'clock every day and began cleaning the house, making beds, doing laundry, and vacuuming. After starting dinner, I would turn on my hot rollers, put a few curls in my hair and apply my makeup. As I changed out of my rumpled clothing into something cute I'd look at myself in the full-length mirror. *Hopefully, Kenny will think I look pretty and think I'm skinny enough.* I had lost all my baby weight and looked better than I ever had. I kept my hair curled and always wore mascara to enhance my hazel eyes, which was my best feature. I hoped I looked cute in my colorful summer dress that hugged my twenty-four-inch waist.

Unfortunately, he rarely noticed what I looked like. I hardly ever received a compliment. But I continued to be the best wife and mother I knew how to be, spending time with my children while waiting and hoping my husband would come home from work and eat dinner with the family.

"Are we going to wait for Daddy again to eat?" My four-year-old asked.

"No, let me put the baby down and we will eat dinner." I'd turn away hoping he wouldn't see the tears escaping. It would be another lonely night wondering where my husband was.

Sometimes we would hear his car pull up when it was still light outside and Jeremy would run to the window. "Yeah! Daddy's home."

He'd pass by Jeremy without saying a word and stomp into the kitchen. "Where is my dinner?"

No matter what time he came home his home-cooked meal was always waiting for him. I'd serve him, pouring his soft drink, buttering his bread and cutting his meat. Jeremy would sit at the table, hoping to spend time with his father while I fed the baby. Sometimes Kenny spoke to him, ignored him or tried to start a fight with me. We never knew how the evening would turn out. Oftentimes, my husband would lie in front of the television set, with Jeremy snuggled up against him, and fall asleep.

Other times he'd come traipsing in the kitchen look down at his plate and scream. "Where's my steak? I'm a meat and potato man. You expect me to eat this? Fix me a steak. I'm cleaning up, and it better be ready as soon as I'm done."

I could hear the shower while I scrambled to find a frozen steak. *It was at times like this that I wished I had a microwave oven.* As I put the steak in a skillet, I willed for it to hurry up and cook. *Is he going out? Is he leaving? I have to have his dinner ready so he won't leave.* Opening a can of baked beans, I'd warm them up put everything neatly on a plate.

"It's ready."

I could smell the cologne before he entered the kitchen. It permeated everything he touched.

"What's this? You think I'm eating this? I'm going out."

"But I made steak. Look everything's ready for you. Why are you going out?"

"Look at this house, it's a mess. Why can't you be a better house-keeper?" Throwing open the cupboard and drawers. "You're a slob just like your mother. Come over here, look at this." Pointing to a spot of dirt on the wall, "It better be cleaned by the time I get home!" Slamming the door, he'd get in the car and I'd hear it roar down the street.

As I crumpled into a chair, hiding my head in my lap, a sweet quiet voice would say, "Mommy, what's wrong. Why are you crying?"

Quickly, I straighten up and wipe away my tears, determined not to let my child see how upset I was. Thankfully, the baby was usually asleep. I had to maintain a sense of normalcy as I bathed my son and helped him pick up his toys. Then I would read him a story till he fell asleep. Soon afterwards Kristy would wake up, she needed to be fed and receive a little attention. Hours later after both kids were sleeping peacefully, I'd lay in my room and cry out to God, *"Why is this happening to me, why am I so bad? I must deserve to be treated like this. Why does he go out? Why does he treat me so bad? How can I change myself so he will love me? Why do you hate me, God?"* All my Alanon teachings had been forgotten at times like these.

I'd play the waiting game and try to fall asleep but I was afraid if I did Kenny wouldn't come home. Perhaps he'd be in a terrible accident and die. I had to stay awake willing him to be safe. It never occurred to me I was repeating the past, only now I worried about Kenny dying, instead of my mother. Sometimes I'd turn on the radio and listen to Dr. Joyce Brothers. She was a psychologist who answered people's questions about their problems. I kept waiting for someone to say something similar to my problems. Nobody ever did. Where did my serenity go?

Usually after two o'clock in the morning I'd hear a key in the lock. Sometimes I'd pretend to be asleep. Other times I'd run to greet him, feeling excited to finally see my husband. Sometimes I'd scream, "Where have you been?" Most of the times I'd clean up his vomit and then lie there while he had his way with me. I'd keep my eyes tightly shut pretending it wasn't happening. After all, this is what a good wife was supposed to do---wasn't it?

One night when Kristy was seven months old Kenny and I went out to a movie without the kids. Standing in the ticket line I noticed an extremely attractive man coming towards us. He was probably the best-looking guy I had ever seen. My heart did a little twitter as I noticed his eyes met mine.

"Kenny, is that you?" He asked.

"Hey Randy, how the hell are you?" said Kenny. "Oh, this is my wife, Debbie."

He shook my hand and I was too busy gazing into his eyes to notice his fiancée standing beside him. "This is Jill," he said.

I hardly heard a word when Kenny explained he and Randy worked together and he was the boss's son.

The four of us sat together in the movie and all the while I found myself daydreaming about wanting to be alone with Randy. I just couldn't help myself. I had the biggest smile on my face coming out of the movie theater.

Days went by and I couldn't stop thinking about Randy. I had only felt like this when I had a crush on some actor on my favorite soap opera. I found myself thinking of reasons to use the car, hoping I'd see Randy when I dropped Kenny off at work. Sometimes I did and we'd make small talk. I also noticed the way he looked at me, or was it just my imagination. Luckily, Kenny had usually gotten out of the car. As hard as I tried I couldn't shake my thoughts, and honestly, I didn't want to. Whenever Kenny said unkind things to me I kept picturing Randy at my side protecting me.

We were invited to Randy's wedding a couple weeks later. I was overjoyed to be able to see him again. After a few drinks and sharing a dance with him I knew I wanted to be with him more than ever. Thinking about Randy and imagining ways, we could be together filled my thoughts throughout the day. I'd bring up his name at the dinner table hoping to hear some tidbit about him from my husband. Finally, I began to notice Kenny looking at me suspiciously when I brought him up.

"Why do you keep asking about Randy? I bet you want to sleep with him?" He screamed at me one day.

I realized I had gone too far in my lustful thoughts about my husband's co-worker. I vowed to myself I needed to stop thinking about him.

26

Jeff

"You saw me before I was born. Every day of my life was recorded in your book." Psalm 139:16

About this time, I was feeling pretty good about myself. I looked nice and was back to my pre-pregnancy weight. I had a boy and a girl and I was done having kids. I think I had one menstrual cycle after Kristy was born. I had read that nursing, combined with spermicidal crème, was a good source of birth control, and I kept waiting for my second period to start. Finally, I started to worry and went to the local clinic and had a pregnancy test. "Congratulations you are pregnant."

I had just had a baby. She wasn't even ten months old. I couldn't have another one. Not yet. I loved staying home with my kids and being a housewife and we couldn't afford another baby. Besides, I was thinking about having an affair with Randy and leaving Kenny. *This couldn't be happening.*

I also felt like Kenny was unreasonable about everything in our lives, every payday he tried to make me feel guilty about only working part-time. "We need the money. You need to get a full-time job. I'm sick of being the only one paying the bills."

He'd cash his check every two weeks and pull out the money, counting out the twenty-dollar bills and curse. "Where did all the money go? I'm sick of living paycheck to paycheck. We have nothing." Flinging the money at me, he'd stomp off yelling. "If I weren't married to you I'd be driving a brand-new Corvette by now."

With tears rolling down my cheeks, I'd gather up the money and pray that we'd have enough to cover our bills.

He'd continually scream at me telling me what a horrible house-keeper I was but how could that be, I spent most of my time cooking, cleaning, washing clothes, tending to the kids, grocery shopping, paying bills, and mowing the yard. I didn't have friends I hung out with and I hardly ever saw my family. The only thing I knew how to do was to be a wife and mother. I felt like I always trying to appease him, it seemed nothing was ever good enough for him.

I constantly felt defeated and continued to fantasize about divorcing my husband especially since I had Randy to think about. But how could I leave Kenny now that I was pregnant again? I was really stuck!

The day I found out I was pregnant I ran into a childhood neighbor of Kenny. Beverly and I had also become friends since her husband Jim had just started working with, my husband.

"Don't tell Kenny, but I just found out I'm pregnant again. I don't want another baby. We were only going to have two and besides Kristy is less than a year old."

"When are you going to tell Kenny?" Bev asked.

"I don't know, but I'm not ready to say anything yet."

"Are you going to get an abortion?"

Although that thought had crossed my mind, I knew I could never really consider it. After all, what if God had some great plan for this baby? At the time, I didn't think abortion was wrong. I did not realize it meant you were killing a child. Something about it just didn't seem quite right though. "No, of course not."

"Well I'm on my way to pick up Jim from work," she said as she started to drive away.

I called after her, "Please don't mention this to Kenny if you see him today."

At home, I went through the motions, taking care of the kids, doing laundry, and making dinner. My Alanon friend was constantly telling me it was wrong to think about Randy, and now being pregnant, I knew there was no way I would go through planning a rendezvous with him.

A couple hours later Kenny came stomping in the door. "What's this about you being pregnant," he screamed.

"What?"

"Beverly came to pick up Jim from work and she said congratulations."

"I told her not to tell you. I wanted to tell you myself."

"When were you going to tell me? Is it even mine?" He eyed me distrustfully.

"Of course, it's yours. I can't believe you'd even ask me that. I just found out today," I said, trying not to cry.

The yelling started, me trying to defend myself, he accusing me. After showering, he shoved me out of the way and left for the night. This is how he handled a problem. Sobbing on my sheets, I once again cried out to God. *Why is this happening to me?*

I was occasionally going to my 12-step program but was getting more and more disillusioned with it. After all, Kenny was still drinking and going out and was still blaming me for everything that went wrong in his life. I was trying not to feel suspicious every time he went out but my heart told me he was probably going out on me. I just didn't want to believe it. I wasn't completely innocent in my thoughts either. Who was I to talk?

Life resumed, and after a few months I began to feel the baby kick and forgot all about my fantasy life with Randy. Although I was still having a difficult time believing I was pregnant again so soon after Kristy was born.

I was about five months pregnant when Kenny informed me he had to go on the road for his job, and he assured me we would talk every few days. He would be traveling to the East Coast for up to six weeks. We had never been separated more than a few days except fourteen months ago when I had stayed at the County Farm. My fearful thoughts began to kick in. What if something bad happens to him? What if he goes out with someone else? What if he wants to leave me?

Finally, the day came and I said goodbye and carried on with my daily routines, taking care of the children and our home. Interestingly enough, life seemed more peaceful with Kenny gone.

After a few days, I found myself enjoying the freedom of not having to make a three-course meal every night and keeping the house spotless. I liked not having to share the car. But after a couple weeks I eventually began to miss my husband.

I was glad I had my meeting every week to go to. One day on the drive home Rosa said, "You know the program is based on the twelve steps of AA and Step 2 says: 'Came to believe that a Power greater than ourselves could restore us to sanity.' A lot of people in the program refer to their Higher Power as God. We've been going to the meetings for almost four years and I was wondering, is Jesus your higher power?"

"No God is. I really don't know much about Jesus even though I went to the Catholic church while I was growing up."

"You know Jesus is God's son, don't you? Rosa asked. "Have you ever thought about accepting him in your life?"

"What are you talking about? I'm spiritual, not religious. I don't need Jesus in my life. I already have God."

In spite of my beliefs, I began to think about what Rosa had said and started listening to sermons on television every Sunday morning while Kenny was gone. What Rosa had tried to share with me began to make sense. Each week I found myself getting on my knees, asking Jesus to come into my heart. There was no emotional feeling attached to it. I just repeated the prayer I heard on TV. I also thought about going back to church.

At about the same time I had been reading a book about Luke, the Apostle. He was the only disciple who had never met Jesus. He wrote his gospel after speaking with Mary and the other disciples about their experiences with Jesus. Mary, the mother of Jesus knew what it was like to experience an unplanned pregnancy. Looking down at my growing belly, I finally began to enjoy being pregnant. I was no longer angry or scared about having another child. Walking outside one night while the kids were sleeping, I looked up towards the sky, beautifully lit up by the glistening stars, and called out to Mary, "Help me to be a good mother to this baby, and please help my marriage to get better."

On our drive home from our next meeting I shared my experiences with Rosa. "I love attending my weekly meetings it has become a way of life for me, and I am always reading self-help books. I have also been listening to Christian radio shows, hoping I will feel better about myself. But I still feel like something is missing."

"I know what you mean," Rosa said, "I've been thinking about starting a rosary group and praying to Mary once a week. Will you join me?"

"I do love Mary and I want to pray more, but right now I just want to have this baby. Can we talk about it after the baby is born?"

"Sure, I can wait."

One night, a few weeks later, I heard a truck pull up in front of our house. Running outside, I watched as my young, handsome, muscular husband came striding towards me. He picked me up in his arms and smiled at me. "I missed you. I really missed you."

"Me too," I gazed into his eyes. I was in love again.

The next day, after watching the kids play, Kenny patted my belly, and said, "Something happened to me while I was gone. But I can't tell you yet. First I need to see a doctor."

No matter how much I begged him he wouldn't tell me. Crazy thoughts went through my head over the next couple days wondering what his secret was.

A few days later after he returned from his doctor's appointment, he drew me aside.

"Remember a few months before you got pregnant you flirted with Randy, and you swore you never had an affair with him?"

Hanging my head in shame at the memory, "Yah, I told you I was sorry. I guess I was mad at you because you started drinking again. I lost weight after Kristy was born and I thought I looked really good. You never even noticed. I swear to you nothing happened, really!"

"Well I was at a truck stop over Labor Day weekend and met another driver. He talked me into going to a bar where nude women danced. I never intended anything to happen really, but I took this dancer back to my motel and one thing led to another and we had sex. I immediately felt bad about it and kicked her out in the middle of the night. I left the motel and stayed at the truck stop for the next few days. She came by to see me and we just talked. I felt sorry for her and wanted to do something to help her. Honestly, I just listened to her talk about her problems. Anyways I thought I caught a disease, that's why I went to see the doctor. Thank God, he said everything came out negative. I just wanted to get revenge on you, but I'm not mad at you anymore."

I was speechless! I stood there trying to process what I had just heard, trying to think of something to say while anger, hurt and resentment boiled up inside me.

"Why did you want to get revenge on me?"

"I know you had an affair with Randy."

"I told you I never had an affair!"

He walked out of the room believing he had done the right thing, convinced he had reason to commit adultery. I felt like no amount of me defending myself made any difference, I knew Kenny wholeheartedly thought I had been unfaithful so I did what I always did—what came easy to me, I kept my thoughts to myself, pretending what he said didn't bother me.

But over the next few weeks an array of emotions consumed me. Because of my infatuation for Randy I just knew I was to blame for Kenny's betrayal. I was consumed with guilt for allowing myself to entertain thoughts of an affair even though it had been over a year ago. *If only I had been a better wife.*

I also felt suspicious every time Kenny was late coming home from work believing he was fooling around on me. Then I would feel guilty for thinking such things. I can't even explain the hurt I felt that he had chosen to have sex with someone else. It's one thing to imagine it but to actually know he went out on me made me feel extremely angry towards him. Outwardly I treated him like I always did but inside I was filled with rage and resentment towards him for breaking his marriage vows. I kept everything quiet in my mind and didn't tell anybody about the things that were going on in my head. I don't know how I kept it together, taking care of two kids under the age of five and pregnant with a third while knowing my husband had committed adultery.

A few months later while Kenny was getting ready to go to work, I said. "Why do you have to drive an hour away today, my due date is in a week, besides our other two babies were early I'm afraid this one will be too."

"I can't help it, the boss told me I have to go to Pueblo today. What am I supposed to do?"

He kissed me goodbye and I fell back to sleep. After I got up I felt some slight pain but dismissed it and began feeding the other kids and then started cleaning up. The pain intensified and I began to feel uncomfortable. I knew I was in labor. Panicking, I called Kenny's boss. "I'm in labor and I need Kenny to come home to take me to the hospital right away."

"Okay, I will make sure Kenny gets home. Just in case he runs late what's the name of the hospital you'll be at?"

Feeling afraid he wouldn't make it for the birth, I reluctantly I called my little brother, Rob and asked him to drive me to the hospital. Then I called Monica and asked her to come over and watch my kids.

After being checked into the hospital, I was immediately wheeled into the delivery room with still no sign of my husband. I watched the clock, hoping and praying I wouldn't have to deliver this baby all by myself. The pains were coming closer together. Moments before the baby was born, Kenny came running into the room. He made it just in time to see our son born.

It was an easy birth and I was home within twenty-four hours. My new baby had fat, rosy cheeks and a contented demeanor. We named him Jeff.

Even though Kristy and Jeff were only eighteen months apart and a lot of work, I found myself enjoying my new little one. While I read a book to Kristy I was able to nurse Jeff. Jeremy helped after school and I found a routine that worked for me.

Because Kenny had been feeling guilty after his affair he had even begun helping me with the kids after Jeff was born. He was coming home at decent hours and he seemed to be less angry. He always acted better when he was wracked with guilt, I would come to realize later.

When Jeff was two months old, Rosa and a couple of her church friends began to meet at my house to say the Rosary and pray to Mary. While Jeremy was in school and Kristy played with her toys, the baby was usually napping, we began saying our Hail Marys' and the Lord's Prayer. Because both our fathers had molested us, we were trying hard to believe God was a loving father, who we could trust and who would never hurt us, but we felt safe asking Mary to take our prayers to God, our Heavenly Father.

I continued to watch Sunday services on television and asked Jesus into my heart each week having absolutely no idea what it meant. All I knew was, every time I did, I began to feel peaceful and I liked the feeling. I started attending Mass with Rosa. Kenny refused to go, but he gave me permission to take the kids. I assumed he wanted the luxury of sleeping in with no one to disturb him.

A couple months later as I was out shopping I ran into one of my cousins whom I rarely saw. "Have you ever heard of Calvary Chapel?" Carl asked.

"No, what is Calvary Chapel?"

"It's a non-denominational church I've been going to and it's really good. You should go sometime."

"What does non-denominational mean?"

"It just means following the words of Jesus Christ in the Bible and it is not related to any specific religion."

Later in the week my brother Rob, who was the first one in our family to attend another church besides the Catholic church, came over to my house. "I started attending Calvary Chapel. It's downtown, you should go sometime. It's great. Here, listen to these cassettes."

Not long after that, my girlfriend called, "My husband and I went to this awesome church called Calvary Chapel. You can even wear jeans. Your husband would probably go with you. You want to go with us some Sunday?"

After three people in a row mentioned Calvary Chapel, I was convinced God had a message for me. Popping the cassette into the machine one afternoon when the kids were napping I listened to Pastor Larry. I loved what he said, along with his sense of humor. The worship music that played was something I had never heard before. I felt a wonderful sense of peace. I began to pray that Kenny would go with me, or at the very least give me permission to go without him.

A few weeks later, Kenny reluctantly agreed to go after a night of drinking and arguing. *Was it guilt that motivated him?* We walked into the old refurbished courthouse that had been turned into a church and dropped the kids off in their Sunday school classes and nursery. Following the sound of the inspirational music led us to the auditorium where I saw the band playing while the congregation sang. Closing my eyes, I swayed to the music. I had never heard anything more beautiful. It was as if angels themselves were singing.

While my eyes were closed, the pastor who I had been listening to for weeks began to pray. *Am I really here? Am I listening to a tape? Is this really Pastor Larry in person?*

Timidly, I stood in line afterward to touch the hand of the man whom I had grown to respect through the words he had spoken on the cassette. Kenny stood away from me and watched. For me there was something sacred, almost holy about being near the pastor. I didn't know it then, but he would eventually help me to understand who Jesus was.

"You're new. I'm so glad you're here. I hope you will come back again." Larry said with a genuine smile as he reached out to hug me.

As soon as we got into the car Kenny started screaming at me. "I don't think I'll ever go back to that place again. I didn't like it. And that preacher was flirting with you. I saw the way you looked at him too."

I was crushed! How dare he accuse me of wanting to be with a man of God? As tears rolled down my face, I turned and looked out the passenger window. His words only quickened my resolve to detach myself from him. Things really hadn't changed at all. I added a few more bricks that day to the wall I had begun to build up against him.

27

Finding Faith

"Teach me your ways O Lord, that I may live according to your truth! Grant me purity of heart so that I may honor you. I will give glory to your name forever. For your love for me is very great." Psalm 86:11-13

I knew my feelings had changed about Jesus after a few more visits to Calvary. I couldn't wait to share with Rosa. "I understand clearly now what you had tried to tell me so long ago. Jesus is God, and He left the safety of heaven to enter our world and breathe our air and share our pain and walk in our shoes. Jesus Christ knows what it means to be human and to suffer disappointment. That's why He understands our weaknesses and our prayer needs. He came to earth to sacrifice his life for all of mankind's sins. He died and rose again so I could get into heaven and have a relationship with God the father. I understand the verse in the Bible: *"For God so loved the world he gave his only begotten Son, that whoever believes in Him shall not perish but have everlasting life." John 3:16*

Soon I began to realize that being a Christian was about building an intimate relationship with Jesus while religion was man's idea of being good enough for God. I still didn't understand everything, but I went forward and accepted Christ as my Savior the following Sunday at my church.

A few weeks later, Rosa shared with me. "I don't feel like we need to go to Mary to pray anymore. We can go directly to her Son. Why don't we turn our rosary group into a prayer group?"

"That is a great idea, I was thinking the same thing. I am starting to believe how much Jesus loves me and wants me to get to know him more intimately. In all the years, I attended the Catholic Church I never realized that."

I decided it was time to stop going to my Alanon meetings. I felt like the group encouraged divorce, and now that I was a Christian I would not allow myself to think that way anymore. Immediately, I promised God I would never again threaten divorce. There were many verses in the Bible that talked about being a submissive wife and I had heard several sermons about the subject. None of them ever mentioned living with an abusive husband, it was all about how the wife should change for her partner. I had come to the conclusion, submission meant that I should never speak up or give an opinion or disagree with my husband, and I mistakenly believed I was inferior to him. This coupled with my unhealthy way of thinking, led me to erroneously assume being submissive meant allowing myself to be walked on and that's what God preferred. What I didn't realize at the time was I had been living that way and giving it a name just reinforced what I was already familiar with.

When Kenny came home late just like before I always had his dinner ready but now I decided I wasn't going to be resentful. Keeping my mouth shut about his drinking and having a better attitude no matter what time he came home was something I tried real hard to accomplish.

I made a vow that I would quit feeling suspicious every time he left thinking he was interested in other women. Swallowing my fears and my insecurities, I prayed more and sought Jesus to help me change. I laid aside my own desires and feelings. I wanted to make life perfect for him. (I did not realize I was just stuffing down everything I felt.) I presumed I was doing the right thing and was convinced that this time, things would be different because I was doing what I falsely believed the Bible said. I also thought I was doing what pleased God.

After I had been attending church for a few months with Kenny's permission, he came home from work pulled me into the other room and demanded, "I don't want you going to Calvary. You can go back to the Catholic Church. No more Tuesday prayer group, either!"

No amount of arguing convinced him to change his mind so I shut my mouth and obeyed my husband, once again believing I was doing the Lord's will. Halfheartedly, I went to the Catholic Church the following Sunday. The minute I walked inside, I felt I had lost the freedom to raise my hands to praise God. The music felt uninspiring and the sermon was too brief. I felt empty when I left, but I didn't complain and went back, week after week. After all I was pleasing God by obeying my husband.

On Tuesday mornings, I'd pray with Rosa on the phone asking for Kenny to allow me to go back to Calvary Chapel and have my friends over again. *Of course, at the time I didn't realize I needed to learn to stand up for myself.*

After a few weeks, Kenny motioned to me, "I thought about it, you can go back to that church if you want to and you can have your prayer group come over on Tuesdays."

Not for one moment did I think he was unreasonable, controlling or manipulative, I just assumed I had done something wrong. Looking heavenward I silently said, *thank you, God,* and reached out and hugged my husband. I began to believe God would also make Kenny stop drinking. It became my number one prayer. All I had to do was go to church, pray, be the perfect wife, and trust God and surely things would be different.

In my spare time, I started writing short stories about the kids. One day I noticed an ad in the local newspaper; '*Readers send your stories in about your special Valentine. If we pick your story we will print it on Valentine's Day*'. Feeling inspired, I wrote about Jesus being my Valentine. I was so in love with him. I didn't tell anyone what I was doing. I completed my story and sent it in the mail.

The morning of Valentine's Day, I grabbed the paper, flipped through the pages and saw my story in print. I was overjoyed. It was the only one written about Jesus. Kenny had already left for work and I couldn't wait to tell him the good news after he returned home from his job. My mom, sister, and brothers all called to congratulate me.

That evening Kenny walked in after a long day at work. Holding the newspaper article in his hands he shoved it at me. "What is this? Why did you write down that you are worried about our finances? Now everyone thinks were having money problems. People at work are going to think I'm not capable of supporting you. You make me sick!"

"No, no that's not what I meant. I only said when I worry about things I go to my secret place, get on my knees, and pray for Jesus to help me. I wasn't trying to make you look bad."

"Get out, go to your mom's I don't want you here."

Reluctantly, I loaded the kids in the car and calmly walked in my mom's house, praying all the way there. *God, you inspired me to write this story and I believe with all my heart you will help Kenny to change his mind and let me come home.*

Less than an hour had passed when the phone rang. "I'm sorry I said those things. You can come home now."

Somehow, I wasn't surprised. I knew God would work everything out. I wrote several stories about my children over the next few months and they were all printed in the newspaper. I was finally feeling like I could become a writer. Kenny even bought me an electric typewriter that Christmas. Not only was writing a hobby of mine, but it was perfect for a stay-at-home mom, and hopefully a way to earn extra money. After the kids were tucked in bed, I pulled out my typewriter and pounded the keys. I began to fantasize about becoming a famous writer, signing autographs, having a best seller, and making lots of money. Of course, I kept all my pages hidden away as I was still afraid Kenny would read what I had written down. I couldn't handle any of his rejection or criticisms I also enjoyed writing a journal and I kept it hidden away, too.

Some days were fun when Kenny arrived home in a particularly good mood. After a home-cooked meal, we'd take the kids to the department store and buy brand new shoes. Later he would encourage them to race each other in the front yard. "Look Mommy how fast I can run with my brand-new shoes," Jeff would holler.

Other times after a spring rainstorm Kenny and the kids would collect new fallen leaves. "Let's pretend they are boats and have a boat race," he'd say as he placed the leaves in the puddles of water. Some weekends when the weather was nice he'd grab the basketball and shoot a few hoops with Jeremy. I always hoped those times would last forever I never wanted them to end. I loved seeing him play with our children. But unfortunately, they were too brief and too infrequent during our marriage.

Being home with my children was a privilege I absolutely loved. After Kenny left for work, while feeding the kids their breakfast, I'd take out my Bible and ask the kids to repeat, *This is the day the Lord has made, let us rejoice and be glad in it.* We'd all say it together. They always enjoyed learning about Jesus. Excitedly, they would share their Bible stories with Kenny and, depending on his mood, he'd sometimes listen, ignore them, or explode with anger. I never discouraged them from sharing with their father but I would often change the subject when Kenny was near, not wanting the kids—or me—to have to face his unpredictable behavior.

I recently stopped watching soap operas, and felt bad for all the time I had wasted over the years. (I eventually wrote a short story about it and it was published in our church flyer.) But I knew God wasn't mad at me and I began to use my time more wisely. Spending my spare time reading the Bible, praying with others over the phone and sharing encouraging words with my friends and family members became a priority for me.

In the early years the two little ones kept me occupied as soon as Jeremy left for school. On cold days, we'd gather in the living room and play Duck, Duck, Goose then chase each other around the house. They sat on my lap as we read bible stories and flip through picture books. Singing Bible songs and nursery rhythms was a favorite thing for us to do to.

Gathering up every pillow off all the beds and removing the couch cushions, my little ones pretended to make an imaginary house. It was a special game Kristy and Jeff played often. "I love watching you two plays," I'd say as nestled my toddlers in my arms.

It was an exciting and sad day when Kristy started kindergarten, sad for Jeff and me but she was only to eager to follow her older brother out the door. Afterwards when school was over I'd fix treats and we'd sit at the table munching our snacks. I'd encourage my children to share their day with me and we would laugh together. Jeremy was pretty quiet, and in order to get him to open up I learned to ask him questions that did not require a simple yes or no. He was always a good little helper and did whatever I asked him. Kristy would run in the door, bouncing with enthusiasm, eager to share her adventures. We enjoyed listening to her funny stories while she crammed carrot sticks or celery and peanut butter into her mouth. Kristy was a little chatterbox and I didn't have to coax her into talking. Jeff loved to entertain us with his jokes and remarks. He was fearless. Sometimes he would be the first one up and I would find him standing on the kitchen counter his chubby cheeks full and white powder on his lips.

"What were you eating?" I'd ask.

"Nothing, Mama." Shaking his head

I'd scoop up my youngest and dust the evidence off his pajamas. Once again, he had found the powdered white donuts that I had been saving for his Daddy's lunch. The other kids always asked permission when they wanted something sweet, but Jeff knew what he wanted and always found a way to get it. I couldn't help but laugh about it.

Chores came next and afterwards, I'd prepare dinner. I always sat with them while they worked on their homework. Scribbling on a piece of paper, Jeff pretended he had homework too. Continually looking for ways to teach my children about God, as they got older, we read Bible stories, listened to worship songs, memorized verses, and attended church when Kenny allowed it.

Sometimes, we'd gather around the TV and watch age appropriate program. There was a lot of junk on television I didn't want them to watch, but as soon as Kenny walked in the door he threw my rules out the window. No amount of pleading would convince him to turn off the television or change the channel. Instead, I'd gather up my brood and we'd sit on my king-sized waterbed and read books. Rolling around on the bed, laughing and talking, was a favorite activity before bath and bedtime.

Autumn would bring the promise of cooler nights and shorter days. Every year we looked forward to the annual Chili cook off at the kids' elementary school which was right across the street from our house. Smelling the chili brought mouth-watering appetites to us all. Halloween soon followed as I dressed up the kids for their school parade. Being in their classroom as a room mother allowed me to see the smiles on their faces during holiday parties. In the evenings we'd sit together on our plush couch and watch the last of the orange and pink rays before twilight beckoned the shiny stars.

Winters in Colorado were enjoyable when my children and I hung out together. Sitting in front of our large picture window we'd watch the snowflakes drop and collect on the ground. Snow days, when the kids were called off from school, were the best. My children and I would bundle up in our warmest clothes, hats, boots and mittens. Walking up the hill, dragging our sleds behind us, we would slide down. Finally, it would be time to head inside for some hot cocoa. Oh, how I wished we had a fireplace to warm up to instead, I'd turn on the oven after preparing a fresh batch of chocolate chip cookies the sweet smell of them permeated the house. Then we'd stand in our small kitchen warming up near the oven waiting for our delicious treats reminiscing about all the fun we had just had.

Finally, the winter months would be over, walking outside we'd notice the first glimpse of spring, robins rooting on the ground looking for a fat worm, tulips peeking their tiny buds up, and leaves appearing on the once-empty trees. Spring would bring rain and ear-splitting thunderstorms. Sometimes it even hailed, and the kids and I would run outside afterward and gather up the little white balls of ice. We spent many days and nights huddled together on our cozy, soft couch sitting close to each other and thanking God for all our blessings.

Every May the kids helped me plant a small garden. Watering was easy for them and I did the weeding. They were always ready to collect ripe produce and enjoy fresh crispy vegetables. Their favorite pastime was picking stalks of pink and green rhubarb, rinsing it off with the hose and chewing on it. The tart taste of it brought laughter as they watched each other pucker their lips and make funny expressions. Childhood friends liked hanging out at our house while Kenny was away at work. We'd play across the street where the kids went to elementary school after classes were over. I'd push my little ones on the swings and sing silly songs with them. We'd play Hide and Seek with the other kids from the neighborhood. I preferred to spend most of my time hanging out with my kids and their friends it wasn't often I hung out with the other moms in the neighborhood.

On hot summer afternoons while Kenny was at work, I'd open the windows and turn on fans then we'd play monopoly for hours in our somewhat cool house. When the heat would get the better of us we'd run out back turn on the hose and have water fights. Sometimes in the afternoons I would prepare crispy fried chicken, grab a bag of potato chips and homemade cookies and take my kids on a picnic. We'd walk over to the school and cover the lush green grass with a blanket while we ate our delicious meal. Many summer nights were filled with the smoky warm whiffs of neighbors barbecuing. Sometimes I even grilled burgers and dogs while the kids stood around watching our hotdogs turn black around the edges. Afterwards it was the perfect time to take our nightly walks. Always hopeful when we rounded the corner we would see the pale yellow, Ford Granada sitting in the driveway, it rarely was. We never knew what time their daddy would be home.

Our home was peaceful until Kenny arrived, then everything changed. He'd make sure to let me know the house was not clean enough and dinners were never good enough. I was never skinny enough and the kids didn't do their chores properly. It was always something.

Weeks turned into months, months turned into years. Kenny stopped hitting me, although he'd still occasionally shove me. He continued to criticize me for just about everything that went wrong, when money was tight, when his boss yelled at him and even when the kids acted up. Although his drinking abated for a while it never completely stopped. "It's your fault I drink," were familiar words I heard often. Fortunately, I continued to pray every week with my group, attend church and sneak away to pray when things got to overwhelming. I was able to make new friends and even went to a couple of Christian concerts. But I still asked his permission every time I left the house. I thought every wife did that.

Taking my kids to church on Sunday mornings was something I looked forward to. Sometimes my husband even attended church with us. I would have loved to go on Sunday nights but I knew Kenny wouldn't allow it and I didn't want to rock the boat. I was trying hard to be the perfect, submissive wife and mother and tried not to think about all the things that were still wrong in our marriage.

Even though I tried to fool myself into believing things were better, I knew nothing had really changed except my attitude. As I continued to try to keep peace in the household, I kept noticing more and more inexcusable things Kenny had been doing. I thought back on our ten-year high school reunion that had occurred a few months earlier.

My old friend Myrna had moved out of state years earlier and right around the time of the reunion she was in the process of a divorce.

She flew out for the big day and stopped at our house. After putting the kids to bed, she shared her sorrows with Kenny and me as we listened to music play softly in the background. We both hugged her when she left. I was filled with compassion for her.

"It is obvious Myrna is still hurting over her divorce." I mentioned to Kenny.

Right after she walked out the door Kenny looked in her direction, snapped his fingers and said, "She wanted me, and I could have had her like that." Then he walked into the bedroom.

I couldn't believe he could say something so awful and at that moment I lost all respect I might have had for him. *Who was this man I was married to? Who would say something like that especially to me, his wife!*

One Labor Day weekend ten years after Kenny and I had been married, a friend of mine from church pulled up in front of our house. Kenny and I were outside doing yard work (as we did most weekends.)

Pat called me over to the car. "Do you want to go to Prospect Lake with our church? They will be baptizing people today."

"I don't know if Kenny will let me. I'm afraid to ask him. Will you?"

"Kenny, can Deb and the kids go to the park with me today? The church is having a picnic and my daughter and I are going to get baptized. It would mean a lot to me if she was there."

He glared at her, "She's not going anywhere. She has yard work to finish."

Pat left quickly. I knew better than to plead my case. I didn't want to ruin the day by having my husband mad at me. Instead I smiled and grabbed the rake. Inside I was dying, wondering why I was being treated so unkindly. After all I was always nice to him. I felt angry with him for not allowing me to go with my friend but even more angry with myself for not standing up to him. I had never gotten over my fear of Kenny and I hated myself for it.

I kept things organized in our home so when Kenny came home everything was in its place. I made sure I was always in a good mood and the kids were on their best behavior. I never told Kenny about things that I struggled with. I talked to my girlfriends and would pray throughout the day. It didn't occur to me that a wife could talk about her feelings with her husband.

I never expected him to watch the kids. They were usually with me, although by now, Jeremy was old enough to babysit the younger kids for a few moments if I was late running an errand. Sometimes I'd ask my mom for help, but I rarely went anywhere without my kids.

Jeremy was nearly ten and he was extremely responsible for his age. He did his daily chores and helped me with the younger kids whenever I needed his help. Jeremy would often take his siblings with him to his friends' while I cleaned the house or when Kenny and I got in a disagreement. He was fearful of his dad as we all were, except Jeff. Maybe he was just too young to realize what a bully Kenny was. Sometimes when Jeremy forgot to do a chore, he would tense up and bemoan the fear he felt about his dad. One time when he heard Kenny's car pulling into the driveway, he came running up to me. "Mom, I forgot to pick up the dog crap in the backyard. Dad is going to be so mad at me. What should I do?"

"Hurry, run out there now. I will keep him busy in here." *Please God don't let him notice.*

I would do whatever I could to protect my children from Kenny's wrath. *Why was I so afraid? What was I afraid of? Now I had taught my children the same thing.*

Kristy, who was five and a half, laughed easily and for a while seemed to have a special place in her daddy's heart. He'd pick her up when she was a toddler, tickle her and sit her on his lap. She was loud, funny, and always tried to get her father's attention. Kristy kept herself busy playing alone or with one of her friends. She had an active imagination and we all benefited from her singing and role-playing.

Jeff, who was only four, didn't demand as much attention as his sister. He seemed content getting an occasional hug or a pat on the head. He had several friends around the neighborhood who were always hanging around with him at our house. Later, when Jeff started kindergarten, they would knock on our front door and walk together across the street to the elementary school. He kept himself occupied and out of Kenny's way.

In our house, the world revolved around Kenny. If something made him mad, the kids and I suffered. We all learned it was best just to try to maintain the peace and stay out of his way when he was in a foul mood.

In my prayer times I begged God to make sure Kenny got a raise so I wouldn't have to leave my three children and go to work full time. I was still working at a nearby elementary school as an on-call substitute teacher's aide. I enjoyed leaving the house occasionally and helping out with the bills but I certainly did not want to work full time. My husband was away from home so much either working or drinking and I didn't want to be away from my kids too. They didn't need two parents gone.

Although my mother only lived ten minutes away, I rarely went to see her unless we went over for dinner. Mom was pretty busy with her job, attending school part time and her AA friends. About twice a month my mother-in-law invited us to eat with her and my brother- and sister-in-law. There were barbecues, picnics and birthday parties; we'd spend with our siblings and their kids. My sister and I hung out as often as we could. I was close to all my sister-in-law's and I loved Kenny's family as well and enjoyed spending time with them. Going out to dinner with family and friends was something we did a few times a year. Of course, holidays were always spent with our extended families. Spending time with family was always a highlight in our home. The kids loved hanging out with their cousins, aunts and uncles' grandma's and grandpa.

We did not have many friends who we hung out with. Don who was middle-aged, Kenny had befriended at work would sometimes stop by unannounced. I got the job at the elementary school because of his wife. We occasionally had dinner with them and their two girls. Often times when Don came over Kenny would make sexual jokes to me and grab me in places that should have only been done in the bedroom. Squirming away from him, I'd excuse myself, and go in the other room until Don left.

"Why did you touch me like that? You really embarrassed me. And I'm sure Don wasn't very comfortable either."

"Oh, don't be such a prude, Don didn't even notice."

It didn't matter how disrespected I felt, Kenny would not change how he treated me.

I didn't ask for much, I was content without spending money on myself. I rarely bought makeup and made my mascara last as long as I could. My clothes didn't need to be replaced too often. I went years only owning one bra and a few pair of underwear. The kids wore hand-me- downs and I didn't make a big deal out of getting new things. It was more important for me to stay home with my kids and sacrifice where I could. One time, after I had Jeff, I badly needed some new clothes and I prayed really hard for God to provide me with clothes, knowing our funds were low. The next day I went to my part-time job at the elementary school and the secretary, reached out to me. "I noticed we are the same size and I have a whole bag of clothes I was going to give away. Would you like them?"

"Thanks so much, I was just praying about getting new clothes." I knew God had answered my prayer.

Some paydays Kenny would take us to Kmart and he would decide he needed a whole new wardrobe. After he'd try on pants, shirts, belt, socks and underwear he'd turn to me and ask, "Is there anything you want?" Since I mentally counted the money he had just spent on himself, and I was the one who paid the bills, knowing that after diapers were bought as well as all the things the kids needed, there was no way we would have any money left over, I politely declined. So, I always learned to be resourceful with the household budget, the kids shared plenty of hand-me-downs as well as trying to make things last as long as I could.

Most days I never knew when Kenny would be coming home from work and I spent my time hanging out with my children, keeping busy waiting for him to arrive home. One summer, I begged Kenny to buy me a 10-speed bicycle. I was tired of borrowing bikes from the neighbor kids. I just wanted to go bicycling with my children.

He refused. "You just want to show off your butt in those short tight white shorts as you cycle around the neighborhood. I'm not buying you a bike."

Where were those crazy words coming from, I thought back about the recent times Kenny had gone out with the neighbor's son who was only twenty-one. My husband's moods seemed more erratic than ever then and I found myself constantly praying for peace in our home.

One night he came home visibly high and he confided a secret he had been keeping. "I have been snorting cocaine with Chris. I swear I'll never do it again. I feel so bad don't be mad at me."

Of course, I told him I wasn't angry but I was thinking about all the money he had wasted and all he had put the children and me though. I had no idea he took drugs. But I still felt compelled to remind him of Jesus's love. "I just read a book about BJ Thomas, the singer, and he took drugs but he became a Christian and he stopped taking them. Maybe you should read the book."

He seemed to feel so badly about what he had been doing that I wanted to console him. After ten years of marriage I felt like I could trust him with my secrets. "I have a secret to tell you. My dad molested me when I was a little girl."

After hearing the details, he said in an angry tone, "Why didn't you tell me sooner?"

I almost had the feeling he didn't believe I was telling the truth. Later when he wanted to hurt me, he would say hateful things to me about my secret and throw it back in my face. "It was your fault he did those things to you. You probably wanted him to."

Although he was a Dr. Jekyll and Mr. Hyde, I wondered what was wrong with me. At times, he made me feel as if I was the crazy one. I tried to remember all the things I had learned in Alanon: The alcoholic is a master manipulator. He will try to blame you for everything. The alcoholic will always try and destroy his mate. You become sick right along with him. You make excuses for him. The world revolves around the alcoholic.

I thought things would change after I had become a Christian. *Didn't my prayers make any difference at all?* I still tried to do everything in my power to keep my family together, even when I realized how fearful my children felt towards Kenny. I believed it was what God wanted for me. I thought this was my lot in life. I just needed to be happy in spite of being mistreated. I was still so confused!

28

It's Over

"Deceit fills hearts that are plotting evil: joy fills hearts that are planning peace!" Proverbs 12:20

I had spent nearly eleven years with an angry, abusive man and I found myself imagining what my life would be like without him. It would be so much easier, I reasoned, with nobody to hit me and call me filthy names, nobody to accuse me and criticize the kids and me. I worried my children would grow up to become an alcoholic or marry one. I did not want them to make the same mistake I had. Since becoming a Christian, I always prayed that God would choose their mates for them when it came time for them to marry. I hoped I hadn't jinxed them by staying married to Kenny.

I knew I had a reason to leave my husband because he did commit adultery, one that he had admitted to. We never went to counseling about it or even talked about it among ourselves or to anyone else. Sometimes when he would go out I had such strong feelings that he was actually going out on me. Always, I'd dismiss my thoughts and cry out to the Lord. *Why am I so insecure? Surely, he wouldn't really sleep with somebody then come home and have sex with me the same night!* I would beg God to change my thoughts and help me to trust my husband.

Even though he continued to verbally abuse me I was grateful he hadn't hit me in a while. But I still wasn't sure if all those things added up to divorce. No matter how much I tried to convince myself that I had given my marriage to God, I started looking for a way to leave my husband while trying not to feel guilty about it.

A year later, on Labor Day, once again, my friend Pat stopped by to ask me to attend the church picnic with her. She parked and got out of the car. The whole family was outside doing yard work.

"Kenny," she called out, "Can Deb and the kids go to the park with me? Our church is having a baptism."

Without hesitation as he had done a year earlier, Kenny glared at her. "No, she has to finish raking the yard."

Angrily, I shrugged my shoulders and watched Pat drive away.

"Why can't I go? The yard work is almost done. Why can't the kids and I just go with her?"

"Because I said you can't. That's why!"

Suddenly I didn't feel afraid anymore. "I'm going anyways."

As I turned towards the house, he lunged after me. "You are not going anywhere."

I started running from him. He chased me and caught my shirt in his hands, ripping it until my bra was exposed. Holding the front of my blouse, I escaped his grip. When he finally caught up with me he started shoving me. I broke free again and was able to get far enough away from him. Running to the front door, I slammed it shut. Luckily, he did not follow me inside.

I sat in the bedroom, looked in the mirror at my ripped shirt and replayed the ugly scene over in my head, feeling terrible that my three children had witnessed the whole thing.

"What's wrong with me? Why do I put up with this?" I yelled to know one but myself. *What have I done to deserve this? Where are you, God?*

I changed my shirt, washed the tears off my face and went back outside to take care of the kids. Kenny ignored me as he finished the yard work. I tried to act like everything was okay. I wasn't hurt and I wanted things to go back to normal. *What was normal anyways?*

"Come on Kristy, you want to help me rake the grass?" Fuming inside I had really wanted to go to the picnic with my friend instead I swallowed my hurt and got to work. I knew I still wasn't brave enough to go against Kenny.

A few months later a friend asked me if I wanted a part time job. I asked Kenny's permission. "Do you mind if I work every other weekend passing out samples of food in local grocery stores?"

"Yea, we need the money, just make sure you don't talk to any guys."

He wasn't opposed to me making money and I was excited to get out of the house on Fridays and Saturdays. I enjoyed the interaction with other adults and the attention I received from the customers.

My first Saturday I came home. "Where are the kids?"

"I took them over to your mom's earlier, I had things to do."

"I had so much fun today. I'm glad I'm working."

"Is that because you were flirting with all the men who came in to buy groceries? Or were you making plans to secretly meet up with one of those young, grocery clerks?"

I couldn't believe what I was hearing, "No that's not it. I don't flirt with anyone."

He flew into a rage. "You're lying, you b____h, you need to quit that job."

I did not want to argue with him. I just wanted to be left alone. "I'm going to pick up the kids," I said and left quickly.

After his blow up, I decided to keep my job and tried to avoid his angry accusations every time I came home. I was relieved when most of the time he wasn't even there.

Shortly after the Christmas holiday, my little brother came over late one night to visit me. Of course, Kenny was out drinking.

"Rob, I'm thinking I want to get a divorce." Immediately after the words came out I felt guilty for saying it and regretted that I had actually verbalized the word. Visibly shaken, I ran to the front door. I looked out then ran to the back door, swung it open and looked out.

"What are you doing? What are you looking for?" Rob asked.

"I'm feeling like Kenny is out there and he can hear what I'm saying. I'm so scared right now."

"Come here, Sis, quit being so paranoid. Kenny isn't here. He does not know what you're saying. You are having a panic attack. Try and relax. Take a deep break come sit down by me. You need to realize he does not have any power over you. You have to get strong and take care of yourself and the kids."

I sat down next to Rob and felt the panic slipping away. "Thanks for calming me down and helping me to figure this out."

I told him what had been going on the last few months, about my new job, and all of Kenny's accusations against me. For the first time, I was totally honest about the way Kenny treated me.

"He has hit me and shoved me around since we have been married. Sometimes it will end for a while and when he feels guilty about something he treats me nice. Otherwise he is always accusing me of flirting or sleeping around. I never even go anywhere and the kids are always with me. I am getting so tired of being treated bad. I don't know why I still put up with it and I am afraid of him. I feel suspicion every time Kenny is late coming home from work, I keep thinking he is going out on me. Sometimes he doesn't come home until 2 in the morning and he just says he falls asleep in his car. I am also worried he might be taking drugs. I never see a paycheck he just throws the money at me so I can pay the bills."

"Don't you realize you're always walking on egg shells? All of us can see it, you live in fear. Can't you see how dysfunctional your relationship is? Have you noticed we don't like coming around when Kenny is home. We can't stand the way he treats you. We all love you so much and it hurts us. You don't even realize that you deserve to be treated so much better."

"Have you ever heard rumors that Kenny has been unfaithful?"

"I think you should know I heard he was having affairs."

"I've thought maybe he was but I can't really picture it. I only know of the one time he confessed. Honestly, I don't even know who I'm married too."

"You need to consider your future. Do you really want to keep going on with this guy? It sounds like things have just gotten worse throughout your marriage."

"You're right. I've been fooling myself all these years. It has gotten so bad sometimes I just wish he'd die in an accident so I wouldn't have to make a decision and actually divorce him. I can't believe how awful my thoughts have become. I feel so guilty for thinking that way. And the Bible says, God hates divorce so I don't feel like I can even leave Kenny."

"You have to quit feeling guilty about everything and believe in yourself, you can take care of your kids without him. God does not want you to live in fear and be abused, physically and verbally, and treated with disrespect. That should be enough reason to leave him. If you want to get legalistic, Kenny is an adulterer. So, there is your reason."

"I guess deep down I must have known. Why do I stay only to get mistreated? I am so scared for the future."

"The whole family is here for you. We will help you anyway we can."

I was so afraid of Kenny and I did not know how I could ever leave him. What if he somehow was able to keep my children from me? What would he do to me physically? And I had no money of my own!

Weeks passed and I kept thinking about what my brother had said to me. I picked up my Alanon book again after many years and realized the wisdom that it held for me. I spoke to my friends that were divorced and tried to draw strength from them. For the first time, I spoke openly to my sister, mother, and other family members about what I was contemplating. They gave me the courage to start making plans to leave my abusive husband. As much as I felt guilty, I knew I had to think about it and make plans to protect my children and myself.

First, my sister convinced me to make an extra key for my green Ford sedan. Kenny always kept the key unless I asked to drive the car. Next, I met a lawyer at my church and talked to him on the phone. He helped me to find peace about my decision. He told me he would take payments if he handled the divorce. Instantly, I felt like it was something I could handle.

One day early in March, Kenny met me at the door when I came home from my part-time job handing out food samples. "You're late. Who were you talking to this time? Get in the car we are going to the hospital to visit my dad."

As we got in the car my mind was in turmoil. Kenny continued to badger me with accusations while my children, sat stone faced, in the back seat. I don't remember exactly what he said to me but as we drove down the street, I summoned the courage to stand up to him. "Stop the car, I'm not going with you."

After arguing with me he finally pulled over. "Get the hell out b____h." He shoved me towards the door while screaming obscenities at me.

Quickly, I ran towards the house. Tires squealed as he turned sharply and sped out of sight. Shaking with fear, I knew I had to act fast, so I telephoned a friend, "Can you come pick me up? I'm leaving Kenny. I can't take the car because his is in the shop so he is driving my car."

"You know I will come pick you up I've been waiting for this day." *I could almost hear her applauding.*

I spent the night with my friend and I was so keyed up I couldn't sleep. Instead, she and I stayed up most of the night and talked. "Are you really going to divorce Kenny?" Pat asked.

"Remember the older gentleman I met at church? He is a lawyer. He said he would represent me. Can you take me to his office in the morning? I need to do this fast before I chicken out."

"Of course, I will do anything I can to help you. Have you thought about how you're going to pay for a divorce?"

"I have been stashing my last few paychecks from my part-time job at the school and passing out food samples on the weekends. Kenny doesn't know how much I've worked. He's rarely home."

"What are you going to do about getting the kids?"

"I will take them out of school later, hopefully Kenny will be at work. He was so mad at me when we were in the car I was afraid he was going to hit me. I didn't want to leave the kids, but it all happened so fast. I do regret the way I left. But I'm kind of glad it happened the way it did, otherwise I probably would have talked myself out of leaving him."

It was Monday and I anxiously walked in to see my lawyer while Pat waited for me in the parking lot. When I left his office, I felt a mixture of relief, guilt, and fear. The words "God hates divorce" kept ringing in my head, but I quickly dismissed my thoughts and planned a way to get my kids. Patting my pocket, I felt the extra key and was hoping my car would be at the house.

My friend stopped in front of the elementary school and I was relieved to know my two older kids were there. After withdrawing my children from school, I gave the principal strict instructions, "Please don't let my husband take them out of school from now on. We are in the process of a divorce."

"To be honest with you, I don't think I've ever laid eyes on your soon-to-be ex."

"You're right, I can count on one hand how many times he's been involved with the kids' school programs."

After hugs and kisses, Jeremy and Kristy calmed down. They were glad they would not have to go back with their father.

"Did you get Jeff?" Jeremy asked, as we headed to Pat's car.

"Where is he? Didn't your dad go to work today?"

"No, he stayed home with Jeff," Kristy said.

"Well, let's go home and get him."

"No Mom, we're afraid. What if Dad tries to take us."

"I won't let that happen. Pat is going to drop me off in front of our house so I can get my car. If we don't see your dad, maybe I can get Jeff at the same time. If that doesn't work, I will have to figure something out. You stay in the car with Pat, I will meet back up with her in the school parking lot and hopefully have Jeff."

"But Mom we are scared. What if Dad hurts you?"

"Don't be afraid, everything will work out. I will be right back, I promise." I tried to reassure them but I was shaking on the inside.

Pat dropped me off across the street from my house. Running up the driveway to my car I quietly unlocked the door and got in.

I could see my youngest standing in front of the huge picture window pointing towards me, tears streaming down his face. Suddenly, I saw Kenny standing behind my five-year-old. He started for the door.

Putting the key in the ignition I quickly backed out. I had to leave Jeff behind and my heart ached, but I knew I couldn't take the chance of having an altercation with Kenny.

We spent the night with my sister and I hardly slept. I kept trying to figure out a way to get my youngest away from his dad. I decided to keep my two kids out of school the next day.

Something told me Kenny had taken Jeff to his friend Beverly who lived right around the corner from us. She was the one who had betrayed me and told him I was pregnant when I was expecting Jeff. She was never really my friend and was only loyal to him.

Later that day, I quietly pulled up in front of her house, peeked in her window and saw Jeff sitting at the dining room table eating lunch.

I pounded on the door and when Beverly opened it, I ran past her and grabbed my son. Beverly was a big lady and she blocked me like a football player. Yanking Jeff out of my arms, she started screaming at me and raised her hand to hit me I turned and ran out the back door,

I jumped the fence, afraid of what she'd do to me if she caught me. My wedding band caught on the fence and broke in half. I saw it as a good omen that my marriage was over.

"I'm calling the police on you," she yelled.

I sat in my car not wanting to leave without my son, contemplating what to do next.

Within minutes Kenny showed up. He held onto Jeff and stood outside taunting me.

Getting out of my car I said, "I just filed for divorce and I want my son."

Just then a policeman showed up "Is he the father?" pointing to Kenny. "Because if he is then he has the right to have his son and there is not a thing you or I can do about it."

Kenny stood there, quiet, with a sarcastic grin on his face.

There was nothing I could do as I watched my son squirm in his father's arms crying the whole time. I left feeling defeated.

Later that night, after I tucked the kids into bed, I went out to talk to my sister.

"What are you going to do about getting Jeff?"

"I think I will call Tiffany. She is the teenager that lives across the street from me and she babysits for me."

I dialed her number. "Tiffany, is anything going on at my house? Do you know where Jeff is?"

"Actually, Kenny came over looking for a gun. My sister gave him my dad's. He said he was going to kill himself."

"What! Your sister gave him a gun? Where's Jeff?" Visions of what he might do played in my head.

"Ray, the old neighbor is over there trying to talk him out of it. Wait, I can see them standing at the window. Kenny is waving the gun around and he and Ray are drinking beers. I see lights and I hear a siren. I think the cops are coming. Give me your number, I'll call you back."

I could feel my heart pounding out of my chest. *Where was my baby? Is he going to kill him too?"* I kept dialing my neighbor's number. Finally, she answered the phone.

"I ran across the street and saw the cops talking to Kenny but I didn't see Jeff anywhere."

I hung up and tried the other neighbors. They knew something was going on but they had not seen Jeff either.

I was ready to get in the car and drive back home to find my little one, when my sister yelled that Mom was on the phone.

"I have been trying to call, but the phone's been busy. Kenny called and asked me to come get Jeff. He had been drinking when I got there."

"The neighbor said he had a gun."

"Everything's okay I have Jeff, he is safe."

"Oh, thank God. I was so worried."

"Do you think he will really kill himself?" My mom asked.

"To be honest with you, at this point I really don 't care. As long as my children are safe I don't care what he does."

A few hours later my teenage spy called to tell me the police had returned the gun and left our house. Of course, Kenny didn't go through with it. I almost wished he had, and then I wouldn't have to make any difficult decisions. That's how sick my own thinking had become.

I drove to pick up my son and he ran into my arms as soon as he saw me. I was relieved to have all of my children with me. A few days later Kenny was served with divorce papers and the kids and I moved back into our house.

The first few months Kenny did everything he could to make my life miserable. *But that was nothing new.* He also bought a brand-new, sky-blue corvette. *I remembered it was always something he had threatened to do.* He took the kids for rides in it until his lawyer persuaded him to get rid of it. "Buying a brand-new car won't look good to the judge when you go to court."

He did stupid things; like the time he broke into the house and stole my knickknacks, throw rugs, and houseplants. He had moved in with his parents and the children saw him every other weekend. Then he decided he wanted them to come one at a time because he claimed it was too much to have all three kids at Grandma's for the whole weekend. He even petitioned his lawyer to give him the washer and dryer. Obviously, that didn't happen.

I was glad to have him gone. In spite of the trials I felt a sense of peace because I didn't have to deal with him on a daily basis. All the while, I still fought feelings of guilt and shame for filing for divorce.

The last straw came when Kenny decided to quit his job. One thing I had always respected about him was that he was a hard worker. I found out later my dad had made the suggestion to him, if you quit your job you won't have to pay child support. *Thanks Dad!*

29

New Job, New Friends

"Humble yourselves before the Lord, and he will lift you up in honor." 1 Peter 4:10

My brother Rob suggested I put my application in at Safeway grocery store where he worked. I was hired at minimum wage shortly afterwards at a different store near my house. One of the neighborhood teenagers would stay over and watch the kids when I worked the late shift.

Things were still tense with Kenny, he broke into the house several times and threatened me. I found out he lied about me to all his friends and family members saying I had had an affair. He called at all hours of the night spewing accusations at me and cursing me. I was afraid, and I kept asking God to protect my children and me from my angry, drunk husband. Eventually, we struggled through the usual divorce proceedings, deciding on visitation rights and making a property settlement. I was able to stay in our house, but I owed the first mortgage as well as a huge second mortgage. Although I worked part-time, money was always tight, I struggled to the pay the mortgage. Cleaning houses on my days off and doing other odd jobs helped to bring in extra money, however I still had to trust God to somehow provide for us.

Kenny got another job but rarely paid child support and as time went on he saw the kids less and less. Shortly before the divorce was final Kenny decided to date my just divorced neighbor across the street *the mother of my teenager spy.* Tiffany was mad. I consoled her and told her it wouldn't last long and it didn't. Unfortunately, while they dated, he paid more attention to the neighbor's children then he did his own, it really hurt them.

It was the little things that gave me a sense of freedom and power after my divorce. One of the first things I did was to connect a second phone in the bedroom. I would never have to worry about anyone listening in on my phone calls and making untrue accusations against me.

I was able to write in my journal and leave it in sight without being afraid of anyone reading my private thoughts. I could go to church on Sunday nights without having to ask permission. I didn't have to give Kenny the last five-dollars I earned by mowing Old Ray's lawn. Best of all I could drive whomever I wanted in my car to run errands, without being reprimanded for doing a good deed for somebody. A friend gave me a small, black puppy and she became my new companion, I even let her share my bed at night.

I loved working at the store and met lots of people, and soon a co-worker, Jon, took an interest in me. I had not dated anyone since I was seventeen. It was exciting to know someone actually liked me. I wanted so badly to be loved by someone, anyone. After talking with my Alanon friend, she wanted to know all about my relationship with Jon.

I told her, he drinks in the morning and he will buy cases of beer when it's on sale.

"Those aren't good signs. Do you think it is a very good idea to get involved with someone who might have a drinking problem?"

"He works all night so his morning is really like his night. He seems pretty intelligent so I'm sure if he thought he was losing control of his drinking he would realize it and stop. Besides he is just trying to save money." I just excused it away. I didn't really want to believe I was actually involved with another alcoholic. *Denial is a strong force to be reckoned with.*

Regrettably, I spent many nights with Jon while my babysitter stayed with my children. I justified my actions telling myself I was still going to church with my kids on Sundays and Wednesdays. I was still praying and talking about God. I actually thought I was falling in love with my new boyfriend.

In reality, I had left one alcoholic and immediately gotten involved with another. I should have remembered all the things I learned in the program. At the time, I felt that without Jon in my life I surely would have let Kenny sweet talk me into taking him back, and he did try. But because I was with somebody else, it was easier to say no to his advances. I was still so weak!

The phone rang late one night. "I just called to say I love you," Kenny sang.

"You're not even original." I said in a disgusted tone. "Stevie Wonder sings that."

"Let's try it again," my ex-husband pleaded. "I can't believe you really divorced me. I never thought you would. I thought you'd always stay with me like my mom stayed with my dad."

"I won't ever go back to you."

"I promise I'll do things differently this time," he slurred, obviously he'd been drinking.

"Like I said, it doesn't matter what you say anymore because I will never go back to you."

"You've changed. I don't even know you anymore. You're so mean!"

"You're right I have changed. I'll never put up with your abuse again." Slamming the receiver down, I felt good finally standing up to him.

Jon reached for me and I felt safe and loved. I couldn't afford to let Kenny's words tempt me. I was just beginning to understand I had been mistreated for a long and I didn't want to be miserable anymore.

During the next several months I tried hard to be a good Christian, even dragging my boyfriend to church with me. Finances were always tight and a neighbor helped me pay my electric bill and she provided day old bread and treats for the kids. The few friends I had, continued to pray for me without judging me, even though they did not approve of my relationship with Jon. Unfortunately, I didn't realize that by becoming involved immediately with someone else I did not give my children or myself time to heal.

I felt helpless to stop seeing him even though I lived in a constant state of guilt and shame. On the other hand, I felt free. I left my abuser and didn't have to worry about being threatened, accused, or hit anymore. As time went on, the angry threats ended and my ex-husband quit begging me to take him back. Kenny got involved with someone else and he stopped coming by to pick up the kids and eventually moved to Texas.

My children and I continued to attend church. I encouraged all their friends to go and even picked them up and took them to youth group. Rosa and I had stopped praying together on a weekly basis, but I stilled called her and other friends, and we prayed together often. I continued to berate myself for my shortcomings and felt guilty for repeating the same bad choices over and over again. I still did not know God saw me clothed in His robe of righteousness. I did not realize he delighted over me with singing. *He will take delight in you with gladness. With his love, He will rejoice over you with singing. Zephaniah 3:17*

Within a few months of being single I met a young girl who worked at Safeway. I walked out with her to the parking lot one night when we both worked the late shift. I noticed she had blankets, pillows, and laundry in her car. "You're not living in your car, are you?"

"Yes I am. If my parents find out I'm pregnant, especially with a black child, they will kill me," Laney said.

"There is no way I'm going to let you live like this. I have a small, three-bedroom house you're welcome to sleep on my couch. Sometimes you could help me with groceries and watch the kids. Is it a deal?"

Laney moved in and we became good friends. When she'd experience one of her pregnancy cravings, like cream cheese on soft white bread, we'd make a dash to the nearest market that was open all night. She made ordinary things feel like an adventure.

Laney's boyfriend, Max, came over often and played basketball with Jeremy and Jeff. We'd regularly have meals together and sometimes competed in board games afterwards. My kids loved our new roommate. She was fun to be around and helpful. She hummed familiar tunes and she was always singing and swaying back forth while putting on her makeup and doing laundry. (She had been in choir when she was in school.) She was always in a good mood and brought positive energy to our home and her boyfriend was good to the kids.

The Christmas immediately following my divorce was a holiday I was not looking forward to. Money was still tight, and I didn't have any idea how I would buy presents. My family couldn't help either, everyone had kids of their own and financial struggles as well. Since Kenny moved out of state he had stopped all contact with the kids and my occasional child support promptly ended, although I still continued to take my children to visit Kenny's folks on a regular basis.

Unbeknownst to me, my roommate called a meeting at work one day when I was off and shared my dilemma. All the employees gave generously and Laney collected enough money to buy Christmas presents for my kids. She asked her boyfriend's mother to make Kristy her very own Cabbage Patch doll. Kristy was delighted! I was so touched by the generosity of my co-workers and all the people that helped me that Christmas. I was beginning to understand that God still cared about me, even though I had gotten a divorce and oftentimes continued to feel guilty about it.

About this time, I met another teenager who worked with Laney and me. Dee often babysat for me, did my laundry, and would hang out at the house. One day she showed up unexpectedly. "I haven't told anybody, but I think I'm pregnant, and I can't let my parents find out. Will you take me to get an abortion?"

"I don't believe in abortions. I can't do it."

"You don't understand, my parents will kick me out if they find out please, please take me," she pleaded.

"Dee, I know you're only eighteen and I will help you out anyway I can. But you can't kill the baby. Please listen to me."

Laney woke up from her bed on the couch and interrupted. "I'll take you tomorrow. Now let me go back to sleep."

"I wish you both would reconsider. It's wrong and I don't want any part of this."

Dee left. Laney went back to sleep and I went into the other room and dialed my best friend's number. "Tracey, I just found out a friend is getting an abortion tomorrow. Would you pray with me that somehow she won't go through with it?"

"Of course, I will, I would give anything to have a baby." Tracey prayed, "Father in heaven, please block Dee from getting an abortion, and keep this baby healthy."

Early the next morning before I left for work my friend and I again prayed for Dee. I also urged Laney to change her mind about taking her, but she wouldn't. As soon as I got home the two of them met me back at the house.

"They won't do it. I'm so angry. They said I was twenty-five weeks. What am I going to do?" Dee cried.

I was so happy! I couldn't wait to call my best friend and share the good news with her. *Thank you, God!*

"Dee, I will help you anyway I can. You can even stay here if you want."

I wouldn't see Dee again for months although I worked with her we always had a different schedule. When we did have the same shift, she would barely look my way and I could hear her bragging about partying and taking diet pills to lose weight. My heart ached for her and the life of her unborn baby. There was nothing I could do; she refused to let me in her life. Tracey and I kept praying for her and the baby.

In February 1985, my phone rang early in the morning, while it was still dark, and woke me from a deep slumber. "Deb, hurry, call my dad and ask him if I can baby-sit for you." Something is happening to me and I'm having really bad pains," Dee whispered.

"Do you think you can drive? Leave him a note and just get in your car now and come over."

I called Tracey, "Please pray for my friend. I think she is in labor."

Unfortunately, I had to go to work while Laney dashed out the door with Dee and rushed her to the hospital.

"Call me at work and let me know what happens."

Less than an hour later I received her call. "I just had the baby and I am going to put him up for adoption."

"Wait, wait before you do that. I have a friend who has been married for a while and she can't have kids. Tracey had an infection and had to have a complete hysterectomy when she was twenty-three. Can she and her husband adopt your baby?"

"Of course, any friend of yours is a friend of mine," she assured me. "I don't want my parents to ever know."

Dialing Tracey's number, "Guess what? Dee had a baby boy and she said you can adopt him!"

I could almost feel her tears of happiness through the phone.

"God is so faithful. My husband and I have been praying for a baby for years. And you and I have prayed. This is a miracle."

The adoption was set in motion. It would take a full year before everything was legal and my friend would be the mother she always wanted to be.

Shortly before the baby was born, my boyfriend had broken up with me. I grieved the end of our relationship, as stormy and unhealthy as it was. I eventually came to realize the tears I cried were really tears of mourning for my failed marriage, not for my boyfriend. I had never properly mourned the end of my marriage and all the hopes and dreams I had had. Slowly, I began to heal, or so I thought.

30

Second Time Around

"Don't waste your breath on fools, for they will despise the wisest advice." Proverbs 23:9

Soon after baby James went home to be with Tracey, I paid her a visit. It was wonderful to see my friend with her newborn son. A friend of hers showed up while I was visiting.

"Lee, this is Debbie."

"Hi," he said, staring dreamily in my eyes. "Didn't we go to different high schools together?"

Laughing, I said, "I don't know about that."

We spent a lot of time talking and joking with each other while holding the new baby. Later that night Tracey called. "Lee wants your number. Can I give it to him? He used to date my sister so I've known him for a while. He had some problems, but he is a Christian now."

"Sure, go ahead."

The next day he called. We talked for hours. I invited Lee over to watch the Academy Awards. He was late, but the kids and I didn't mind because he walked in the door carrying four different boxes of candy.

Lee told funny stories while feeding my hungry brood those sweet treats. What kid wouldn't like that? After I tucked them in bed we spent the whole night just talking.

Lee came over every day after that and we talked for hours. It was refreshing, he seemed interested in me, there was never a lack of conversation, he always had something to talk about and he acted like he wanted to be around me all the time. Kenny had rarely engaged in conversation with me unless it was to ridicule or accuse me of something. Lee quickly swept me off my feet with promises of a quick marriage and wanting to become a father to my kids. I was thrilled to actually have someone interested in me who didn't have a drinking problem.

I found out he had two boys from a previous marriage. Because he was unable to pay child support he had given his boys up for adoption to their stepfather thirteen years earlier.

"How did you feel about giving up your kids?"

"Of course, I regret giving them up. I still feel terrible, but I was in a bad situation at the time. I had just gotten in a car accident. My buddy was driving and he fell asleep at the wheel. We hit a parked car and he was killed instantly. "Look!" He pointed to his injured leg. As he pulled off a piece of white gauze I noticed a small hole in his calf with clear fluid oozing out.

"I have to wear a bandage every day of my life, day and night. And now I walk with a limp. Why did I survive? I don't know. Maybe God has something else for me. I still struggle with survivor's guilt. Maybe you're the answer, you and your kids. I can be a husband again and your children can replace the ones I was forced to give up."

Finally, I thought, somebody had come into my life that would love me and take care of us. It was the love I had been looking for all my life. I appreciated that Lee actually opened up about his feelings, regrets, and his dreams. It seemed to me he had learned from his mistakes. And the most important thing of all, he talked to me, constantly!

Laney moved out shortly before I met Lee. She had a little girl and was so happy her parents finally accepted her interracial relationship. She was able to move back home. Laney and Max were making plans to marry after he graduated from high school.

Lee and I met in March exactly one year after I had filed for divorce. We were inseparable and spent every spare moment together, although he went home every night to his own apartment.

Lee's job was to take underprivileged kids door-to-door to sell candy. He worked whenever he wanted to. He seemed to love kids, and appeared responsible. He had a great rapport with my children, and Jeremy began working for him. Jeremy enjoyed making his own money and meeting new friends.

Lee was a charmer and he seemed to say all the right things. He radiated confidence, and gave the impression he had the ability to overcome obstacles and move forward in his life despite his past setbacks. I felt he had integrity too. He seemed too good to be true. He was always ready to go to church with us and he was never at loss for words. Best of all, he didn't have a drinking problem.

"We can live in your house and I can help you fix it up. I can build a recreation room for the kids. I'll help you take care of the yard. I can even make a tree house in the back yard. If it means I have to work more hours and help with the house payment I'm ready to do it."

It seemed like a dream come true!

Everything was moving quickly and I thought it was because he was in love with me and couldn't live without me. Within weeks he asked me to marry him and we decided to get married right away. I got in touch with my old pastor, (who had recently divorced and had left the church) and asked him to perform the ceremony. Lee and I secretly eloped near the scenic red rock formations, known as the Garden of the Gods, only a few miles from our home. It was simple, quick, and romantic. Jeremy and my sister stood up with us. Because we kept it a secret from everybody else, it seemed so exciting. Four months later we decided to have a small wedding and invited our family and a few friends.

A couple weeks after we were married Lee proposed a plan. "I want all of us to go camping. Doesn't that sound like fun?"

We had never been camping and we were all looking forward to it. The kids and I were up at the crack of dawn, ready to load the van, excited to leave for our trip.

"We all need to clean the van before we load it," Lee began barking orders.

"It will be dirtier when we get back. Can't we just clean it then? The kids and I are ready to go now."

"Nope, it has to be cleaned first," He said, adamantly. "That's just the way I do things."

Hours turned into all day, as Lee was very particular about how the van had to be cleaned and packed. By five in the evening the joy and enthusiasm about the trip had waned. Nobody was excited anymore, except Lee. I began to realize the cute way he was late on our first date was really a lifelong bad habit of his. He always kept people waiting and he procrastinated on just about everything. I just thought he was spontaneous. I liked it before we were married; now it wasn't so cute anymore!

We took more camping trips, and although the kids and I loved being out in nature, Lee simply turned the ventures into disasters. We kept hoping each trip was the last one, but it never was. Lee would fly into fits of rage over the smallest things. On one trip, Lee's two brothers joined us. All of us sat by the campfire. "Look up, there's a planet," Lee pointed upward.

"I can't see no planets, those look like stars," Jeremy stated.

"That's a double negative Jeremy. You said it the wrong way," Lee corrected him.

"No, I didn't," Jeremy said.

"You don't even know what a double negative is? You're just stupid!

"No, I'm not," said Jeremy.

"Come on, Lee, leave the kid alone," Ray, Lee's younger brother said. "Don't make it a big deal?"

I also asked him to leave Jeremy alone, but Lee wouldn't shut up. He continued to belittle Jeremy for not understanding what a double negative was. *I just wanted him to shut up.*

"You're supposed to take my side and you're always taking the kids side. You probably don't know what a double negative is either!"

I tried to reason with him. "Just leave my son alone. You sound so self-righteous. Please don't call Jeremy names. You're embarrassing him in front of your brothers."

All of a sudden Lee screamed. "Let's go. We're leaving. Pack up! Get in the van now."

Finally, his brothers calmed him down. But the trip was ruined for the rest of the weekend and we did our best to stay out of his way. We even stopped making comments when he was around. Later the kids and I talked about it when we were out of Lee's earshot. "I am sick of Lee correcting me about my grammar and just about everything I do." Jeremy said angrily.

"Me too," said Kristy. "I'm sick of being criticized for everything I say and do."

"I don't like Lee making jokes about me," added Jeff.

"I'm sorry, you guys. I'm just glad his brothers are with us. It makes it easier to be stuck out here. Unfortunately, they are leaving tomorrow."

A few days later Lee decided it was time to go home. It took all day to pack up.

"I want you to drive the van. I'm tired."

I had only recently learned how to drive it and I was nervous. It was so big and I was inexperienced. "Please don't make me drive. I'm not that good at driving a stick yet. I know you're tired, but I'll keep you awake, I promise."

"I said I was tired and if you don't drive we will just stay here for a couple more days."

"But I have to go back to work, and I am really nervous about driving your van. Please don't' make me drive it."

My pleading did no good so I climbed into the driver's side, put my foot on the pedal and prayed all the way home that I would be able to drive and not make any mistakes.

Within months after we had our wedding ceremony, I knew I had made a terrible mistake by marrying Lee. Although he brought some new adventures into our lives it was evident he wasn't the man he had portrayed himself to be. His demeanor changed as soon as he moved into my home. I was constantly confused with his mannerisms and his display of unruly behavior and rages and particularly the way he treated my children. I felt like I was going crazy. I had never dealt with anyone like him before. I had no idea who this man really was! I soon realized I had jumped out of the frying pan into the fire. I felt guilty for my first divorce and even guiltier for what my children were enduring because of my quickie second marriage. Feeling helpless to change the direction my life was going, I felt like such a loser.

The real Lee proved he had no self-confidence and was filled with insecurities that he began to display daily. Lee hardly worked at all. I realized the only reason he drove kids around to sell candy was because it was an easy job for him and he was lazy. Mistakenly, I believed he enjoyed hanging out with kids. Now my children seemed to get on his nerves most of the time and he always found ways to criticize them. I noticed Lee would spend hours lecturing the kids and me. All he wanted to do was argue, he just had to get in the last word. No one could reason with him. *What had I gotten us into? I felt stuck!*

Unfortunately, my husband had a strong sense of entitlement and was content to let me carry the burden of paying the bills. "After all, I didn't get to spend any of that money you took out on your second mortgage, and therefore it's your responsibility to pay it." He often stated.

At first the weekend trips in the van whenever Lee worked was fun, but after a while all of us grew tired of the hearing the same jokes over and over and listening to his exaggerated stories. It wasn't long before I noticed all conversations were about him. I had thought he enjoyed talking with me but in reality, he was a compulsive talker. He hoarded the conversations and was quick to interrupt my attempts at joining in. One of the other things I began to notice was his lying. I began to catch him in lies all the time.

When I went to work, I had to leave the kids with him. I hated the way he wasted time. He had grandiose ideas about how he would win the lottery one day and he would spend countless hours writing down how the money would be spent. Then he'd show us the list during dinner and try to get us all excited in his unrealistic fantasies. Fruitless hours were spent wasted by Lee whenever his magazines came in the mail. I dreaded the day when he would receive his beloved Reader's Digest. He would stay in bed all day reading the magazine from cover to cover, never acknowledging the kids or me. Sometimes I'd leave for work before the mail arrived and I would find him, still in his pajamas, holding on to that stupid magazine, when I'd get home from work. Finally, I began hiding the book if I checked the mail first.

Jeremy was the one that got everyone ready for school and made dinners when I worked the late shift. Lee ignored the kids, and if he wasn't ignoring them, he was nagging them, forcing them to do their chores to perfection. He never praised them but was quick to point out any shortcoming on their part. He usually ended up grounding them. There were certain things in the house that belonged only to him, such as his desk. He was always accusing the kids of touching his things. "Get your grimy, dirty hands off my stuff. I will put you on restriction if you touch it again. If your mother lets you then she is going to be in trouble too."

I tried to stick up for my kids.

Lee only argued with me, "We're married. You should take my side not theirs."

He even had his own special boxes of cereal. He'd meticulously tape up a box of Captain Crunch so my kids wouldn't eat it. When I accidentally washed his money, and checks he marched me into the laundry room to teach me the appropriate way to check the pockets and do his laundry. I had been washing clothes since I was ten. It was absurd!

I thought things would get better financially after we got married, but because he rarely worked money was always tight. He had stopped working for the candy company and went from job to job, or, more to the point, he hardly ever worked. I was the sole breadwinner and he did absolutely nothing to help out and child support was virtually non-existent.

Growing tired of waiting for Lee to bring some money in, I applied for food stamps. He didn't think anything of using my food stamps to help himself to food but he refused to go with me to apply each month. I kept bugging him about getting a job, but he wouldn't listen. Thinking I was helping, I'd read the morning paper and circle jobs in the classified section hoping he would apply for them.

Before we got married he had bragged about working for a real estate agency, owning his own waterbed store and working in his dad's wrought iron shop. Now I wasn't sure if he had done any of those things. I never met a man who could spend all day doing nothing. The only thing my first husband had going for him was he worked hard. Mistakenly, I thought all men did. I realized what the word lethargic meant when I married Lee.

I had never been around someone like him and was so confused about his behavior. Just when I thought he was fun to be around he'd act unreasonable and fly into rages. Like the time we were driving home from a camping trip and I started my period. Realizing I forgot to bring tampons, I stuffed an old shirt between my legs. "It's five hours till we get home can you stop at a store?"

"No, you should have come prepared. We're not going to stop."

No amount of pleading and bargaining would make him change his mind. Shocked, I wondered who this man was and why was he so damn mean.

Most times after our camping trips Lee expected me to drive part of the way home. I began to refuse to give in to his ridiculous demands. He knew how anxious and uncomfortable I felt about driving his big, blue van, but that didn't matter to him. He would head towards home then stop about 45 minutes from our house, then he would order me to get into the driver's seat. Sometimes, I stood my ground and said no. I was more afraid of having an accident than submitting to Lee. I didn't care that he would make us spend the night at a rest stop. He thought he was punishing me, but the kids and I just got comfortable and fell asleep for the rest of the night. This would be repeated many times throughout our marriage. He knew when I had to be at work, thankfully, I was always home in time for my job.

When I was at work, Lee would hassle the kids and send them to their rooms. My two younger ones often crawled out the window and would run to the neighbors. Petie was grandmotherly and had no kids of her own and always made my children feel welcome. They would call me at work. "Mom, Lee is being mean to us again."

"Okay, you can stay at Petie's until I come home. I will deal with him after work."

Unfortunately, I couldn't reason with Lee and he would continue to put the kids on restriction and scream at me later. "You're always taking their side, you should take my side now that we are married."

There were times I had to work and couldn't prepare dinners for the family, fortunately Jeremy was very responsible and had learned to cook. He took care of his brother and sister. Lee rarely cooked for the children. He'd open up a can of soup for himself but he seldom offered any to them. Lee would go to the store and buy himself warm, just-baked French bread and lunchmeat and order my kids not to touch HIS food.

Jeremy was good-natured, but a few times he and Lee argued and it almost came to blows. Stepping in, I'd beg Lee not to hit my son. Luckily, these kinds of heated arguments only happened when I was home to intervene.

Lee would often spend all day, sitting at a local coffee shop, flirting with the young girls who worked as waitresses.

"Why are you at the coffee shop letting those girls hang on you? We are married. You shouldn't be doing that."

Even though we fought constantly I desperately wanted to be loved by him. I believed if I was prettier, skinner, or more fun that Lee would prefer me instead of hanging out with the girls at the coffee shop.

One night we even planned a date and I came home from work showered, dressed up and waited for Lee. When he didn't come home, I finally asked the kids, where they thought he might have gone and when he had left.

"I don't know Mom, right before you got home he got in his van and drove away."

Angrily, I stomped out to the car and drove around until I saw his blue van parked at the Kwik Inn, his local hangout. Walking in, I saw him surrounded by teenage waitress. "Lee," I hollered. "What are you doing?"

He turned to look at me and then followed me outside. "I thought we agreed that you wouldn't go to the coffee shop and hang out with those young girls anymore, and besides we had a date planned. Isn't this important to you? I have been home getting ready and waiting. Why are you hanging out with those girls?"

"They make me feel young." Staring straight at me, he rolled his eyes. "The novelty has worn off with you?" *What the heck did that mean?*

I shook my head. Was I too proud and too guilt-ridden to seek help? I don't know. How could I let other people know what I had gotten myself into? I felt helpless to change the mistake I had made. I wasn't even thirty-one. I wasn't about to get another divorce. How would that look to other people? Selfishly, I didn't consider how my children were suffering. All my Alanon teaching went out the window. I seemed to have forgotten all the ways in which the Lord had worked in my life earlier.

My mom even tried to talk some sense into Lee, but he twisted everybody's words and blamed everyone but himself, refusing to admit he had any problems at all. I often questioned my sanity while being married to Lee. Sometimes I felt living with an alcoholic was minor compared to the verbal and mental abuse the kids and I suffered from him. Some of the things he said to me were so cruel. Kenny would have never said those awful things. *Did it have a name? Is this what mental illness looked like? Was I going crazy? Was he crazy?*

Lee was small in stature and I wasn't afraid of him physically like I had been with Kenny. But there was something about the way Lee manipulated things that made me feel as if he had control over my kids and me. Because there was no alcohol involved I had erroneously believed that this time things would be different. Boy was I wrong!

During the times, we fought it became evident we were both a couple of pessimists.

"I'll never lose the extra fifteen pounds I've put on. I feel so fat," I'd say.

"You probably won't, and I will never be able to stop smoking."

"You probably won't. We are just a couple of losers, aren't we?"

"Yes, we are," Lee agreed.

We brought out the worst in each other. Lee and I fought like cats and dogs. Because I wasn't afraid of him, I yelled as loud as I could and said things to hurt him. He, in turn, would let a torrent of cruel words explode from his mouth. We both seemed helpless to control our anger. Thankfully these altercations only happened when the kids were at school. It would take me a long time to realize that not only was I mad at Lee, I was unconsciously mad at every man who had ever hurt me and I took it out on him. Nonetheless, I didn't want to be a failure for a second time and I continued to try and make the marriage work.

Eighteen months after we were married Lee and I listened to a speaker talk about co-dependency and dysfunctional relationships, but we were both so blinded we didn't even relate it to our own lives. We were too busy pointing the finger at each other or everyone else. Denial still had a stronghold over me. I spent my time at my job, raising my kids, and trying desperately to figure out what was wrong with my marriage and thinking of ways I could fix it. We continued to go to church on Sundays and mid-week services. Once again, I believed I was doing the right thing. But I was gradually losing hope in my marriage.

31

Ashley

"You watched me as I was being formed in utter seclusion, as I was woven together in the dark of the womb."
Psalm 139 15

Jeremy asked me on a number of occasions why I continued to stay with Lee. Shaking my head, I was filled with despair for the stupid mistake I had made. I felt as if I was trapped and couldn't find my way out. I made excuses for his actions while trying to encourage my kids. "He didn't mean it. His own mother didn't treat him very well. Please try and forgive him. Don't let his words bother you."

About two years after we were married, I was convinced maybe having of a child of our own would fix our relationship and Lee and I talked about trying to have a baby. I thought it would bring us closer and that it would somehow replace the children he had lost. I still felt sorry for him. It would take me much longer to realize Lee had really given up his kids because he had refused to take responsibility for them.

"I'm not sure I want a child. I feel like at thirty-six I'm too old to start over again," Lee said.

We didn't come to any conclusion after several conversations, but I did end up getting pregnant shortly after one of our talks. I was thrilled to be after the shock wore off. Of course, I worried about our finances since I was basically the one who was supporting the family. I was grateful I had insurance and the kids seemed to be excited as well. My boss at work refused to let me carry heavy boxes and treated me as if I had never been pregnant before.

All and all things seemed to be going well but we still fought constantly. Once, when I was about seven months pregnant, Lee became so angry with me after an argument he raised his fist and hit me.

I exploded and punched him back. "I will never let another man hit me again."

"It's all your fault! I've never hit a woman, you made me do it."

"You're crazy! You chose to hit me. I didn't make you."

He never hit me again.

Sometimes Lee would get so depressed and self-condemning I was immediately moved to feel sorry for him. I felt my role was to do whatever I could to make him happy. I believed if I focused all my attention on his needs I would be able to make a difference in his life and he would be joyful and content. I was so consumed with fixing him. I failed to think about the emotional needs of my children. Although I did not neglect them and I paid attention to them I should have been making them my top priority instead of trying to fix Lee. Unbeknownst to me at the time, I was repeating what I had done with my mother and Kenny.

I was eagerly awaiting the birth of my fourth child. My last baby, Jeff, was already eight and I longed to hold another baby in my arms. The kids were excited too. Kristy desperately wanted a baby sister and finally in March of 1987 I went into labor.

Ashley was born several hours later in a birthing room at our local hospital. All the kids were in the room, and they watched in fascination as I gave birth to my baby girl. She was beautiful with a full head of dark hair. I held my little bundle close and thanked God for the new life he had given me. I was thrilled she had become a part of our family and each of the kids looked in awe at the tiny baby in my arms. I'm sure it was a moment in their lives they would never forget.

When I had been pregnant, Lee would pat my tummy and talk to the baby and fall asleep with his arms around me. After she and I came home from the hospital, I expected him to continue to cuddle me.

"Why aren't you holding me like you did when I was pregnant?" I asked him one night.

"You had the baby," was all he said. With no other explanation, his embracing stopped.

Immediately following Ashley's birth, the other kids and I ceased to have any importance in Lee's life. At least before, on his good days, he acted like he cared somewhat for the kids. I dreaded going back to work after taking my maternity leave. I had never before had to leave any of my children at eight weeks and it was killing me. Thankfully, I was able to nurse my baby and freeze my milk in between shifts. Lee was also kind enough to bring Ashley to work so I could still feed her on my breaks. Between him bottle feeding her my frozen milk and bringing her to the store I was able to nurse her for over a year.

Lee was a very attentive father, always taking care of her when I was at work. But unfortunately, he discouraged any relationship between Ashley and her siblings. In fact, he acted like he resented my kids and he made sure they knew it. After she was born, Lee borrowed his brother's brand-new video camera and it became a permanent fixture on his shoulder. Ashley was on camera from the time she was a tiny baby. *This was before cell phones with great cameras were invented.*

Jeremy took an immediate liking to his new sister and watched over her when Lee wasn't around. He continued to be the man of the house taking care of the rest of his siblings while I worked. He found time to hang out with his friends in the neighborhood and he and I often spent time together throwing the basketball, playing catch or getting involved in a card game whenever we could steal a few minutes from daily life.

Kristy, who had turned ten shortly after Ashley was born, was my creative child and she had quite an imagination. A favorite game of hers was decorating the dining room table with colorful material. "Mommy, can I take your order?" she'd ask. Some afternoons when I came home from work, she'd run to greet me at the door with a plate of homemade cookies and lemonade. Sometimes Kristy imagined she was a mommy and mother her little brother. Lee didn't trust her with Ashley and made sure she didn't spend any quality time with our new addition. She was brokenhearted. All she wanted was to be a big sister to our baby. She just wanted to please me and make me happy and she did whatever she could to receive attention from her stepdad. Incredibly he just continued to ignore her or belittle her. I spent most of my time worrying about my children's feelings.

I worked different schedules, and when I had to leave before the kids got home from school, I'd walk across the street looking for my two younger ones who were usually at recess.

"Kristy, I have to go to work now. I will miss you. I love you very much."

She'd reach out to me through the fence and we'd spend a little bit of time together before I had to leave. "I love you too, Mommy. Wish you didn't have to go."

Jeff would wave. "See you later, Mommy. Hurry and come home."

He was happy-go-lucky and was popular with his little friends. But the longer Lee was in the picture, the more it affected Jeff. He seemed to lose his good-natured personality and he began to act fearful and insecure. He'd come home from school wearing his jacket zipped up under his chin and refuse to take it off no matter what the weather was. Lee would belittle him about taking off the jacket. I came to realize later it was his security blanket. Jeff spent hours playing with his friends or his brother and sister and he kept himself out of his stepfather's way as much as possible. They all did well in school, and I didn't notice any disciplinary problems. In fact, they were a joy to be around. From all outward appearance, you'd never know the scars that were forming in their young hearts.

We celebrated Kristy's 10th birthday by having a dance party at our house with several of her girlfriends and neighborhood boys. We'd laugh and act silly, although Lee would get angry when the kids or I got more attention than he did. He wanted to be the star of the show. The kids and I had more fun times when he was out of the house, which unfortunately, wasn't often enough. Since he rarely worked he always seemed to be around except when he would leave to take Ashley to parks and restaurants around town.

When I'd come home from work he and Ashley would usually be gone. I missed my baby. After a long day at work I wanted to hold her in my arms. His relationship with our new daughter became obsessive. It was evident to the other kids that she was the star. When I was away at work Lee often dressed her up in frilly dresses and took her to restaurants where the waitresses swooned over her. He loved the attention! In fact, he hardly took the kids and me anywhere after she was born. He bought stuffed animals and toys and presented them to Ashley while my children stood by and watched. I felt helpless to do anything. I couldn't understand his behavior and I didn't realize at the time how much it was hurting my kids.

32

Restoration

*"Don't be afraid, for I am with you. Don't be discouraged,
for I am your God. I will strengthen you and help you. I will
hold you up with my victorious right hand." Isaiah 41:10*

When I was pregnant we took a trip to California to visit my older brother, Mike and some of my old friends. One of Mrs. Kinzer's boys from my neighborhood had recently bought my childhood home. I asked him if I could walk through my house where I had lived when my father and mother were married. As I entered each room, memories of the abuse flooded my mind. I could see myself as a little girl and it brought me to tears. I knew it was time for the little girl inside of me to be healed.

My father lived nearby and shortly before Ashley was born, he had begun to stop by frequently and would randomly visit me at work. Even after all the time that had passed, I still needed his love and acceptance. I never blamed him for the sexual abuse because I had long ago convinced myself it was my fault, even though my mother told me it wasn't. I started to notice that being around him felt uncomfortable and

I found myself cringing when he'd reach out to hug me. Afterwards, I'd feel guilty for feeling that way.

Rosa and I still prayed together but not as often after I married Lee. She helped me to understand that God wanted to heal me of the deep hurts in my heart that I had hidden away. I continued to ask God to show me how I could change. I had recently begun listening to a Christian radio program where several psychiatrists answered questions about life issues. I started to read their books. They taught that we are all products of our childhood. It was if the blinders were slowly coming off and I began to understand I had a lot of unresolved anger and resentment towards my father, ex-husband, Lee, and God. I thought the past could no longer hurt me. I began to realize the choices I had made in my life were a direct result of being sexually molested. I felt like a child reacting to situations the same way I had as a little girl. Erroneously, I still blamed myself for what my father had done to me, believing it was my fault and I was filled with shame, guilt and self-loathing. The Bible said my Savior, Jesus Christ loved me unconditionally but all I could focus on were all the bad things about myself that I hated. *How come He didn't see them?*

I was beginning to understand that because the relationship I had with my earthly father was abusive, it was hard for me to accept God as a kind and loving father. I know at certain times in my life I had tried to believe it, but I don't know if I ever really accepted it. I still hadn't realized what could transpire in my life when I fully acknowledged the real healing power from the Lord and the power God had to change my life. *"He brought them out of darkness and the deepest gloom and broke away their chains." Psalms 107:14*

I went to visit Rosa after my vacation and told her how I had felt when I had walked into my old house again.

"I'm also feeling uncomfortable when my dad pays me a visit and he hugs me when he leaves. I hate the way it makes me feel when he touches me, it makes me cringe," I explained.

"I know you still blame yourself for what happened. I think you're feeling uncomfortable with your dad's touch because it's time for you to confront him," Rosa said.

"Why did God let it happened?" I questioned. "He had the power to stop it."

"I don't know the answer to that," she took my hands in hers. "Let's give this to Jesus and ask him. Now close your eyes and imagine the homes you grew up in where the abuse occurred. Describe to me what you see."

"I can see the room and can also picture the bed it happened on. I am lying there and I can see myself as a little girl. "My dad is coming in. He pulls back the covers and lies down with me. He begins to touch me and I ask him to stop. He won't."

"Can you see Jesus? Is he there with you?" Rosa asked.

"Yes, yes he is. He is sitting near the bed and he can see what is happening to me."

"What is he doing?"

"His head is in his hands and big tears are rolling down his cheeks. I think he is crying for me."

"Debbie if he is there with you, why doesn't he stop it?"

"I can see him shaking his head sadly, crying the whole time, and He looks toward me and says, 'your father has his own will and I cannot stop a person's free will."

"What else is Jesus saying to you?"

With my eyes tightly closed I felt as if I could hear Jesus say, "I chose you. I was always with you. I am here with you now. I will never leave you." It wasn't as if I heard an audible voice but instead it was an impression in my mind.

Opening my eyes, tears streaming down my face, I understood for the first time why God did not stop my dad. He hurt for me, he watched it all, tearfully knowing he couldn't make my dad stop. The vision the Lord put in my head would become instrumental in my future restoration.

No longer mad at God, I found myself feeling angry towards my father. I finally felt strong enough to confront him. I knew it was the right time. I realized I hadn't really trusted my heavenly Father to take care of me because I had been so deeply wounded by my earthly father. "Please help me to really trust you," I asked God in my prayers.

My father liked to buy old, broken-down used cars. Because I lived outside the city limits, he used my address to receive the titles of the cars he was buying, so he wouldn't have to pay sales tax. I began to feel used and taken advantage of. It reminded me of how I had felt as a child. I asked my mother if she would sit with me while I confronted my father.

"I'm so angry at that man for what he did to my girls. I will tell him myself how he messed up your lives."

"No, Mom, this is something I need to do. I just need your support and I need courage."

"Okay. I'll be here for you."

Nervously, I dialed his number. "Daddy, I don't want you using my address anymore and if anything else comes in the mail I will throw it right in the trash. I feel like you're using me just like you did when I was a child to satisfy your own desires."

"Oh, honey please, please do not throw my mail away. You know I would never do anything to hurt you."

Those were the exact words he had said to me as a child while I laid helpless in my bed in the darkness of the night. And he did hurt me, physically, as well as emotionally and spiritually.

"I mean it! I remember everything you did to me when I was little. You better not use my address again. Don't come visit me and don't ever call me. I want nothing to do with you ever!"

"Honey, don't throw my mail away," was all he said.

Click! I hung up on him. I felt like an enormous weight had lifted off my shoulders. For the first time in my life I transferred the blame to where it should have gone in the first place-on him! I had been an innocent child and he violated me. He used my body with no regard to what it would do to me later on. In that instant, all the hatred I had felt about myself transferred onto him. I felt so angry! He had destroyed my trust in a loving God and had destroyed my faith in men. I had believed I was worthless all my life-even after becoming a Christian. The scars were so deep.

Over the years I had read books on incest and talked to people and had been prayed for. Now I was beginning to understand, only God could heal me from the inside out. Each week I was able to comprehend more truths. I began to see that I had chosen men who abused me either physically or verbally. It's what I believed I deserved. It was comfortable in a familiar way and it was all I had ever known. After all, it was what I had grown up with. I was beginning to see the lies I had concocted in my own head because of what had been done to me. I was finally beginning to believe God had always loved me and I was worth loving. That was the truth, not the voices in my head that told me otherwise.

After finally believing how God felt about me, my steps had a new bounce in them. Happy thoughts took the place of anxious ones and I found a new peace. I began to share my feelings, my hurts, my fears, and my joys with God on a daily basis. I received his reassurance by reading and believing what He said about me in the Bible. *"I have loved you with an everlasting love; therefore, I have continued my faithfulness to you."* Jeremiah 31:3

A few months had passed since the day I confronted my father. I began to wonder what happened in my dad's childhood to make him do those awful things to me. Maybe he had been molested too. Eventually, it was God who changed my heart towards him and took away my hatred and anger. He gave me the desire and the strength to forgive my father. After all, God had forgiven me for all my sins. I wanted to reach out to him to tell him I had forgiven him, even though I felt I no longer needed his love, approval, or an apology. After all I was receiving those things from my Father in Heaven.

My dad had moved out of the city and had stayed in contact with my sister. I kept meaning to call her and get his new phone number. I didn't, but the nagging feeling that I should call him wouldn't go away. I kept thinking, *call your dad and tell him you forgive him.*

Ashley was born in March and a few weeks later on Saint Patrick's Day, Lee and I decided to drive to the other side of town and take the kids to the annual parade. I dressed them in green and off we went.

When the parade was over we walked down a neighborhood towards the parking lot. Suddenly, I noticed a familiar face, a gray-haired, bearded man, standing on the sidewalk, in front of somebody's house.

Briskly, I walked towards him. "Daddy," I called.

With a frightened look, he stood motionless. Our eyes met, but he quickly turned away from my stare.

Striding over to him, I immediately hugged him and whispered, "Daddy, it's okay. I forgive you now. You can call me anytime."

My father embraced me tightly. "Honey, I'm sorry for what I did to you."

I knew it was a divine appointment God had arranged. It was no coincidence; in fact, I called it my God-incident. There was no other way to explain running into him like that.

Even though I was feeling good about the healing I had been working on for myself, my relationship with Lee was still at odds. When Ashley was just a few months old most of the time I could count on coming home from work to find Lee and Ashley gone. Panic would seize me and I would worry that one-day they might not come home at all. Not only was I afraid of being abandoned, but I was also fearful that Lee would run off with my sweet, little daughter and I might never see her again. His unhealthy attachment to her scared me. Our arguments always sounded like this. "Why don't you treat me like I'm special any-more? I feel so alone. You are always leaving with Ashley within min-utes before I'm supposed to get home."

"What do you mean?" Lee asked. "There's always kids around."

"I miss you and my daughter when you're not here. I just want you to pay attention to me."

He'd just laugh at me and make me feel stupid for sharing my feelings with him. Finally, I began keeping my thoughts to myself while resentment rose up in me. I wondered why he had lost interest in me and continued to beat myself up for not being good enough. My feelings were growing numb towards him. But I was so terribly afraid of being alone again. And I desperately wanted to be loved.

I continued to feel abandoned by Lee every time he left the house. It was my sister, who had recently become a Christian, who pointed something out to me what I hadn't realized before. One day after com-ing home from work and finding Lee and Ashley gone again, I panicked as usual. Sobbing uncontrollably, I called Monica. "Why does he leave right before I get off work? He knows what time I'm due home and the kids tell me he leaves about ten minutes before I'm supposed to arrive. I went driving around to his favorite coffee shop and I didn't see his van and I drove over to the other coffee shops and by the park where he hangs out and I couldn't find him. Where is he? What is wrong with me? Why doesn't he want to be with me? Why does it hurt so much when he leaves me? What if he runs away with Ashley? I'm so scared."

"Deb, you have abandonment issues. In fact, you're the one who told me that God would never abandon you. People will come and go, but God won't. You can choose to detach yourself from Lee and learn to trust Jesus one day at a time. Then you take away Lee's power to hurt you."

She was right of course and I began to start and end my day with prayer more often and read the verses about God being with me over and over until I memorized them. The stronger I got inside, the closer I moved towards God and the more detached from Lee I felt. I no longer felt afraid when he left. The Lord also showed me I was mistakenly reaching out to Lee to fill that empty spot in my heart that only God could fill. As I meditated on the verse "I will never leave you or forsake you" I felt God reassuring me that He was with me. I knew I would never again need Lee in an unhealthy way. I continued to grow apart from him.

I looked forward to my days off, when I would have time to spend with my little toddler while the older kids were in school. Regrettably, I wasn't able to spend much alone time with Ashley because Lee was always around. He had nowhere else to go, with no job and no friends.

"Lee, can't you take a drive? Just go somewhere, please. I want to spend time with just Ashley. I only have a couple days off a week and I would really like some alone time with her."

"No, I don't have anything to do. Let's take her to the park today. Come on, it will be fun."

Some days I grew so tired of fighting him and gave in. After all it was the only way I could spend time with my daughter on my days off.

At other times, when I felt like I could stand up to Lee I'd take Ashley outside to my burgundy Subaru and lift up the hatchback sit in there just to get away from her dad. I knew he wouldn't follow me to my car. I'd turn the heater on in the winter and the air conditioner on in the summer. We'd play with her toys and then I'd read a story to her. I had to be creative to steal precious time with my little one.

Early in our marriage, Lee had introduced me to his friends who lived an hour away from us. The wife, Sharon and I had become close. We were both pregnant at the same time. Only weeks after she had the baby, my friend found out her husband was having an affair. After the divorce, he had custody of their child fifty percent of the time. I saw how hard it was for Sharon and I felt sorry for her. When I allowed myself to think about divorcing Lee, the anxiety I had about splitting time with my daughter and the fear of him possibility running off with her caused me to put the thoughts out of my mind.

Even though my second marriage was free from the problems of alcohol, the daily verbal abuse towards my children and me continued. Seeking counsel at our church, I begged Lee to go with me. Reluctantly, he went one time.

At our meeting, I spoke openly to the Assistant Pastor, Coleman, "Lee constantly says unkind things to my children. They are painful to hear and I believe he is wounding them. But instead of consoling my kids I make excuses for him. He also favors Ashley and it's evident to the other kids. He brings her presents and ice cream but brings nothing for them. The older kids say they don't care, but it is really hard on Jeff. I worry about what is happening to my children and how he is affecting them. I've tried to stop it and I'm mad at myself for letting it continue and I blame myself."

Lee yelled loudly and began making excuses for himself. "Well, Ashley is my own kid. The other kids aren't even mine. Besides, you always take their side over mine." Angrily, he stomped out of the room and left me to find my own ride home. I'd worry about a ride home later.

"Have you ever heard the word co-dependent?" Coleman asked. "People that are co-dependent have low self-esteem and look for anything outside themselves to make them feel better. You were co-dependent with your mom, your ex-husband, and now with Lee. Your caretaking has become compulsive and defeating. When you take care of that other person you began to feel like a martyr. You also rob people of taking responsibility for their own lives. These are all the things you learn in a twelve-step recovery program," Coleman explained.

"Mistakenly, I thought you could only be co-dependent if you were in an alcoholic marriage. How I wish I had stayed in Alanon," I said regretfully.

Coleman helped me to understand I could still be co-dependent even though I was not married to an alcoholic anymore. That was eye opening to me. I really believed that dysfunctional marriages were always due to addiction.

"No regrets! Romans 8:1 says; 'There is no condemnation for those who belong to Christ Jesus.' Remember, God's timing is perfect. Here is a paper I want you to read. Think about joining a group and pray for

God to change your unhealthy patterns. You can keep counseling with me if you want to."

"I'm sure Lee won't ever come back," I said sadly.

"It doesn't matter. You need to concentrate on what you can do to grow. Let God worry about your husband."

"What do I do about the cruel things he says to the kids?"

"Ask the Lord to guard their hearts."

I sat outside, after calling Jeremy to come pick me up, and read through the material Coleman had given me.

Characteristics of co-dependents are: An exaggerated sense of responsibility for the actions of others. A tendency to confuse love and pity, with the tendency to "love" people they can pity and rescue. The co-dependent will do anything to hold on to a relationship to avoid the feeling of abandonment. A sense of guilt when asserting themselves, difficulty in making decisions and identifying feelings is also another sign. Co-dependents view themselves as victims and are attracted to that same weakness in their love and friendship relationships. (Mental Health America)

I kept reading and the more I read the more the scales fell from my eyes. Why had I been in denial for so long? As I thought about what I had read I kept hearing Coleman's words, "There is now no condemnation, God's timing is perfect."

Another year passed and with it my slow but continued recovery from my past. Each day was a new adventure as I prayed for growth. I was learning to say no, to be self-reliant and to assert myself. I also felt like I had dealt with my abandonment issues. Even so, Lee continued to verbally abuse all of us except Ashley.

As he continued his domineering and controlling actions, I adamantly defended my kids and he in turn tried to make me feel guilty for choosing them over him. I still supported the family while Lee pursued his own interests and worked whenever he felt like it, which wasn't very often. He refused to act like a father (except to our daughter) or a decent husband. I realized the kids and I couldn't live with him anymore and I seriously contemplated leaving him.

I went in to see Coleman. "Nothing has really changed. In fact, Lee has gotten worse. He is so unkind to my kids. He favors Ashley and it hurts her siblings. I can't reason with him. How do I help my kids?"

"Can you share with me what he has done?" Coleman asked.

"He is always videotaping Ashley and that's fine but the only time he tapes the other kids is when they make a mistake or he catches them in an embarrassing situation. He always finds ways to make them feel stupid. When Ashley was two, Kristy was carrying her around and she accidentally dropped her. Ashley was fine but he aimed the camera at Kristy and made her apologize to Ashley over and over. He made her cry and he said she was stupid, clumsy, and irresponsible. I tried to get him to stop but he wouldn't listen to me. Then he took the camera over to his mother's house, and while we were there he played it for her over and over. They just laughed at Kristy and she was so embarrassed. I was so angry but I couldn't do anything to help her. He constantly belittles the kids and I am so worried about what this is doing to them."

"Bring your children in and I will talk to them," Coleman said.

One by one I brought the three oldest kids to see Coleman and he talked to them separately. Afterwards he called me into his office. "I didn't understand what you were telling me a year ago, how difficult and harmful it's been to the kids. I'm so sorry. With the things, you and your kids are telling me it sounds like Lee might have a Narcissistic Personality Disorder. Now I'm no psychiatrist, but here is an article I want you to read. You can draw your own conclusions. It might be a good idea for you to separate for a time from Lee. Just think about it. Now I am not advocating divorce, but that man is destroying your children. You need to get him out of their lives, at least until he decides he needs help."

I also shared my fears about Lee running off with Ashley. He prayed with me and helped me to trust God for Ashley's future.

Lee and I already had planned a camping trip for Kristy's thirteenth birthday a couple days after my appointment with Coleman and Kristy was really looking forward to it. She had already invited four of her closest friends. I figured I'd let my kids have a little fun before I brought up my thoughts about separating from Lee. The boys were going to stay with their cousins.

I kept the girls company in the back of the van while Ashley snoozed in her car seat. The trip started out fine, but as soon as we set up camp Lee kept finding reasons to yell at Kristy. I tried to keep things peaceful and every time he yelled I'd grab Kristy and her girlfriends and we'd take a walk or go hang out by the river to get away from him.

On the last day, he called out to Kristy. "You and your friends take the dirty dishes over to the river and wash them. Then you can pack them up and put them away."

"Okay, Lee," Kristy said.

"Take Ashley, too. Me and your mom are busy."

Lee and I stayed back and packed up the rest of the belongings. "Hey, let's fool around. The girls will be over there for a while."

"No, I wouldn't be very comfortable doing that." *I felt disgusted, I never wanted him to touch me again.*

Coming over to me, he slipped his hand underneath my blouse.

"Come on let's have some fun."

"No! Stop it!"

He turned away angrily.

Just then I heard Kristy call out to me with a fearful tone in her voice. "Mom, Come here quick. Ashley fell in the creek and now she is all wet."

I could see by the scared look on her face she was hoping her step-dad wasn't in earshot.

"It's okay. I have some dry clothes."

Lee ran ahead of me and scooped up Ashley. His face was purple with rage. "I told you to keep an eye on her. You're so irresponsible. You can't even watch your little sister for five minutes. I can't trust you with anything."

I got the feeling he overreacted more than usual because I had just spurned his sexual advances and he was taking it out on Kristy.

Kristy grimaced and cringed while Lee berated my sweet daughter and her face grew red with humiliation. Looking towards the ground she clenched and unclenched her fists while trying to hide her tears.

"Get over here and change her into some dry clothes. If you think you are capable of doing that?" Lee continued to yell at her.

"It's her birthday and you are embarrassing her in front of her friends. Leave her alone."

"You're always taking her side. Just for that she is grounded when we get home."

Kristy's friends stood by watching, obviously feeling uncomfortable while Lee continued calling her names and making her feel worse than she already did.

I stood their feeling helpless, as he continued to belittle her. I could see my words didn't make any difference and I did not want to keep arguing in front of Kristy's friends. I just wanted him to shut up. Kristy's friends followed her to the van and I continued to glare at Lee.

She had already been through enough. Leave her alone I was silently screaming. *God, please do something! I'm sorry but I hate this man. He is destroying my children!*

Later as we finished loading the van, Lee poured himself a bowl of cereal. "Kristy where is my big spoon?"

She came running to him carrying a small, white plastic spoon, still eager to please him.

"What's this? I'm a big boy. I need a big spoon." He threw it back at her. "I told you to keep my big spoon out when you were washing the dishes. Once again, you prove you have no common sense. You're irresponsible and you don't listen! Now find me the big spoon. I don't care if you have to go through everyone one of those boxes."

With tears pouring down her face Kristy and I quickly rummaged through the boxes while Lee stood by watching with a smirk on his face.

"Mom," she whispered. "He ruined my birthday and keeps yelling at me in front of my friends. I hate him. I hate him."

"Shush, don't let him hear you. Don't say that. It's wrong to say that. Let's just hurry and find the spoon so we can leave this place." *Why didn't I let her talk about her feelings? She had a right to feel that way. I felt the same way she did.*

"Mom, I never want to go camping with him again."

"I know, me too," I said as I stroked her hand.

Holding Ashley in his arms Lee said in a loud voice, "You'll never be stupid like your sister is."

"Just leave her alone," I shot back.

But he wouldn't shut up and he just went on verbally abusing my precious daughter while I stood by feeling powerless to do anything.

That was the last straw! Once again, I had failed to stand up for my children. I knew I would never be strong enough to defend them or myself with him in our lives. As we drove away from the campgrounds, I knew in my heart it was over.

33

A New Start

"The Lord is compassionate and gracious, slow to anger, abounding in love." Psalm 103:8

I read and re-read the material Coleman had given me and it seemed to me that Lee had all the symptoms of a disorder called NPD.

Narcissistic Personality Disorder is a mental disorder in which people have an inflated sense of their own importance and a deep need for admiration. Those with narcissistic personality disorder believe that they're superior to others and have little regard for other people's feelings. They react to criticism with rage, shame or humiliation. But behind this mask of ultra-confidence lies a fragile self-esteem, vulnerable to the slightest criticism. (Mayo Clinic)

All the things I read really summed him up. Now I understood why he so easily disregarded my children's and my feelings and he reacted with rage over the most insignificant things. For the first time, I realized it wasn't me. I wasn't crazy! I finally had a name for the way Lee acted, and I couldn't live with him anymore or put my children through it. They had suffered enough. Several days after we returned from the camping trip I demanded Lee move out of my house.

He gave me one excuse after another why he couldn't leave. "I have nowhere to move."

"Your mother owns a five-bedroom house less than thirty minutes from here. I'm sure she won't mind you living with her."

Weeks went by and Lee still wouldn't budge. I tried to keep the kids away from him as much as possible, and when I worked I took them over to my mom's so they wouldn't have to stay in the same house with him. At night, he slept on the couch, but still he wouldn't leave.

My oldest son had left for Hawaii several weeks earlier to spend the summer with my brother Rob. I was glad he wouldn't have to put up with Lee anymore. And I was hoping Lee would be out of the house by the time Jeremy returned.

A few weeks later, out of desperation, I called Lee's younger brother, Ray. We met for coffee, "I am ready to leave Lee and I can't get him to move. Is there any way you can help me get him out?"

"What took you so long? He can stay at Moms."

"He refuses to. He says he wants his own place."

"I care about you and the kids I always have and I've noticed the way Lee treats you guys. What can I do to help?"

"Would you lend Lee some money to move into an apartment? Although you know you will never see it again."

Ray gave me a hug and assured me he would get Lee out of my home. He wouldn't mention to Lee he and I had talked.

A few days after my visit, Lee began packing his belongings while I sat on the porch watching him. Peace resonated through me. I felt no guilt watching him move out, my only regret was that he hadn't left earlier.

"Do you know what day it is?" He asked.

"Yea it's Saturday."

"Today is our fifth anniversary."

"It couldn't be more perfect," I said, with a huge grin on my face.

Later that day after putting Ashley to bed the other kids and I celebrated. We ate pizza and laughed, it was wonderful. We all felt a sense of peace something we hadn't felt in a long time. I couldn't wait to call Jeremy and share the happy news.

"Guess who finally moved out?"

"Is Lee finally gone? I can't wait to come home. What a relief. I'm so glad I will never have to live with him again."

"That's right, you won't because first thing Monday morning I am going to the courthouse to file for divorce."

"That's great, Mom. You made the right decision, I'm so proud of you, and by the way I love you."

One of the first things I did shortly after Lee left was to call my old prayer partner, Rosa. We talked about everything we had been through and how our Tuesday morning prayer sessions had led us on a path that helped us heal, confront and forgive our abusers.

"True recovery involves hard work, but all the time and effort is worth it. I never realized how much the past has to do with the choices we make in our lives and even though I have made a lot of mistakes I have learned that God loves me just as I am. Recovery is an ongoing process and I am willing to look at myself and change in the areas where God shows me I need to. I know I'll probably never have another chance to be in a healthy relationship and do it the right way. But I sure hope I can change the future for my kids so they won't make the same mistakes I have."

"Thankfully, you starting believing that God loved you unconditionally and it helped you to stop hating yourself. You were able to begin to love the person God created you to be and to see yourself as God sees you." Rosa shared with me. "You are only thirty-five, still a young woman. Don't give up on relationships. I know God will somehow repay you for all that's been done to you.

> *"I will repay you for the years the locusts have eaten. You will have plenty to eat, until you are full, and you will praise the name of the Lord your God who has worked wonders for you; never again will my people be shamed." Joel 2:25-26*

"Seriously, I am not interested in another relationship at this time in my life. I just want to be the best mom I can be for my kids and grow in my love for the Lord."

I had always been honest with my children about my struggles. They in turn shared their hearts with me. They had watched me faithfully attend church and Bible study over the years. They saw me pray and they listened as I shared answered prayers with them. My journey with God continued to bloom. There were no secrets in our home. As soon as my children were old enough I told them about their Grandpa Bob and how God was continuing to heal me. I knew my dad and I would never have a normal father-daughter bond, but I continued to pray for him. We saw each other infrequently, throughout the years.

Time passed as I waited for the divorce to become final. I reluctantly got used to sharing my three-year-old with Lee, although I didn't like being separated from her. I found myself occasionally worried he would run off with her. However, I knew I had to put my trust in the Lord.

"Don't worry about anything; instead, pray about everything. Tell God what you need, and thank him for all He has done. Then you will experience God's peace, which exceeds anything we can understand. His peace will guard your hearts and minds as you live in Christ Jesus." Philippians 4:6-7

The kids felt a huge sense of relief with Lee being out of our home. Just having him gone helped to heal some of the damage that he had done to them. They began to relax, and I could sense a real peace in their lives. Jeremy would be coming home in a couple weeks and we were looking forward to his return. In just six short weeks, autumn would bring cool rains, red and gold leaves, and early nights.

34

My Brother's Friend

"No eye has seen; no ear has heard and no mind has imagined what God has prepared for those who love Him."
1 Corinthians 2:9

"Trust in the Lord with all your heart and lean not on your own understanding; in all your ways acknowledge him, and He will direct your paths." Proverbs 3:5-6

Shortly before Jeremy was due to come home my younger brother Dave called. "Bring the kids over to my house on Saturday. You remember my old friend, Cary Wheeland? He will be in town. I'm having a barbecue for him, his mom and brother."

"I'm off on Saturday. The kids and I will be there."

"Cary just got back from Hawaii. He went with our old high school friend, Becky and they stayed with Rob. He met Jeremy and has a photo of him he wants to show you."

As I hung up the phone my thoughts drifted back to the childhood friend of my brother, I hadn't seen for twenty years. Dave had given me updates on him throughout the years. He graduated from a college in Colorado, then immediately accepted a job in California. He had been living there ever since and he and Dave had remained good friends.

Saturday came quickly, gathering up my children, I headed out to spend the day with my brother. The kids and I were walking to the front door when an older woman approached us.

She immediately introduced herself. "Hi, I'm Lorraine, Cary's mom."

"I'm Dave's sister, Debbie, glad to finally meet you."

"Cary and Becky were in Hawaii together. Maybe she is the one!" Lorraine said.

"After all he is thirty-two, it's about time he got married.

"Who knows, maybe she is the one," I smiled.

My mom greeted me as soon as I got inside and the kids instantly took off to find their cousins. It felt good to be surrounded by my family. Just then a handsome, distinguished-looking man reached out and shook my hand.

"Hi, it's good to see you after all these years."

"Hello, you must be Cary, I would never have recognized you."

"Even though I haven't seen you in twenty years, I would've known you anywhere. By the way, I have a photograph of Jeremy. Do you want to see it?"

"Of course, I do. I really miss him." We made small talk and I found myself enjoying him.

There was something about the way he looked at me, his eyes never left mine. It felt as if he were hanging on to every word I said. In just a few seconds he made me feel like I was the most important person in the room.

"It was a pleasure meeting your son, he's a good kid. Jeremy is a good-looking boy and well mannered. He looks so young, he must take after his mom," Cary laughed nervously.

"Thank you," I blushed. "This is the longest I've gone without seeing him. I can't wait for him to come home."

I studied the picture, Cary and Becky stood side by side, Rob, was next to them with his arm around my son, who would turn seventeen in a month. I handed it back to him.

"Keep it. I brought it for you, and I was looking forward to seeing you."

Holding it to my heart, "Thanks I appreciate your thoughtfulness."

Over the course of the evening I introduced him to the other kids and shared a little about what I had been doing the last twenty years. I met his brother, Lance and family who had driven seventy miles from Denver to be there.

While the children mingled with their cousins, I could hear music playing in the background. My mother called me over. "Cary's such a nice man. You should ask him to dance!"

"But, Mom nobody's dancing. He's not going to want to dance with me."

"Just ask him!" Mom was very persistent.

Always trying to please my mother, I walked over to Cary and gestured toward him. "Hey you want to dance?"

"Sure," he said, taking my hands in his.

I was surprised he had agreed so quickly. He twirled me around in the middle of the living room. All the while his pesky, eight-year-old niece tried to break in between us. We laughed and continued dancing. I can still recall the song that was playing that day, *All I want to do is make love to you, by Heart.*

After our hamburgers were eaten, the night was still young and Dave suggested we go to a local club to dance. I was in the downstairs bathroom reapplying my make-up when Becky walked in. We made introductions.

"Did you have fun in Hawaii with Cary?"

"Are you kidding? What kind of guy goes to Hawaii and forgets his bathing suit? Truthfully, I would have had more fun with one of your brothers."

Chuckling, we headed out the door.

While the music was blaring and the lights grew dim I began swaying to the rhythm. After a few songs, Cary made his way towards me, holding out his hands to me. "Would you like to dance?"

Spinning me around the dance floor he kept repeating, "Keep your arms taut, keep your arms taut!"

"That must be a college word. Since I didn't go to college, I don't know what "taut" means," I joked.

"Keep your arms tight, I'm trying to teach you a dance move."

He continued to spin me, dip me, and twirl me around the dance floor. The evening proved to be a lot of fun dancing with my brother, Cary's brother, and a few more times with Cary.

"Thanks for the lesson. It was a lot of fun," I said to Dave's friend as the last song played.

Early the next morning Cary, Becky, Dave, his kids, my kids and I made plans to drive to Denver and eat at a historical Mexican restaurant, *Casa Bonita*. While sitting around the table, I decided I should get to know Dave's best friend a little better. After all, he was a good dancer. I laughed at my thoughts.

"Over the years my brother would bring your name up and I often asked him about you. The last memory I have is right after your dad died. My sister and I were walking back from your house. I was pushing Jeremy in a stroller. You and Dave walked in front of us. Do you remember that?"

"Yes, I do. It was a pretty hard time for me. My dad had just passed. It was two months before I graduated from high school."

"I felt so bad for you. What did you do after that?"

"My mom and dad had been divorced for about three years, Mom remarried and moved to Nebraska so my oldest brother, Rod and his wife moved in with me till school was over."

"Dave said you graduated from a University, where was that?"

"Western State, it's about three hours from Denver. It was a great experience for me."

"So, what are you doing now?"

"I work for a food management company and I feed college kids, we provide food for museums, and corporations too. But enough about me, I want to hear about you."

Cary moved a little closer to me and looked me straight in the eyes. I began to feel giddy. There it was again. He was totally focused on me and once again made me feel like the most important person in the room. Shivers ran down my spine and I started to speak as if my tongue was tied. "I'm, I, I'm sure my brother told you I'm divorced, twice, actually. You knew Kenny, my first husband, right? He lived around the corner from both of us?"

"Of course. Who doesn't remember him? Back in high school he had a reputation for being a bully and a fighter."

"Yea, that's him. Unfortunately, he never changed. I finally realized the kids and I deserved to be treated better. I am blessed because I have three great children from him. My relationship with Ashley's dad was pretty dysfunctional, too." I said, pointing to my three-year-old who was sitting on my lap.

"I work at Safeway in the meat and seafood department and I really enjoy my job. You know my family and now that you've met Jeremy, you know everybody."

"They seem like great kids. You've done a good job with them. Jeremy was very considerate. Both his uncles bragged about how responsible and generous he is. It was nice getting to know him."

"Mommy, can we go see the puppet show now?" Ashley asked, tugging at my shirtsleeve.

"All right, let's go and have some fun!"

Cary walked with me as I rounded up the other kids and we went to find the puppets.

Soon the evening was over and we headed to our cars. Cary hugged me. "Thanks for coming, it was great spending time with you and your children."

I watched him drive away with Becky. On the drive home, the kids said, "We had a good time. Cary is so nice."

I nodded my head in agreement. *He was easy to talk to and I felt so comfortable with him. I wish the evening hadn't ended so early.*

I clocked in at work for the first shift shortly before the store opened the next morning. Putting on my apron and hat, I set up the meat and fish counter while cheerfully greeting my customers, most of them by name. Soon I found myself daydreaming about the events of the last couple of days. Just then a shrill ring interrupted my pleasant thoughts.

A harsh voice screamed at me from the telephone. I cringed as I recognized the voice of Lee. "I'm tired of you giving me the run around. I want to see my daughter more. Why didn't you let me have her while you worked today? I swear I'll hire a new lawyer and get full custody," he threatened.

Recoiling, my heart went numb. Fearfully, I said, "I should have called. I'll try harder to work things out with you. I'm sorry. No, no please don't call a lawyer." *Why was I giving in again? What was I afraid of? I had never learned how to stand up for myself with the abusive men in my past. Why did I allow them to still have control over me?*

After hanging up the phone and wiping my tears, I tried to put on a friendly smile while I wrapped fish for the customers.

A few minutes later, I looked up and saw Cary with a big smile on his face coming down the aisle towards me. Strolling in his direction, I could tell he was visibly nervous. He stopped, looked at me and fumbled in his pocket. Pulling out his business card he extended it towards me. "Debbie Griswold, there's something about those eyes. There's always been something about your eyes." Gazing steadfastly at me he continued, "I have to admit I asked Dave about you pretty often. I had the biggest crush on you when I was in junior high and high school. Whenever I would come to your house I was secretly hoping you would be there too. I was glad I stayed with Rob for a couple of days. It gave me a chance to meet your son and look at pictures of you and your kids. You're still as beautiful as you were when I first laid eyes on you twenty years ago!"

I blushed, "thank you."

Cary paused and repeated the words that moved me. "Like I said, there's something about those eyes. He reached out to me and his eyes never left mine. "Will you call me?"

"Of course, I would welcome a nice man in my life." I took the card.

"I'm heading back to California late tonight and I wanted to come and say goodbye."

He hugged me and looked at me in a way that I had never been looked at before. "Please call me."

I watched him walk away. *Wow, what a nice guy. I've never met anyone like him before. Why would this successful, kind, attractive man be interested in me, a twice-divorced mother of four?*

It was nearly quitting time when the phone rang again. Remembering my last conversation, I was almost too afraid to answer it.

"It's Dave. Hey you want to come to my house tonight for some homemade chili and say goodbye to Cary? He and Becky will be here to eat before she takes him to the airport."

"I don't know. I talked to Sue earlier and she asked me to bring the kids over and have supper with her."

I didn't tell him I had just seen his best friend.

"Come on, it's my famous chili. You know you'd rather come to my house."

"Okay, you're right, I will swing by and pick up the kids from Mom and head over after work."

There was a soft, warm breeze blowing on that serene Colorado evening in the middle of August, as I walked swiftly up the steps to my brother's house later that night. After we ate we looked through some old photographs, laughed, and made small talk until it was time for Cary to go to the airport. I was leaning against the counter in the kitchen when Cary walked over to me and embraced me tenderly.

"It was so good seeing you after all these years." Again his eyes never left mine. He hugged each one of the kids and turned around and hugged me for a second time.

Standing on the porch, waving goodbye to him, I could still feel his arms around me. For some unexplained reason I felt warm and treasured.

Three days later, Dave drove me home from work because my car was in the shop. As I was putting the key in the lock, I heard the phone ringing. Running into the kitchen, I picked it up.

"Hello," I said, cradling the receiver.

"This is Cary. How are you?"

"Who is it?" Dave yelled as he turned to leave.

"It's your friend Cary," I mouthed to him.

"Why is he calling you? Call me later and let me know."

"I haven't stopped thinking about you since I left."

The rest of the conversation was a blur as I found myself thinking about the way Cary had looked at me and embraced me the last time we were together.

Although I had only been single for a few weeks the last thing on my mind was another man. I was content to enjoy the peace that came with the end of my last dysfunctional marriage.

After the phone call ended I found myself thinking about the way Cary had looked at me and the words he had spoken to me and I walked around the rest of the day with a big smile on my face.

The next day after I got the kids to bed I received another call from Cary, this went on for a few more days. He was so easy to talk to. It felt as if we had been friends for years. I found myself looking forward to our late-night chats. Finally, Cary said, "I like you a lot and I need to tell Dave how I feel about you."

Later he called and shared the conversation with me. "I told your brother I have been talking to you every day since we got reacquainted at his house. Then Dave said you like my sister? Are you crazy? Do you know what you're getting yourself into? She's been divorced twice and has four kids. Then he laughed you know your brother he's a big joker. Finally, he asked about Becky."

"What did you say?"

"I told him there was never anything serious between Becky and me and she feels the same way. I told him I like your sister and I have enjoyed getting to know her. I think about her all the time. I can't help myself. I tell you its destiny, it's destiny, man."

Later I called Rob. "Guess what? Cary's been calling me since he left your place, and he even gave me his business card. I've never known anyone with their own business card."

"What! Doesn't he know you've been divorced twice and have four kids? Is he crazy?"

"Ha, ha, that's exactly what Dave said to him. Maybe he is a little crazy."

Rob laughed. "He's such a nice guy. Did you know Cary is a Yuppie?"

I giggled. "What is a Yuppie?"

"A Young Urban Professional. And he sends his clothes out to get dry cleaned!"

"Have we ever known anyone who goes to the dry cleaner?" I joked.

Rob and I laughed a lot during our conversation. Later that night Cary chuckled as I repeated Rob's phone call to him.

Walking into work the next day, I checked my schedule for the week. It was the Monday before Labor Day and for some strange reason I would have the holiday weekend off. Later as my shift was getting ready to end the phone rang in my department.

"Thank you for shopping at our friendly Safeway store, this is the Seafood department. Can I help you?"

"Hi, Darlin', I know I told you I don't believe in calling while you are at work, but I just had to call this time. Will you go out on a date with me?"

Did I hear him right; my head started spinning while my heart did flip-flops. Nobody had ever called me 'Darlin' before, and we had only known each other for a couple of weeks. "I'll just hop on a plane and be there tomorrow night," I laughed.

"No, I will come to you. I already have a plane ticket for Saturday morning."

My knees went weak. "What, what? Are you serious, you're coming here?" All the feelings of the last couple weeks came flooding back. His smile, his outstretched hands, his embrace, even the way he had gazed at me intently made my heart pound. I was sure he could hear it over the phone.

"Yes. Can you pick me up from the airport in Denver?"

"Of course," I replied, "as luck would have it I have the whole weekend off. And that rarely happens. If I didn't know any better, I'd say you and my boss planned the whole thing."

"I'll never tell," Cary laughed. "Now get back to work. I will see you Saturday. Expect a call tonight."

I walked around for the rest of the morning dazed, with a big grin on my face. *What was going on with me?* Even though we still didn't know each other very well I found myself increasingly thinking about Cary. We had talked every day for the last two weeks. After getting home, I'd feed the kids, when they were tucked into bed the phone started ringing. I talked about my children's daily escapades, my work day and my emotional state. I mentioned how hard it was to leave my little girl with Lee and how much I missed her when he had her. Cary was always upbeat and he never told me what to do or gave me unasked-for-advice.

He listened attentively to my every word. He encouraged me to talk about the rough time I was having with my ex-husband and how cruel and controlling he still acted towards me. I was astonished. I had never met anyone like him before who seemed more interested in the kids and me than himself. But his responses to me made sharing my day easy with him. I always looked forward to our evening chats.

My oldest son had been home from his summer trip from Hawaii for a couple weeks. He was the first one I told about Cary's planned visit. "Cary wants to come out and visit this weekend. How do you feel about it?"

"First of all, it was great to come home from my trip knowing Lee will never live in our house again. I really liked Cary from the moment I met him at Uncle Rob's house. I think it's great. Although it might be a little weird, first I saw him with Becky and now he's with my mother," Jeremy chuckled. "But seriously, I am looking forward to seeing him again."

Early Saturday morning I cashed my paycheck and bought some snacks for a picnic lunch. Later, I curled my hair, put on make-up and chose a black and purple summer dress to wear on our first date. My hazel eyes, the feature Cary liked most about me, sparkled.

During the seventy-minute drive to the airport I had plenty of time to think. Even though I had been looking at the pictures Cary had sent me, I wondered if I would recognize him after he stepped off the plane. What was I feeling for him? It had been a little over two weeks and I did not have a very good track record for judging peoples' character. I thought Cary and I had gotten to know each other pretty well since the barbecue at Dave's house. He didn't have a problem opening up to me and I trusted him enough to tell him about my mistakes, my childhood, my fears, and some of my insecurities.

At the airport, I stood at the gate, waiting for him, *in 1990 you still could*. One at a time I inspected each person coming off the plane. Suddenly, he was rushing in my direction, with a huge smile on his face. Dressed in a navy-blue business suit, he was even more handsome and distinguished looking then I remembered. My heart was beating so hard I thought it would jump out of my chest.

When Cary hugged me, I knew I would never forget the feel of his touch. Something about his embrace melted my heart and healed it at the same time and somehow, I knew I would never be the same again. I had never felt so loved and protected. Cary held me close and gazed into my eyes. He once again repeated those familiar words, "Debbie, there is something about those eyes!" He lingered over his words, watching me intently. Interrupting his thoughts, he said, "Sorry, I didn't have time to change. I had a meeting this morning before my flight and I didn't bring any shorts. Can we stop at Kmart?"

"Of course," I said as my heart fluttered. He was so good-looking in his suit all I wanted was to stare at him as I held his hand.

Changing in the bathroom at Kmart, Cary was ready for our first date. "What's the plan, Darlin'?"

"I brought some food and I thought we'd find a place to have a picnic somewhere here in Denver. Would you mind driving?"

"No, I don't mind driving. Surely there will be a park nearby," he said.

I scooted over as he got in the driver's seat of my burgundy Subaru wagon.

"My name's not Shirley. Wasn't Shirley last week's date?" I giggled.

Cary threw his back his head and guffawed. It was such a stupid joke, but I liked the way he laughed at my quirky sense of humor.

"Autumn is my favorite time of year it's absolutely gorgeous." I pointed to the leaves on the aspen trees that were just beginning to change to shades of gold."

Cary reached out and touched my shoulder. "I'm so glad to be sharing this time of year with you."

Blue spruce fir trees lined the freeway. There were lush green meadows and secluded alcoves hidden along the roadside. As Cary and I drove up the mountain highway we found a hidden spot. The barb wired gate was open, inviting us in. We drove the car in several yards and the noise of the traffic faded away. The road turned to the left a few hundred feet away from the main road. To our surprise, on the other side of a four-foot wooden fence, there were several horses grazing. Without thinking, I climbed over the fence in my knee-length summer dress and hopped on the back of one of the mares. Grabbing onto the mane I playfully smiled at Cary.

He took a minute to just watch me. "You look beautiful with your long, brown hair blowing in the wind. I could stare at you all day. Your big, sparkling hazel eyes are bewitching me."

Blushing shyly, I turned away. "Thank you. I just love horses. This is perfect. Can you help me get down now?"

We spread out a blanket, brought out the food, and he popped open a beverage. Taking a sip, he said, "I can't believe you remembered my favorite drink."

"How could I forget? It was one of the first remarks you made to me when I met you at my brother's house?"

"Oh yeah, when I saw you standing there after twenty years, I was so tongue-tied and nervous and that was the first thing that popped in my head."

Looking intently at me he took my hands in his. "All these years my priority has been my job. It's as if I was married to it. But now I find myself wanting to go in a different direction. And that direction is you."

Now I was the one who felt shy and tongue-tied. My head started to spin. Cary drew me close. Laying my head against his chest felt like the most natural thing in the world. A sense of peace enveloped me and I never wanted to move from that spot. Moments passed and we didn't say anything while the silence of the countryside surrounded us. There was no need for conversation.

I don't know who broke the quiet first, but soon we took out the lunch. I dropped a few luscious, green grapes in Cary's opened mouth; he dropped and missed my mouth a couple times. We laughed together and found plenty to talk about. We stole a few kisses as we gazed into one another's eyes. The scene would have made a great first chapter of a romance novel.

As the late summer sun was beginning to set we gathered up the leftover food and loaded it in the trunk. "Look, the horses are gone," I said as we drove around the corner towards the gate.

Slamming on the brakes Cary stared straight ahead. Just then a hearty laugh exploded from his mouth. There was a sign on the closed barb wired fence and it read, PRIVATE PROPERTY. "How could we have missed the sign?" he asked.

"Oh no, somebody shut and locked the gate! How are we going to get out of here now?" I was beginning to feel like I was going to panic. I waited for him to start screaming at me for getting us into the predicament. After all, I was the one who had suggested the secluded spot. And my ex-husbands surely would've blamed me. Silently, with my head tipped down, my eyes to the ground, I waited for the onslaught.

Instead, Cary calmly turned to me, lifted my chin and said, "Don't worry Darlin', we'll figure this out," and he chuckled again!

His laugher was one of his most enduring characteristics not just to me but as I would come to find out later, to all who knew and loved him. I felt myself starting to relax.

"I wish we had some wire cutters. They would come in real handy right about now," Cary said calmly.

"I'm sure they would, but unfortunately I don't carry wire cutters around."

He started glancing down the highway "There is a sign down the street and it has the same kind of gate as this one. Maybe there is a number written on it that I can call. Darlin, everything's going to work out."

Looking down the divided highway, I did not see any phone booths and I was wondering how he was planning on calling somebody. Back in 1990 most people didn't own cell phones, neither one of us did. His plan seemed as good as any. I watched him cautiously step over the fence and cross the road.

I did what I always did whenever I found myself in a situation that was beyond my control. I began to pray. "Jesus, please help us out of this mess we got ourselves into." Opening my eyes, I started rummaging through the glove compartment, and the pockets behind the seats. Looking down on the floor, trying to find anything that might work, I pushed the driver's seat all the way back. There, staring up at me was pair of rusty pliers.

Cary returned and was standing on the other side of the fence, holding a piece of paper with a phone number written on it.

"Look what I found in my car." Excitedly, I handed him the rusty pliers through the fence. "Do you think this will help?"

"All right!" Cary shouted exuberantly. He began to carefully unravel each piece of wire from the post. It wasn't difficult, just time consuming.

Watching him apprehensively, I still waited for any sign of a temper to flare up. Thankfully, he remained calm. The more I observed him the more I liked how he handled himself in this mini crisis. Afterwards he laid the blanket across the fallen wire and drove the car out, put it in park and reconnected each piece of wire to the post.

"Wow, I am impressed. Not only did you figure out a way to get us out but you straightened everything up and made it look like no one had even been here." Immediately, I was amazed at his thoughtfulness. I had never met a man with such integrity.

If I had been keeping score, Cary had passed the first test in our relationship. Number one: He didn't blame me for the predicament we had gotten ourselves into and that was big in my book. Number two: He cleverly figured out a way to solve our problem. Number three: He had a great sense of humor about it. Number four: He was positive and encouraging to me and number five he put things back the way they were.

As we drove away Cary asked, "Do you always carry pliers in your car?"

"That's the crazy part, I don't even know how they got there. One of the kids must have used them for something and I'm glad they forgot to put the pliers away, who knows how long they've been in my car."

"Now that that's over, where would you like to go?"

"I love nature and honestly, right before the sun goes down is my favorite part of the day. I would rather be outside than inside, even if it's just riding in the car." As the sun began to descend, Cary and I decided to take the scenic road back to Colorado Springs.

There was never a lull in the conversation between us as we drove, and the landscape was breathtaking too. On either side of the road there were forests of Aspen, Ponderosa pine, Douglas fir and Blue spruce trees. The sprawling Platte River zigzagged on either side of us. The greens, gold's and orange colors danced before us. We could not have asked for a more perfect day. I didn't want our car ride to end.

It was late when we pulled up in front of my house. Obviously, all the kids were awake and looking forward to spending time with Cary. Jeremy would now see a different side of the man he had spent time with in Hawaii. Cary walked in the house and gave all the kids a big bear hug. He spent time talking to each of them then later helped me tuck them in. Jeremy stayed up late and conversation came easily between the two of them.

As each hour passed, I continued to feel as if I had known Cary forever. He was different than anyone I'd ever met. I was still thinking about his sense of humor, optimism, uprightness and integrity when he interrupted my thoughts.

"You know Darlin', my boss, Michael paid for this trip. He encouraged me to come and spend time with you. After Dave's barbecue, I couldn't eat, couldn't sleep and couldn't work. Michael took one look at me and said go back and look that woman in her eyes and figure it out. Then get back here and start working."

He reached over and held me close. "I'm here to look you in the eyes and figure it out and I'm not going to leave until I have."

Sunday came too quickly. Cary, the kids and I spent the day visiting my mom and all my siblings.

Later our family had an intimate dinner out. On the drive home Jeff farted the whole time. Suddenly, Cary slammed on the brakes. "OK who cut the cheese?"

All fingers pointed to Jeff.

"Ha," Jeff laughed, and he did it again!

"We are going to teach your brother a lesson. Who's with me on this?"

All hands went up as Cary marched Jeff out of the car and fanned his hand back and forth in front of his butt, pretending to air it out. Everybody laughed the rest of the way home.

We ended the evening chasing one another through the house with small water pistols. Everyone sighed when I announced it was time to go to bed.

Eleven-year old Jeff asked, "Mom, can Cary take us to see the hot air balloons at the park tomorrow since you have to work?"

I looked to Cary.

"Of course, Dave and I have already talked about it. I will drop your mom off in the morning then we'll head over to your uncles and we will all leave together. How does that sound?"

"Yeah," the kids yelled in unison while raising their hands in a high five towards Cary.

Nobody was ready to go to bed. Cary sat with me while I read a story to Ashley. Then we both took Jeff and Kristy in their rooms and listened to their prayers. Jeremy went to visit a friend while Cary and I went over the day's events.

"I think your kids are great."

"They were all so comfortable with you. They really like you, and so do I."

"It is going to be real hard for me to leave tomorrow night." Cary reached over and held me close.

Before we knew it, the weekend was over. I drove Cary to the airport and we hugged goodbye. Cary handed me the cutest, small blue box. I opened it and it was an expensive bottle of perfume.

"I've never received such a nice gift before. You make me feel special. Thank you! You are my Prince Charming." I hugged him even tighter.

"Darlin'," he said looking deep into my tear-filled eyes. "I've enjoyed these last few days with you and the kids. I am even more determined than ever to continue our relationship. I don't know when I can come back, but I assure you I will be back soon!"

35

The Chase

"Like a lily among thorns is my darling among the maidens."
Song of Songs 2:2

The kids looked up at me and noticed the tears in my eyes as I watched the airplane take Cary over thousand miles away from me.

"Don't cry Mommy, Care-Bear will be back," my three-year old said, as she reached out to wipe my face.

"Well you guys," I said composing myself. "What do you think of Cary?"

"We like him Mom. He is so nice to all of us."

"How do you feel about me seeing him? I don't want to hurt you by rushing into anything again."

"Mom it's okay, we like Cary. He's different, and he seems really sincere," Jeremy spoke for all of them.

Within a few hours Cary called me, "Darlin', I made it home. I'm already planning my next trip. I hope you and the kids will be ready to see me in a few weeks."

"My children really liked you. We can't wait to see you again. Can you hear them calling your name in the background?"

"Let me talk to Care-Bear, Mommy," yelled Ashley, as she pulled the phone away from me. Days and weeks went by, we continued to communicate through letters and daily phone calls. After I'd get home from work and spend time with my kids, we'd often talk until well after midnight.

One night after he flew into town for a date, we took a drive and stopped at a nearby elementary school. Holding hands, we walked to the swing, Cary pushed me on it and we laughed. It was so romantic, just like in the movies and I knew I was falling in love. He continued to show sides of him that made me melt. He was always so thoughtful and enthusiastic; quick to encourage and seemed to genuinely care for each of my children. Cary flew out to see us about every three weeks. Time always seemed to end too quickly whenever he was in town.

For whatever reason if Cary went two days in a row without calling me, my insecurities got the better of me. Old fears began to plague me. I wanted desperately to believe that all the nice things he said to me were true. I'd wait anxiously for the phone to ring, determined that I wouldn't bug him by making a call to him first. *If he really liked me as much as he said he did, then he would call me, right?* I'd think to myself.

And then the phone would ring, "Sorry I haven't called for a couple days, it's been crazy with work."

"It's okay," I said sadly, during one of those calls.

"Darlin', is something wrong?"

"Nothing! Everything is fine, really."

"You need to tell me what you're thinking. I can tell something is bothering you."

It was hard for me to admit my insecure feelings but with some coaxing I finally admitted to Cary what I had been thinking. "Since you hadn't called for a couple days, I was convincing myself that my problems were too overwhelming for you. I was having doubts about how you said you felt about me. I understand if you want to end this now before it goes any further.

"What are you talking about? Don't ever say that again."

"I don't deserve someone as amazing as you. I feel like I have too much baggage."

"Hold on a minute. You never have to worry about me abandoning what we have together. I'm falling in love with you. I'll do anything I can do help you with your problems. And the truth is, I keep asking God what I have done to deserve someone as wonderful as you. I'm here for you and the kids. *You can take that to the bank.*" It was a phrase he would use often in the early days of our romance.

"What does that mean?"

"That means you can count on me and you can believe everything I tell you. Everything's going to be all right," explained Cary. "Promise you won't think the worst if I miss calling you for a couple of days. No, scratch that, I promise you I will call you every day. And you can pick up the phone and call me anytime."

"I'm sorry, I guess I need to be reassured of how you feel about me. I know you are pretty busy with work and I don't want to take up your time."

"If you need reassurance from me please don't hesitate to call me anytime believe me, I understand because of the way you were treated in the past. But I'm here to tell you I'm not like those other guys. I appreciate your honesty about your feelings. I wish you would realize what a blessing you are to me. Any time spent with you on the phone or in person makes me happy."

I decided it was time for me to get serious about my issues and rise above them and trust what Cary had been telling me. As time went on, I realized how healing our long-distance relationship proved to be. It seemed easier to talk about everything when we weren't seeing each other face to face. I wasn't afraid to hold back in fear of his reaction because I couldn't see him. He always encouraged me to open up to him. I worked at having a positive attitude and to get rid of negativity. Knowing that Cary and I would share our day's events, I wanted our talks to be uplifting. But I also knew I could count on him to hear me if I was having an emotionally difficult time. Although it was challenging when we weren't together and the kids and I missed Cary terribly, we knew God was using our time apart to teach us both something.

It was getting easier to be honest with Cary about everything in my past since he had been my brother's best friend for over two decades. He knew all about my family, all the good and the bad. He knew what he was getting into. I was glad he liked all my siblings and he was especially fond of my mother. I felt lucky to have found a friend like him.

I was depending more and more on the Lord to heal my deep-seated feelings of self-doubt, insecurities and my unrealistic fears. It was getting easier to feel worthwhile when I had a man who constantly said kind things to me and showed me how much he valued me. It was something I had never experienced before. Most of our conversations ended with him saying, "You're stunning, you are awesome, or Darlin', you're incredible!"

Sometimes when I was feeling discouraged, I'd try and convince him I wasn't any of those things. "No, I'm not. I still get easily discouraged. And yesterday I was anxious and yelled at the kids."

"Stop it! I see your heart and I love who you are."

Soon I began to have a newfound confidence. I talked myself out of jealous or envious feelings when Cary informed me the client he was meeting happened to be a woman. I started to believe that he was different from the other men in my life who had needed constant affirmation and attention from the opposite sex. I started believing him after hearing him mention countless times how much he was committed to me. Cary continued to make me feel like I was the most important person in the world to him, it made me feel special and significant.

As our relationship continued, I approached the subject of religion. "Cary, you are such a nice person, are you a Christian?"

"I am although, I haven't been to church in years."

"Would you consider going to church with the kids and me when you come out to visit?"

"Yes, I would love to. I know how important it is to you and I want to make it more of a priority in my life as well."

The next trip out, Cary accompanied us to church and it became a ritual every time he was in town. He encouraged me to share my faith with him, and we began to pray together as well. In turn, he began to grow in his relationship with the Lord.

The kids and I always looked forward to Cary's visits. His integrity, compassion, honesty, kindness, patience, and generosity were character traits that would prove invaluable as we weathered the highs and lows of our relationship.

Time and time again, Cary proved to me he was genuine. He was a born optimist. His words to me when I was having problems with Lee were, "Don't worry, everything's going to be all right." He was right of course; things always seemed to work out. His encouragement and stability helped me through the rough patches with my ex-husband. Cary was my strength, but the funny thing was, he was always telling me I was his strength.

Ashley had fun playing silly games with Cary and she always referred to him as her Care-Bear. Kristy was beginning to feel safe and secure with him. He joked with her and spend time just listening to her. He treated her with honor, the way she deserved to be treated. Since she was almost a teenager, I wanted her to realize she deserved respect from the opposite sex by watching the way Cary treated me. I wanted desperately to erase the awful lessons she had already learned from my other marriages.

My boys and Cary watched football games together and often talked about their favorite teams. For Jeff's birthday Cary bought him a jacket representing his favored football team. No one had ever done anything like that for him before. Jeremy felt comfortable slowly giving up his role as the man of the house. It felt good seeing him relax and enjoy being a kid instead of feeling like it was his responsibility to fix everything.

The whole family enjoyed water fights, snowball wars, sharing dinners and playing jokes on one another. We looked forward to going to the movies, bowling and spending time with other family members whenever Cary was in town.

A few months after we started dating, Cary and I were lounging around my house when he asked, "Would you like to go for a ride with me?"

A block away, he unexpectedly pulled into the driveway of a vacant house, turning to me he took hold of my hands. "I love you, Darlin' more than you know. Since the day you walked into my life, you've changed me. I want to marry you and I want to be the husband you've never had. I want to be a father to your children. Will you and the kids move to California with me?"

Not waiting for an answer, he reached over and held me in his arms, looking deeply into my eyes. "You bring out the best in me!"

I was speechless. *He was too good for me. He had never been married. He had a good career. He had no baggage. What was wrong with him that he wanted to spend the rest of his life with someone like me?*

"When I first saw you, I knew then. I had no control over any of this. It's destiny!"

I tried to talk him out of it. "Come on, what's your mom going to think? She was all ready for you to marry Becky, who is single with no kids. What's she going to say about me, a woman twice-divorced, with four kids?"

"You are who you are because of what you've been through. My mom will love you. Everything's going to be fine. The past belongs in the past. You've obviously learned from it and you keep moving forward. I am so proud of the woman you are."

"How did you turn out so normal? I've never met anyone like you. What is your secret?"

"I don't know, both my parents showed their love for me, and my dad was always involved in my life. He took care of me when Mom worked and he often took me to work with him. He was fifty when I was born, but he always made time for me. My dad accepted me for who I was. He supported me emotionally and encouraged me whenever I was down. He was never afraid to say I love you and he hugged me often. But I was thirteen when my mom and dad divorced and it definitely affected me."

"That must have been really hard for you. Did you see it coming?"

"I have to be honest; I went through a tough time. In some ways, I think it was harder because I was older and didn't see it coming. Even though I remember them arguing a lot. It took me a long time to get over the divorce. Then a few years later, when my dad died I went through another rough patch. It was hard. I had to come to terms with my past and how it had affected me. I never forgot how badly the divorce affected my dad and I didn't want that to happen to me. I vowed I wouldn't marry till I was old and gray. I thought, my wife would have to be someone who had a career and I was sure I'd only have one child. I have been married to my career, which has worked out well for me, until I saw you again. I took one look into your eyes and my world changed drastically. All my plans went out the window. Obviously, God had other plans for me."

"I don't know what to say. You've certainly been through a lot and I appreciate the man that you have become."

He took me in his arms once again. "You haven't answered me yet. Will you become my bride? Will you let me be your Prince Charming?"

My heart beat rapidly as I looked deep in his eyes, "Yes, yes, I want to spend the rest of my life with you."

The devotion we felt for each other at that moment exploded, and he held me close while kissing me passionately.

We drew apart and I turned to him with a concerned look on my face. "But, I don't know how the kids will feel about moving."

"I know you and the kids will be giving up a whole lot. You'd have to leave your mom, your brothers, sister, your aunt and uncle, and your nieces and nephews. You'll have to leave your job and your friends and start over with me. It's not going to be easy but we will come back and visit as often as we can. Is that something you and the kids can live with?"

"I can't imagine my life without you. The good thing is my brother Mike also lives in California. I would love to live by my brother and his family. It would be so great to get to know his children better, and my kids could finally hang out with their cousins. I know it won't be as hard for me with my brother close by. But I can't answer you yet without talking it over with the kids."

"I will make a commitment to you right now, I promise I will move you back within five years and find a job here in Colorado Springs, if that's what you need!"

He pulled me close to him. "Darlin,' I have never felt this way before. I want you and your children in my life. I will always be here for all of you. *You can take that to the bank!*"

"You're funny, you make me laugh with your silly phrases."

"I did what my boss, Michael said, and I looked you in the eyes and I fell in love with you. I want to spend the rest of my life with you. Your children are amazing, it's so easy to be with all of you. I've always lived for myself and have done whatever I wanted. I've gone to Hawaii when I wanted, bought expensive suits when I was depressed. You make me a better man and there's nothing I want more than to take care of you and your children."

I could feel the heat of my tears boiling up behind my eyes. "Nobody's ever said anything like that to me before. I am so blessed and I love you." We held each other close for several minutes. I wanted that moment to last forever.

Then reality kicked in. "You know what happened in my past with Lee, I hardly knew him and jumped into marrying him. I can't help but feel a little apprehensive. I don't want to make another mistake. Of course, you are nothing like him. My older kids have been deeply wounded by the men in their lives and the wrong choices I've made.

They were abandoned by their real dad and mistreated by Lee. They lived with alcoholism and verbal abuse as well as seeing me put up with abuse. Ashley was too young to understand what was going on but Lee has continued to build a wall around her to keep her from being close to the other kids. I keep trying to change that. I can't afford to let my children go through any more pain because of my decisions."

"I understand your fears, but put them to rest. I will never hurt your kids. I love you and each one of them, too. I told you before you can count on me. I know God is in this and I'm asking you to trust me. Take as long as you need, but Debbie Griswold, know that I will always be here for you."

"I am scared, but I do want to marry you."

I laid my head on his shoulder and he took my face in his gentle hands and kissed my lips. "Now let's go talk to the kids."

We drove back to the house. All the kids came running outside. "I want to marry your mom. What do you guys think of that?"

"Yes, yes, we want you to marry our mom."

"How would you feel about moving to California, one day?" Cary asked.

"I think it would be great. I've been living in the same house all my life and hanging out with the same people. It would be a nice change," said Jeremy.

"I want to play volley-ball on the beach and lay out and get a tan," Kristy said.

Jeff was a little hesitant. "I'm not sure yet, but I'll think about it."

Ashley ran around giving high fives to everyone even though she didn't understand what was going on.

"I love you guys. Now let's go to dinner," Cary gestured towards the car.

After Cary flew back to California, I couldn't wait to call Rosa and tell her the news. "He's too nice to be a husband. Husbands are not that nice. He's like a best friend."

"Don't you realize that ideally your husband is supposed to be your best friend?"

"That might be true. But I've never known anyone with that kind of relationship. No one has ever been good to me like Cary. Sometimes it feels foreign, even though I know the feelings we have for each other are real. Do you think our marriage will last? I don't want to think about all the reasons it might not work."

"That's where your faith comes in. I believe God brought this wonderful man in your life and he will give you the tools you need to have a long and happy marriage."

"I needed to hear that, thanks Rosa, I value our friendship."

Soon after Cary asked me to marry him we made sure to counsel with my Assistant Pastor every time he was in town. It was easy to talk to Coleman about our plans. He helped me to understand that God had truly forgiven me for my past and he no longer wanted me to dwell on mistakes or feel guilty about them. He too, could see the genuineness that exuded from Cary's heart and the love and loyalty Cary felt towards the kids and me.

At our next meeting, I decided to explore my feelings even further. "I have been reading the co-dependency book you recommended and it said: *Co-dependent people have a greater tendency to get involved in relationships with people who are perhaps unreliable, emotionally unavailable, or needy. The codependent person tries to provide and control everything within the relationship without addressing his or her own needs or desires, which leads to a lack of fulfillment.* I wanted to get your opinion. Do you think Cary or I fit the description?"

"From what you and Cary have shared with me, I can see that neither one of you is unreliable, emotionally unavailable, or needy. Cary encourages your independence and wants you to share your needs with him. What do you think, Cary?" Coleman asked.

"For me, I don't feel like I need to have somebody in my life to take care of, to make me feel good about myself. I have done just fine all these years as a bachelor. I have always been confident in my own abilities. And I certainly don't want to control anybody. But I never knew what I was missing until I found my soul mate." He reached over to me and took my hands into his. Looking deeply into my eyes, "Debbie fulfills my desires and I believe I fulfill her desires as well."

"I agree, I have noticed how Cary encourages you to express your needs and wants. Debbie, you have come a long way since I first met you when you were married to Lee. I can see a real change in you, and I know God has something amazing planned for your life."

As we moved forward in our incredible friendship, Cary continued to bond with the kids, writing letters to them telling each one of them how important they were to him. "Write to me about the kind of house you'd like and that's what we'll try and get."

The kids were beginning to believe they would never have to worry about anything with Cary in our lives. His constant love notes and phone calls continued to bring even more restoration in our lives. I began to see Cary as our healing balm, as he confirmed his unconditional love to each of us over and over, I was even more convinced God had brought this man into our lives.

They wrote their letters often, each one asking for a house with a fireplace and a swimming pool. The kids had grown up with hardly any luxuries, and they often wore hand-me-downs. Their shoes had to last until I could afford to get new ones twice a year. It was a treat for me to be able to take my children to a fast food place on paydays, and then they were only allowed to order the cheapest thing on the menu. Often, after cashing my check, an indulgence was the kids picking out their very own TV dinners. Afterwards, we'd make popcorn or bake cookies and watch movies together. They were always grateful for everything.

The first time Cary took us to eat at a fast food place they asked, "Mom what can we order?"

"You know you'll have to get the cheapest thing on the menu."

"Wait, wait a minute here," Cary interjected. "You can get whatever you want."

"But Cary they don't need…."

"I want to do this. Kids, go ahead and order whatever you want, it's my treat and I'm paying!"

Cary spoiled all of us. For my birthday, he sent me two bouquets of roses, one to my house and one at my job. A few months after we were dating my hours were drastically cut. I couldn't pay all my bills and I was losing my house. It was hard to find another part-time job because I never had the same hours available each day. Calling Cary, I told him what was going on. "This will probably be the last time we can talk for a while because I can't afford my high phone bills. I'm going to let them turn off the phone tomorrow."

"What! Why didn't you tell me, Darlin'? I will not let your phone get shut off. I'm paying the bill. The calls were all made to me, weren't they?"

"Well yea, but I'm not expecting you to pay it."

"Nonsense, don't you even worry about it. I'll take care of it. I can't go one day without talking to you and the kids."

It was hard for me to accept his generosity, but each action thus far had demonstrated that he was honest and caring. It felt good the way he took care of me and I knew I was not taking advantage of his generosity, I was extremely grateful.

One day, on one of our frequent phone calls, I said, "I feel like God is healing me. For the first time in my life I'm attracted to a man who has no unhealthy qualities."

My family was happy for me as Cary and I celebrated our first Thanksgiving together. "Darling, being with you and the kids is amazing. I am certainly looking forward to spending Christmas with you."

36

Third Time is a Charm

"The man who finds a wife finds a treasure, and he receives favor from the Lord." Proverbs 18:20

During the holiday season, Cary made an announcement. "Darlin, I want to take you out to look at rings after you get off work." Later that afternoon, while working in the seafood department, I accidentally cut my ring finger and had to get stitches. Although it was all patched up, we didn't let that deter our plans and we took Kristy with us. Her ring size was the same as mine. I picked out the ring I liked the best and she tried it on. It had a diamond in the middle and surrounding it on either side were two rubies and two smaller diamonds.

"Look Cary, the big diamond represents God and the two rubies are Jesus and The Holy Spirit, the two smaller diamonds are you and me. This is my favorite so far." We looked at many more rings that day and ended our time with a nice lunch.

Our first Christmas together was memorable. After ripping open the presents we spent the morning hanging out then prepared to eat dinner with the whole family at my mother's house. Later that evening we decided to head out-of-town. We threw a few clothes in a bag and drove to Denver to spend the night with Cary's brother and family. All the kids played well together and I enjoyed getting to know Lance and his wife, Lou. The next day we drove to Wyoming and Cary introduced us to his cousins, uncles, and aunts. Cary handled all the kids and schedules with ease and patience. As evening drew near we hopped in the car to head home, the kids had fallen asleep in the back seat.

"Darlin' my life feels complete now. I did not know how lonely I was till I met you. I have my family in the back seat and we're listening to good music. Can life get any better than this?"

I snuggled close to him. "I agree! We are so blessed."

After spending fourteen days together, it was nearly time to end our visit. We had never spent that much time together and it was even harder to say goodbye, when I dropped Cary off at the airport. The weeks passed slowly and for the first time since we met my Prince Charming was not able to come out for a visit. We continued to talk every night and write letters to each other. About a month and a half later the ringing of the phone woke me up from an early sleep one evening. "Darlin' I have been so busy at work and I'm missing you in the worst way. With everything going on right now it would be easier for you to come here for a visit. Is that even possible? It's been six long weeks and I need to see you."

"Yes, I think I can arrange that. Jeremy and my family can take care of the kids and I can probably get the time off of work."

A few days later, I hugged each one of the kids when Jeremy dropped me off at the airport. I boarded the plane that would take me to my Knight in Shining Armor, while my stomach did summersaults in anticipation. After the plane landed, I surveyed the crowd, it felt magical watching Cary walk quickly towards me.

He held me close and looked deep in my eyes. "When I take one look at you my heart does flip-flops. You are stunning. I'm the luckiest man in the world."

Afterward he took me to the University where he had a temporary office, gave me the classified section of a local newspaper, and said, "Do you want to look for a house to rent while I work on this proposal?" (Although we still hadn't discussed a date for our wedding.)

"La Mirada, California that has a nice ring to it. I used to listen to a Christian radio show called the Biola Hour years ago. Where is that?"

"Silly, we're in La Mirada and this is Biola University. Did you find something already?" He asked, gently taking the newspaper from my hands. "Oh, it's right up the street. Do you want to check it out? I can meet you there when I take my lunch break."

He wrote directions for me and I walked up the street a few blocks to the house. Looking in the big picture window I noticed it had a fireplace and a huge dining room, and it was two stories. Excitedly, I strolled across the street where the gated community pool and tennis courts were. Cary drove over at lunchtime and we met with the land-lord. We immediately liked everything about the house.

"It's much bigger than the one I have back home. And the kids will love the fireplace, four bedrooms and three bathrooms. Wow! The pool is an added bonus, too. It's perfect!"

Cary signed the lease that same day. We celebrated our first Valentine's Day a few days later. While we were eating dinner at a nice restaurant, a friend of his walked toward our table holding a beautiful bouquet of red roses. "Happy Valentine's Day. You must be Debbie."

"This is Scott, he works for me, he is also the son of my boss, I asked him to hand-deliver your flowers so you could meet him." Cary said.

"Finally, I get to meet the woman who has changed my boss's life," he said as he reached out to hug me.

Later that evening I expressed my appreciation to Cary. "I am so impressed by your displays of affection towards me. Not only do you wine and dine me and buy me flowers, it's obvious by the way you look at me and tell others about me that you are in love with me. I am so happy."

"Never doubt how I feel about you." Then he took me in his arms and held me close. "You can take that to the bank!"

I was nearing the end of my visit with only one more day to go when Cary suggested we get dressed up and go to an expensive dinner. Later, Cary seemed a little nervous while we shared our dessert. After we ate, he took my hands in his, while gazing in my eyes he drew me close. "Darlin' will you marry me?" He slipped the engagement ring, (the one with two rubies and three diamonds) on my finger.

Without hesitation I screamed, "Yes!" Then we kissed passionately.

Afterwards, roaring laughter escaped his lips.

"What is so funny? By the way, when did you get the ring? I know you didn't buy it the day Kristy tried it on."

"Now, I can tell you what is so funny. There is a story attached to your engagement ring. I sent Jeremy the money a few days ago and he had it shipped to me Federal Express. Did you wonder why I made you wait this evening when I said I had to pick up my dry cleaning and I was gone for an hour?"

"Yes, I couldn't understand why it took so long, I knew your dry cleaner is right near your apartment building. Why what happened?"

"My dry cleaner is also located right next door to my post office box. I went to check my mailbox and the door was locked up tight. Feeling anxious, I looked through the window, knowing your ring was right inside and I couldn't get to it. I didn't understand why the store was closed, then I remembered today is President's Day. Fortunately, the same person who owns the dry cleaner owns the mailroom. I called her up and explained the situation. Luckily she was home and she drove over and opened up the mailroom so I could get your ring."

"What a great story to tell the kids," I laughed.

The rest of the evening was perfect as we dinned and danced late into the night.

The next day I couldn't hide the sadness I felt leaving my love once again. Unhappily, I left Cary's loving arms, and stepped onto the airplane but at the same time, I was excited to get back to my children. I couldn't wait to show off my ring, and share about my adventures in California.

Less than two weeks after I had been home Cary called me with an important question. "Can we get married this Sunday? I've already moved into the house and I can't wait to have you and the kids here with me."

We hadn't talked about a date and my head started to spin. "I can't think of anything better. I'll call Coleman and see if he can marry us in between services."

"Sure, this Sunday before the evening service will work out. One-thirty will be perfect," Coleman said.

We had already talked to Dave about getting married at his house. It was where Cary had looked deep into my eyes and realized his life and mine would never be the same again. A friend baked me a wedding cake. My sister bought me a beautiful dress and made me colorful silk flowers to hold. Hours before, Jeremy had driven all the kids to Dave's house to help get it ready for the wedding. Cary had flown in on Saturday but I had not seen him yet. Lance and his family traveled from

Denver. Lorraine, Cary's mom, couldn't make the trip from Nebraska although she expressed her delight in welcoming the kids and me to the family. Rod, Cary's oldest brother, who lived in Portland and his family were unable to attend but they were all eager to meet us one day. All my loved ones would be there to celebrate the blessed event.

It was finally Sunday, my sister and I drove to Dave's. As I walked to the front door, I heard Kristy playing a song on her flute, *Wind Beneath my Wings*, by Bette Midler. It was time! Never had I felt so loved! Slowly I descended down the stairs to the basement, which had been beautifully decorated. There stood Cary, my Soul Mate, my Knight in Shining Armor, grinning. His eyes never left mine as he watched me walk towards him. It was as if time stood still.

It was over too quickly as we looked into each other's eyes and professed our undying love. We cut the cake, drank champagne, and toasted to our new life together. We danced to the very first song we had first danced to nearly six months previously. My children surrounded me and looked up at Cary with love and trust in their eyes for him.

This time I knew my marriage would be different from anything I had ever experienced before. The greatest gift Cary had given me was unconditional love and acceptance. I knew God was revealing to me through another person how he felt about me and I was finally able to understand and receive it.

The kids were happy, as they had long ago sensed Cary's genuine love for them. The words I had read in the Bible began to make sense to me.

"For husbands, this means love your wives, just as Christ loved the church. He gave up His life for her to make her holy and clean." Ephesians 5:25

That is the kind of sacrificial love Cary had been showing me since the beginning of our relationship. Our wedding was a simple ceremony, but it would change my life, and the lives of my four children forever.

37

California Here
We Come

"The Sovereign Lord is my strength; He makes my feet like the feet of a deer, He enables me to go on the heights." Habakkuk 3:19

We spent the night at an amazing hotel and ordered room service. That was a first for me. While we were gone, Jeremy and his friends loaded the moving van. The next day we said our tearful goodbyes to my family and drove out to begin our new life in California.

Pulling up to the house we had rented, the kids jumped out of the car and explored our new home. It was more than they had asked for. In early March, it was too cold to go swimming in Southern California, but all of the kids put on their bathing suits anyways and jumped into the freezing water at the community pool. Before settling in for the evening, we picked out a strawberry cake, lit candles, and celebrated Ashley's 4th birthday.

A few days later I enrolled my children in school. Jeff was in elementary, Kristy in junior high and Jeremy in high school. Immediately,

Jeremy applied to work at Bon Appetit in the cafeteria at Biola University. Thankfully his school and his job were easy to get to on foot, just around the corner from where we lived.

I was grateful I was able to be a stay-at-home-mom, which is what I had always desired. It felt so good not to have to share Ashley anymore. Or so I thought. Two weeks later, Lee came storming back into our lives. Our peace was shattered! Regrettably, Ashley would be torn apart emotionally for many years, feeling loyal to her biological father yet grasping on to the bond of love she felt towards Cary. But through the years we all learned to deal with it and it wasn't long before he left and returned to Colorado. Fortunately for my older children, Kenny was not ever in the picture. Cary was able to become the loving, nurturing father they never had. Although they continued to call him Cary they referred to him as their "dad."

Three months after we moved to California we arranged to have a second wedding. "Darlin' all our family can come together now as well as my friends and work associates to meet you and the kids. I can hardly wait."

Cary's mom, Lorraine, was flying out to attend our formal ceremony. She would be seeing me for the first time as her daughter-in-law, not Dave's older sister. I was looking forward to finally meeting Cary's oldest brother and his family. My cousins, aunts and uncles on my Dad's side, who I had not seen for over twenty-years were also planning on coming. My old babysitter, Debbie, who remained one of my closest friends, planned to drive two hours to celebrate our happy day with us.

We held our ceremony at an outdoor chapel at Thacher School in the majestic Ojai valley. Kristy again played her flute as Cary and I walked out together. All the kids joined us up front while Cary's friend, who was a minister, led the service. Since Cary worked in food service he was able arrange to have the chef from Biola prepare a delicious meal. It was a celebration that looked like it had been prepared for royalty. I felt like a queen surrounded by family and friends on the arm of my Prince Charming. Toasts were made, and then Cary and I stopped at each table thanking our guests for joining us, while Ashley sat quietly atop his shoulders.

The next day, all the guests met at our clubhouse for a casual time of swimming and barbecuing. We played games and laughed throughout the day. Everyone enjoyed our two-day celebration. For many months, afterward Ashley walked around wearing a scarf on her head pretending to be a bride.

We found a church to attend right away. "Cary, I feel uncomfortable telling people about my past. What will they think when they find out I've been divorced twice? I'm afraid they will judge me and look down on me."

"Don't worry about other people. If they choose to judge you then they have to answer to God. You just keep being the awesome woman I married and they will love you just like I do."

The business Cary was in didn't grow for a whole year, which gave us time to adjust to one another. Often, we looked back on our first year of married life gratefully thanking God that he gave us so much uninterrupted time to connect with one another as a family.

I appreciated staying home the first year we were married then Ashley started kindergarten and I worked part time in Biola's cafeteria. Some days I'd bring my daughter to work with me when she was off from school. The students enjoyed seeing her and she loved the attention from them and my co-workers. Ashley enjoyed going to work with me and she would often swipe the meal cards by herself.

Sadly, even after several months being Cary's wife, my past would overwhelm me and I would often give in to my feelings of insecurities and convince myself that Cary regretted marrying me.

One day he grew concerned. "What's wrong with you? Aren't you happy?"

It was hard to reveal my dark thoughts, but he kept encouraging me to open up to him. "I'm scared you're going to stop loving me when you realize I'm not perfect and I'm moody, anxious, fearful, and insecure. You've been around me when I'm irritable and I get impatient with the kids. I feel like I've brought so much baggage into the marriage and now with Lee being around at least three times a week it feels so overwhelming. Sometimes I am so full of anxiety because I get scared and am afraid you're going to stop loving me."

"Come over here." He took my hands in his, "I know you will never be perfect. I'm not and I don't expect you to be either. Don't you know I see your heart? I love everything about you, even your moodiness. Don't ever doubt my love for you. You can take that to the bank!"

He reassured me that he could handle Lee and all that could transpire because he was in our lives. At those times, when I felt undeserving of his love, God reminded me through his word that he had given me more that I could have imagined.

"Now to Him who is able to do immeasurably more than all we ask or imagine, according to His power that is at work with us." Ephesians 3:20

I called my old friend in Colorado one day, shortly after Cary and I had talked about my fears. "Rosa, I have prayed throughout my life for someone like Cary, never really believing it would happen. God's grace is amazing. I didn't do anything to deserve this but God gave it to me anyway. This has been much better than anything I could have planned for my life!"

"I'm so happy for you. It's obvious he brought a wonderful man into your life to love you and your children."

I finally began to relax and bask in Cary's love. The kids treasured our first year in California. They made new friends and Jeremy liked his job right away. We struggled financially for the first couple of years and we did without many extras but it didn't matter because we all felt loved.

Often after church we'd stop at a nearby grocery store; buy fried chicken, chips, and fresh fruit. Finding a park, we'd eat our picnic lunch. Afterwards, we'd feed the ducks and take long walks. Sometimes we'd all join in a game of catch or take turns playing with Ashley on the playground. Watching Cary proudly push her in the swing and slide down the slide with her filled me with unexplainable joy. After family dinners, there were many nights we stayed up late to finish playing a game of "Risk." Since Ashley was still very young, we all played board games with her pretty often. Even the older kids spent family time preferring to hang out with us, instead of their friends, we watched movies, played games, went out to eat and enjoyed each other's company.

Since our house didn't come with air conditioning, I spent nearly every day in the summers swimming with the kids. Cary always joined us on the weekends and after work. Although I often grumbled about the heat, I was grateful for the closeness we shared at the pool, where we were able to create such wonderful memories. Thankfully, my older brother and his family only lived an hour from us and we had them to hang out with on weekends. My only regret was the rest of my family still lived in Colorado and could not enjoy good times with us.

Two years after we moved to California, my brother, Mike received orders to move to Nebraska. Spending holidays and birthdays with my brother's family had been a blessing for all of us. The kids enjoyed the closeness they experienced with their cousins. After Mike and his family left, we had to make up our own traditions during holidays and birthdays, because we didn't have any extended family close by. Since we had all left our family and old friends behind, I felt like we were able to bond closer as a family since we only had each other.

38

Tyler

"Behold, children are a gift of the Lord." Psalm 127:3

"I praise you for every breath I take and thank You that I was created for good things." Colossians 3:10

Cary and I often talked about having a child of our own. Several years into our marriage, I realized I was pregnant, but unfortunately all my old fears came flooding back. Even my three older children felt it. "What if Cary treats us the way Lee did when you had Ashley? We don't want to go through that again." Finally, we voiced our fears to Cary.

"Don't be afraid. I would never do that to you. I am not Lee. I am your dad and I will always love you as much as I love this new baby." He patted my growing belly and reached out and hugged us. "You don't have to worry about a thing. My love for you will never change. You will continue to be just as important to me even after we have this baby. I hope you will all trust me. You know you can count on me. Have you ever been disappointed in me since I married your mother?"

"No," my children said as they all gathered around Cary.

339

"I can take that to the bank, right?" I laughed. The kids looked at him with tears in their eyes. He had convinced them history wouldn't repeat itself.

When I was five months pregnant the doctors advised us to get an ultra sound. I had never had one with any of my other kids. "You and your husband can find out the gender of the baby if you want," my doctor explained.

Cary and I looked at each other and shook our heads, "No, I never knew the gender of the other kids. We'll wait and be surprised."

The girls were excited to accompany us on the day of my test. It was fascinating to watch the baby kick and move around. After the test was over Kristy took seven-year-old Ashley to the bathroom. While walking back to the room she noticed the nurse looking at my ultrasound pictures. "Tell me if I am going to have a little baby brother or sister. My parents don't want to know but I can keep a secret."

The nurse whispered in her ear.

Being thirty-nine, I often felt uncomfortable with my pregnancy but I still loved the feeling of the baby moving around inside of me and just being pregnant. Cary and I took a birthing class, and he was so supportive as I was going through labor. In the spring of 1994, three years after we were married, we welcomed our fifth and final child, Tyler David Lau Wheeland. I noticed the pride my husband felt as he cut the umbilical cord. Cary and I looked heavenward and thanked God for blessing us with a child of our own. We immediately called the other kids.

Kristy answered the phone. "We had the baby," Cary said.

"You had a boy, didn't you?"

"Yea, how did you know?"

Kristy confessed she had known since the ultra sound and had shared the news with her brothers, all the kids knew except Ashley. They had actually kept the secret from us.

For the first six weeks after Tyler was born, Cary set up his office downstairs in the dining room. I was fortunate to be able to spend much needed time with my new baby. He had his father's nose and lips and my eyes—the bewitching eyes that his daddy was mesmerized with. Cary and the kids took over all the household chores. My husband treated me like a queen, something I had never experienced after childbirth. He drove the kids back and forth to school and made sure there was plenty of food in the house. He was never very good at cooking, but the kids helped out in the kitchen, and we had lots of delivered pizzas and take-out meals.

"I don't want you to worry about anything. You just concentrate on the baby."

"I sure appreciate the way you take care of us." I expressed my heartfelt gratitude to Cary. Each day more gifts arrived from friends, family members, and my husband's co-workers. I felt like it was Christmas in April, I even got to know the deliveryman on a first name basis.

Ashley had desperately wanted a little sister. But after spending time with the new baby she called him her little "brudder" and she adored him. When Tyler was old enough to talk she encouraged him to call her, 'my other mama.' Before he was born I had worried that my young daughter might be jealous because she wouldn't be the baby any-more and she would have to get used to me sharing my attention. But my fears proved to be false as she developed a tight bond with her little brother that still exists today. She learned how to share, to be generous and to take care of someone else. Today Ashley has a special place in her heart for babies and toddlers. Could it that Tyler brought out the nurturing mother in her?

The other kids were excited to have a new little one in the family too. When Tyler was going through his terrible-twos and would throw tantrums in the grocery store, I'd tease my oldest son, who was twenty years older than him, "Discipline your son! He never acts like that with his Grandma."

"He's not my son, he's my brother," Jeremy would laugh.

After not having a little one for many years, I delighted in pushing Tyler in the baby stroller and hanging out at the park or the local library for story time. I didn't have to work and he received my undivided attention. Although I still hated to see her go, having a little one made it a little easier when Ashley spent time with her dad. Since my older kids were all teenagers, I wasn't needed as much by them.

Tyler was two when Cary and I had a serious discussion. "Darlin' it has been five years since I promised you we'd move back to Colorado. Do you still want to go?"

"Well..." I paused, "I love it here and the kids do, too. Although I miss my mom and siblings more than I can say, I don't think I want to go back. And come on, we are only thirty minutes from the nearest beach. We have Disneyland twenty minutes away and Knott's Berry Farm ten minutes from us. Going to the mountains is less than a two-hour drive. We have everything we need right here. Honestly, I don't think I could handle cold, freezing winters anymore. I do love the seasons but we are all spoiled by the year-round warm weather. God has been so good to us. I am truly happy. So, it looks like you're off the hook. We're not going anywhere."

With that said, I knew in my soul that my heart belonged in California. We would never again return to live in Colorado.

The years went by and Tyler seemed to have endless energy from the time he woke up in the morning till his head hit the pillow at night. Along with his fierce independence and stubbornness he had a magnetic and charismatic personality and was extremely friendly, he loved talking to strangers.

As a toddler, Tyler would approach adults he didn't know and start conversations with them. Frequently, I'd meet my oldest daughter at Starbucks after she moved out and Tyler would accompany me. Immediately, he'd seek out an unsuspecting stranger and thrust himself upon their quiet morning. "Mommy, can I go sit with that guy and drink my hot cocoa?" Taking his cup, he'd invite himself. "Can I visit with you? My mommy says it's okay if you want company." *Nobody ever said no.*

Watching from a few feet away, knowing my child was safe, I'd see the face of strangers light up as my four-year-old carried on a conversation with them. Tyler seemed to grow up faster than the other kids; after all he had so many adult role models in his life. With the huge age difference between our children we always had plenty of babysitters so Cary and I could still continue our date nights. When the older kids moved out one by one there were frequent visits, dinner dates, and phone calls.

One of the things we did early in our marriage was to join marriage and parenting groups at our church. Those early lessons only continued to unite us in one accord as we raised our family. As an added bonus, we made lifelong friends with the couples we met in our small groups.

Spending many Friday nights in the summertime at Huntington Beach, lighting a fire and grilling hotdogs and marshmallows was a favorite pastime. Listening to the waves smash against the shore, looking up and marveling at the twinkling stars in the sky, inspired fond memories. Through the years, we arranged birthday parties, cookouts, and Easter egg hunts. We took family vacations and attended attractions close by. We were fortunate to take trips to visit family members in Colorado, Arizona, North Carolina, Oregon, and Nebraska. Life was good!

The other kids continued to be a blessing as they managed to deal with their emotions in a healthy way. When they turned sixteen we taught them how to drive attended their soccer games, took photographs of their proms, and watched them graduate from high school. We tried to attend church as a family as often as we could. *The family that prays together—stays together.* Of course, we had our struggles as most families do, but for the most part the kids learned from their mistakes and felt secure in sharing the deepest part of their hearts with us, knowing that we loved them no matter what. Through it all we have remained close and continue to support each another.

Throughout the years Cary and I made sure we set aside time for each other. He always complimented me in front of the children. You could hear him say, "Isn't your mom beautiful? You have such a great mom. Your mom is such a great cook, wasn't dinner awesome!" How I loved hearing those words. His favorite pet name for me was goddess. We often prayed together and were able to talk about our thoughts and feelings. We were a constant source of encouragement for each other as well as for the kids. We trusted God to meet our individual needs so we could be free to accept and love each other unconditionally without trying to change the other. There were quite a few laughs in our home, we didn't take ourselves too seriously and each of the kids appreciated how easy-going Cary continued to be.

Cary was my best friend and I was his best friend. The kids never had to worry that we would divorce, that was the farthest thing from our minds.

"Cary, I appreciate the way you have loved my children all these years." I often said.

"That is because they are <u>Our</u> children. You know, Deb, we have never struggled through what other blended families have, and I am truly grateful for that. You make my life easy and I appreciate you."

"Thank you, and I value you and all you do for our family. You make my life easy. I've never had it so good." I said as I reached over and planted a kiss on my husband's lips.

Since the kids were getting older, Cary suggested I take time for my hobbies, which included gardening and writing. I had always wanted to be a writer and had put my pen and paper away many years before, after my first divorce. I believed I would never be good enough to write a book since I had not attended college. In spite of my doubts, my wonderful husband continued to encourage me to fulfill my dreams. One day I saw an ad in the newspaper offering a six-week writing course. I took the course and began writing about Tyler when he turned four. Writing short stories about his antics became a passion of mine. I also wrote inspirational stories depicting God's answered prayers. I began to send several of my articles in to different magazines hoping to get them published. A few years after Tyler was born, I received a notice in the mail.

"Open it, Ashley. I'm too afraid to do it myself. I have already gotten so many rejection letters."

"Congratulations, Mrs. Wheeland. We have accepted your story for our publication."

Excitedly, I grabbed the paper from her hands, in the envelope was my very first check, for one hundred and sixty dollars. I was now a published and paid writer!

Later that night the whole family got together to celebrate. "Thank you, Cary, for believing in me and giving me the courage to believe in myself." I raised a toast.

Early in our married life our huge, king-sized bed was chosen as our family meeting place. As a little girl, Ashley loved to climb on the bed and tickle Cary's face while he pretended to be asleep then he would ROAR and scare her as she laughed with delight. When Tyler was a toddler, we'd wake up to the rumble of his footsteps running through the hallway. Throwing open the door he'd jump on the bed and scream, "Mommy, Daddy, I'm awake now!" But most memorable of all were the times in the evenings before we fell asleep, Cary and I were snuggled against our soft, comfy pillows, talking over the day's events, when unexpectedly one of the children would come in. "Mom, Cary, can I talk to you about something?" Soon, one by one, we'd hear the pitter-patter of feet and the rest of the children would join us with Jeff sitting on the rocking chair, Kristy lying across the bed, Jeremy resting at the end, Ashley snuggled close to my side, and Tyler, with his head nestled against Cary's arm. Our time consisted of laughing, hugging, tickling, and sometimes tears.

Often, we found ourselves comforting a hurting child. Holding her close as she cried over a lost boyfriend, or another might receive affirmation for a new job. Or perhaps one of our teenager's cars had broken down and he needed a word of encouragement. Maybe one of our boys was excited about an upcoming prom date. We always urged our children to pursue their passions and often found ourselves teaching life lessons during times on our family bed. It was here where we reached out clasped one another's hands and prayed together. *"Continue earnestly in prayer, being vigilant in it with thanksgiving." Colossians 4:2*

We were all on the family bed when Jeremy made a big announcement. "I have something to tell you, I'm twenty-one and it's time I moved out."

Soon after we helped him carry the last of his clothing to the car, we collapsed on our family bed in tears. "My baby's moving out," I cried as my husband reached over and patted my shoulder.

"Thankfully, he's only moving ten minutes down the road. You know we'll see him often," reassured Cary.

"Mommy, why is Jeremy leaving?" Ashley asked, her eyes misting.

"I don't want Jeremy to leave," said Jeff, sniffling, trying to hold back his tears.

"I'm going to miss my big brother!" Kristy said as she reached for me, bawling. We listened as he started his car, finding comfort in one another once again, on our big, cozy bed.

Afterward Jeff said, "Mom, Cary, do you realize we all seem to end up on your bed?"

"Yea, it's nice we all like hanging out here!" The other kids quipped.

"I hadn't realized, but I guess it's been designated as our special place," I commented.

39

My Dad

"The Lord is good to all; he has compassion on all he has made." Psalm 145:9

One early morning in the fall of 2000, my phone began ringing off the hook. Cary had already left for work and I ran downstairs to answer it.

"Hello, this is Dan from the Montrose Coroner's office. I found your number in Robert Griswold's wallet. He was in a car accident."

"Is he dead," I screamed! My mind raced out of control. What was my brother doing in Montrose, Colorado? I couldn't think straight; all I could do was cry as my thoughts turned to his wife, Mary and his son, Kyle. *No, no, I can't believe my brother Rob is dead!*

"What are you talking about? What happened?" I cried.

"Robert Francis Griswold was in a car accident. I'm sorry, he didn't make it," the coroner calmly said in response to my frantic cry.

"Oh, you mean my father, not my brother!" I said with relief.

Immediately I dialed Rob's number. "I just got a call and Daddy's been killed in an automobile accident. Apparently, he was on his way to California and he stopped to get gas. Then he accidentally drove back up the on-coming ramp and hit a car head on, he died instantly. Luckily, the other driver only suffered a broken leg. One of dad's dogs survived and the ambulance driver kept him. Daddy would have been pleased. I was so scared when the officer called me, he mentioned Robert and I thought he meant you," I explained, still feeling shaken.

"It's okay, Deb, calm down. I'm fine. I will call the coroner for more information. I love you."

Quickly, I made arrangements to go out to Colorado after talking to my sister. "Monica, I always swore I would not go back for Dad's funeral. I feel different now and I want to be there for you and our brothers. I know you and dad were close and I am so happy I was able to see him a few months ago when he came out to California."

"I think he was confused with the medication he was taking. A few weeks ago, he had a feeling he wasn't going to be around much longer and was heading back to California to say goodbye to his brothers and sisters. He must have forgotten he was just there. This was the best way for him to go, driving and being surrounded by his little dogs." Monica mentioned. "I'm so glad Daddy accepted the Lord as his Savior four years ago. After his second wife died such a painful death from bone cancer, I think it helped him get right with the God. He used to watch Billy Graham all the time and he'd drink coffee and talk with a retired priest that lived in his neighborhood."

"I have good memories of him the last few years too. I know he tried hard to do the right thing. I feel at peace knowing he is with the Lord, even though I don't think he ever forgave himself for molesting us."

"Yeah, I think you're right," Monica agreed.

There was a lot to do when I got to my sister's house. We looked and looked and we finally found the right container for our dad's ashes.

We picked out a unique, brown treasure chest. We dropped in the ashes of his favorite dog, Dobie, who had been dead for many years. Dad always said he wanted to be buried with Dobie. My sister made arrangements to have a service at her church. The people there had met our dad many times, because Monica had invited him to barbecues at the church. Since my dad was a real friendly man, everybody was fond of him.

We sent our dad off in style. His favorite music was Scottish bagpipes and we found a CD that played "Amazing Grace" with bagpipes. Dad would have loved it! We draped the American flag near his treasure chest that held his ashes and surrounded the tables with pictures of my dad, who had been a handsome man when he was younger.

Afterwards, my siblings and I gathered at a nearby restaurant and shared funny stories about our father. I could never have imagined that a man who had brought so much pain to his family would be loved at the end of his life. *"All things are possible with God." Mark 23:27*

After I had returned home my sister went to our dad's house to clean it up. While there she found pictures of each of his kids and grandkids above his bed and three World Vision children he had been sponsoring. Monica mentioned he had told her he prayed every night for his loved ones.

Although he never supported us while he was alive, unbeknownst to us, he had signed up for a life insurance plan just six months before he was killed. We each received sixteen thousand dollars apiece. It was like God saying, "Even though he didn't take care of you in life, he did in death." It seemed like it was a big cosmic joke and I liked the punch line!

Less than a month after my dad died, I was at a Women's retreat. As the music played, the words became so real to me, *"The nails in his hands, the nails in his feet they tell us how much he loves us..."* With my eyes tightly shut, I envisioned Jesus; I saw his loving arms around my father. The two of them smiled down on me as they watched from eternity. "It is finished!" Jesus said to me.

Through the vision, God was assuring me that my dad had finally accepted the forgiveness Jesus had offered him so long ago. Gone was the self-hatred and guilt my father had always hung onto. Dad was finally at peace! I felt so strongly God would give me many opportunities to share with victims of abuse that forgiveness and restoration are accessible to all people who carry around shameful secrets and scars. 'Victory from our past' became my motto. I know because I was living it.

"Praise be to the God and Father of our Lord Jesus Christ, the Father of compassion and the God of all comfort, who comforts us in all our troubles, so that we can comfort those in any trouble with the comfort we ourselves have received from God." 2 Corinthians 1:3-4

"Be kind to one another, tenderhearted, forgiving one another; just as God in Christ forgave you." Ephesians 4:32

40

Romance

"My lover spoke and said to me, "Arise, my darling, my beautiful one, and come with me." Song of Songs 2:10

I had been attending a Bible study and Wednesday would be my last day before the summer break. Afterwards, we gals would enjoy a luncheon at our leader's house. I was in charge of bringing the guacamole and chips. Tuesday night Cary and I slipped off to the grocery store and I picked out six, fat, ripe avocados. My mouth was already watering thinking about my lunch the next day.

Early the morning of the Bible study Cary asked me to accompany him to the airport to take Kristy to Oregon to visit a friend for a week. "I promise we'll be back in time for you to get to your study," Cary said confidently.

After a quick shower, I slipped on my shoes and out the door we went. Arriving at the airport we dropped off Kristy. Cary said, "Would you mind if I pick up a ticket for my trip to Denver next week, since we're already here? It's just easier to get it now."

While standing in front of the electronic ticket machine, Cary pushed a few buttons and turned to me. He handed me an envelope with the words, *OPEN IMMEDIATELY written on it.*

Ripping it apart, I read, "*Aloha! You are not going back home today. We are flying to Maui for a week. Sit back, relax, and enjoy. I love you Darlin.*"

Jumping up and down, I screamed, "What? I can't believe this. Are we on Candid Camera? Is this a joke? You're kidding, right? What about the kids? Cary, you sure are amazing!"

"All the kids were in on the surprise, except Tyler, and Ashley is waking him right now to get him ready for school."

"Here, listen to this recording," and he handed me his phone.

"Mom, this is Jeremy. Have a great time. You deserve it."

"Mom, this is Kristy, I'm so happy for you. I called your Bible study leader and she knows all about it. Go and have fun."

"Don't worry about Tyler, we will all take care of him. Go and have a great time. You and Cary deserve this," remarked Ashley.

"Mom you have an awesome husband and you are amazing, I'm so excited for you. Don't worry about a thing. Go and have fun," Jeff said.

I was speechless as tears fell down my face. Finally, I found words. "How long have you been planning this? I can't believe it!" I reached over and hugged my wonderful Prince Charming, affectionately. "But what about my clothes?"

"Kristy packed you a bag and put it in my trunk last night while you and I were out buying those mouth-watering avocados," Cary laughed. "We have about three hours to kill before we fly. Let's go move the car to long-term parking and call Tyler. He should know by now, and he's not going to be happy!"

"Mommy, I want to go to Hawaii, too," Tyler cried! "Why didn't anyone tell me? I can keep a secret."

"Next time Dad does something crazy like this, I promise he will keep you in the loop," I said, reassuring my ten-year old. "I will miss you. Have fun with your brother and sister. Be good! We love you and we'll call every day."

"How long have they known?" I asked Cary, as I thought back on our recent conversations.

"It's been in the works for a few weeks. Maybe a month."

"Wow, I'm shocked! I had no idea any of this was going on right under my nose. Luckily, I showered before I left the house. I was almost going to run out without my bra on. I'm glad I changed my mind at the last minute," I chuckled. "Now it makes sense why you didn't let me bring my puppy to accompany us on the ride to the airport."

Snuggling close to him during the five-hour flight, I thanked God for the gift of my husband, my Prince Charming. This was a dream come true. I had never been to Hawaii. Although Cary had been there numerous times before we were married. It had become a running joke in our house. *You took all your girlfriends to Hawaii, but you've never taken your wife.* I was sure glad he decided it was time to take me.

"Darling, I am so excited to be here with the woman of my dreams for a romantic island getaway," Cary stated, as we rented a jeep for our five-day second honeymoon.

We went exploring, swimming, and snorkeling. We took numerous walks and went four-wheeling in the jeep. Getting up early one morning we watched the colorful sunrise at Haleakala volcano and enjoyed delicious dinners throughout the week. Lying on our lawn chairs while we watched the waves splash on the sand was relaxing. Looking into each other's eyes and professing our undying love for one another filled our hearts with romance. Soon it was over, our time on the island ended too quickly.

"I can't believe you did this for me. It wasn't even my birthday or our anniversary. In fact, it's close to your birthday," I said as we shared our last meal in Maui.

"I love doing things for you. This is what it's all about," Cary said as he reached over and kissed me.

"I have never known anyone so generous in my life. You make me very happy, and I am so grateful to be your wife."

Fortunately, within a few years, we were able to take all of our kids back with us to the scenic Hawaiian Islands. We had dreamed about sharing it with them for a long time.

In the spring of 2002, we were able to achieve a dream of Cary's to take me to Europe. Happily, two of the kids, Kristy and Tyler, traveled with us. Kristy and Cary enjoyed sipping steamy, hot cappuccinos at a riverfront patio on the banks of the Seine River in France. We hopped on a boat on the river Seine which flowed right through the heart of Paris, it was magical. The four of us toured the Queen's Palace in Windsor, England. Tyler begged to sit in the front seat of the gondola as we paddled the canals of Venice. Tyler had traveled with his skateboard, pads, and helmet and to his delight we found a skate park in London. Finally, we met up with friends in beautiful, picturesque Lake Geneva, Switzerland where we rode on an over-sized, 100-year-old barge wearing evening gowns, suits, and ties in our bare feet!

Soon it was time for us to head back to California where the rest of our children eagerly anticipated our arrival ready to hear about our trip through photos and videos.

41

My Heart's Desire

"Delight yourself in the Lord and he will give you the desires of your heart." Psalm 37:4

After returning from our trip, I was fortunate enough to buy a horse. It had always been my heart's desire. I had never given up on my love for horses. Years earlier, before Tyler was born, Cary had taken the kids and me to Pismo Beach, which was about a four-hour drive from our home. "Deb, I've arranged for us all to ride horses on the beach. We are supposed to meet at 1:00 pm. are you okay with that?"

"Are you kidding me? I'm better than okay with that. You've never forgotten my dream of galloping a horse on the beach. Wow! Thank you so much."

I had recently met a new friend named Janice, who had two horses. She invited me to ride while our kids were in school. I loved getting back in the saddle again after many years of not riding. It had awakened a renewed interest in me wanting my own horse.

"Debbie," Janice said one day. "Do you want to go to the horse auction this weekend just to look at the horses?"

"I would love to."

Finally, Saturday came. As we walked through the horse stables, there stood before me a proud, massive white and brown majestic-looking horse. Right away I called him Prince. "Look, there's the horse of my dreams. Of course, I don't have any intention of buying him," I told my friend. "Although, Cary did just receive a bonus," I giggled.

The auction began and out pranced several horses. Since Prince's stall was listed as number 35 I thought he would come in last. Without warning, Prince galloped out with a rider in the saddle. The rider turned him one way, then the other showing him off.

"Debbie, bid on him," teased my friend.

Impulsively, I raised my number. Everything happened so fast!

"SOLD to number 16!"

"What have I just done? Did I just buy a horse?" I screamed.

Reaching into my purse I dialed Cary's number on my cell phone. "Is it okay if I buy a horse?"

"Sure, just use your best judgment and don't spend too much."

"Well," I screamed excitedly. "I just bought one!"

The last thing I heard before he hung up was the sound of roaring laughter. His trademark!

The next morning, we borrowed my friend's horse trailer. Heading back to the auction I could hardly contain my enthusiasm, I was so excited to pick up my prized possession. As we led Prince into the stable in Janice's neighborhood, I kept repeating over and over, "I have a horse. I have my very own horse." All I could think about was climbing on his back.

Later that day Janice called her friend who was a trainer. "Jessica, can you help out? Deb just bought a horse from the auction, we thought he was broken but he pranced around and got a scared look in his eyes when I tried to get on his back."

Jessica worked with my horse three times a week for close to two months and still he didn't seem to improve. Although I couldn't ride him, I loved walking to the stables to feed him carrots and apples. He was like an oversized dog following me around while I offered him treats.

A few weeks later, Jessica said, "It's evident that something else has to be done with Prince. You really need to find someone who lives with horses and can work with him every day. I'm getting ready to go back to school and I won't have the time anymore. Your horse was probably abused in his earlier years. He obviously has issues and he is going to need a lot of work to trust people. I know eventually you'll be able to get on his back. I believe he was probably drugged at the horse auction. That's why he came out of the chute with a rider on his back."

I wanted desperately to be up in the saddle riding my horse. I began to pray, as I did in all circumstances of my life, "Jesus, show me what to do!"

Later that night as I arrived at the monthly Women's Fellowship at our church, I noticed a new lady and introduced myself to her. As we talked, I told her about the problems with my horse.

"Just so happens I have a friend who has about twelve horses. She only lives about fifteen miles away. Why don't we ask her if she can take Prince and work with him? She is a great horse lady. I have also been praying for her salvation," said Lynn.

Lynn's friend eagerly took my horse and promised she would do what she could with him.

Three to four times a week, I made the thirty-mile round-trip to visit my horse, but I soon realized it was more important to spend time getting to know my new friend. I shared my past with her and she too was open about hers. Soon she began to read my short stories, which included how the Lord had intervened in someone's life. She talked about the wounds that kept her from receiving Christ's love. My soul ached for her as I could still see the hurt she had never gotten over, and I prayed faithfully for her.

After six weeks, she told me the bad news. "Prince needs more work than I can give him. My advice to you is to pay someone lots of money because eventually they will be able to figure out his issues. I just don't have the time or energy to do it. Another thing you can do is to take him back to the horse auction and sell him."

Pondering the decision, Cary and I both decided to take Prince back and sell him. Surprisingly, it wasn't painful to see him go. I knew God had arranged everything. I continued to visit my friend throughout the summer. We often went horseback riding on her horses and talked about her newfound faith.

"In the last few weeks I have done a lot of thinking. I know God brought Lynn and you into my life," she said. "I have been praying and I accepted Jesus as my Savior. I think I am ready to go to church now."

"I am so happy for you. It has become clear to me that God had other things in mind when I bought my horse. Having a horse is something I have wanted since childhood. He gave me my heart's desire. But more importantly, he brought you into my life. He showed me your relationship with Him was more important than having my own horse. Although I am grateful for the time I had with Prince, I am even happier to have been part of reaping a harvest for God. *"One sows and the other reaps." John 4:37*

42

My Mom

"Search me, O God, and know my heart; test me and know my anxious thoughts. See if there is any offensive way in me, and lead me in the way everlasting." Psalm 139:23-24

Shortly before I sold my horse, I had been flying back and forth to Colorado to visit my mom who had been in the hospital for some time. She had been on dialysis for almost five years but recently had developed an infection and the doctors couldn't find the source of where it was located in her body. It was a miserable time for her. Not only did she have to spend the summer inside, but also, she desperately missed planting her sweet alyssums, nasturtiums, and lovely white daisies. She wasn't able to see her white and yellow roses bloom and watch spring turn into summer.

Prior to getting sick, Mom could often be seen on her hands and knees, wearing cotton gloves planting, and weeding in her small yard. She had to retire early because she developed kidney cancer and had to go on dialysis. She lived in a small trailer, raised her three, little white, Maltese dogs and spent most of her summers outside. Her cozy fireplace, as well as the television set, had become her best friends in cold winter months. Mom enjoyed her seventeen grandchildren who affectionately referred to her as "Nanny." She continued to stay close to all her children.

My mother had been sober nearly thirty years through the help of AA. Whenever she visited us she willingly accompanied us to church and I believed she had accepted Jesus, although she was very private when it came to talking about her faith.

Heading to Colorado to check on my mom I knew she would be excited to hear about my horse. I went up in the elevator, found her room and hurried to her side. "Mom, remember that year I asked Santa Claus for a horse?"

"How could I forget?"

"Santa Claus didn't bring me one, but Cary did," I laughed and explained all the details.

She was so thrilled, "Oh honey, I am so happy for you. You have always wanted a horse." We hugged and she fell asleep too quickly.

I went back home but less than two months later I flew back to see my mom with my oldest son at my side. After nearly three months in the hospital the doctors finally realized the staph infection she suffered from was called MRSA. It was life threatening because it was resistant to most antibiotics. Since Mom was allergic to antibiotics and her lifelong cigarette habit had also weakened her body, the doctors were unable to save her.

About a week before she died all of her children stood at her bedside. In her last days Mom appealed to us. "Promise me you'll all stay together."

"Of course, Mom, you taught us to take care of each other. We've never forgotten that," we replied.

Fortunately, she had time to say her goodbyes to each of us. Pulling me aside, she said, "Debra, will you be okay?"

"Yes, Mom, because I know where you are going. If I didn't, I wouldn't be okay."

Although doubts still filled my thoughts, I refused to voice them.

I had to leave the next day and I continued to pray for a miracle for my mom. She had endured so much pain for so long. In the last days, she was unable to take morphine because of her allergies, and she endured continuous pain. My heart broke, knowing she was suffering so much. Tears filled my eyes, as I looked skyward, "Don't let my mom suffer anymore, please Jesus. Please help her."

Five days, later, I received the call I had been dreading from Mike, "Monica and I were with Mom till the end. She's gone now."

Weeping, I again appealed to God and begged him to reassure me. "I'm not sure my mom's in heaven. Please give me a sign."

Arrangements were made quickly and we headed back for her funeral. Mike asked my sister and me to pick out a poem to put on her announcement. We chose one called, *In the Garden*. It seemed appropriate, we felt it would convey Mom's love of gardening. Friday, the day of her service, arrived. As we walked through the large mahogany doors to the funeral home the smell of freshly cut flowers permeated the room.

Mike began by reading aloud the poem. "Mom would have loved this, you all know how much she loved to plant and…"

Immediately my mom's sister jumped out of her seat and went running down the aisle. "That's the song your mama, and our daddy and I would hold hands to and sing when we were kids." Then she began singing. "*And he walks with me and he talks with me and tells me I am his own.*"

We were surprised, as we had never heard the story before. Afterward, each person who came forward shared how Mom had positively affected their lives. If only she could have realized how much she was loved while she was alive.

The new husband of mom's best friend went up to the podium carrying a large, red chili pepper. "I didn't know Inez very well, but I loved her sense of humor. The thing I remember most is every time she came to our house she brought a chili pepper." He held it up. "She always made her favorite green chili dish for us." He reached down and placed the chili in a bouquet of Mom's favorite white roses.

It was a balmy autumn day when we drove to the gravesite. While we waited for the rest of the people to arrive, we noticed a graceful, wide-eyed doe and a buck walking timidly on the lush hillside, only a few yards from where my mom would be buried. The deer stood and watched us for several minutes before bounding away.

"Mom would have enjoyed seeing the deer," I said, with a smile on my face.

"It would have made her think of her early childhood when she saw countless deer as a young girl where she grew up," my brother replied.

The days that followed were filled with tears. My heart ached for my mom. I would burst out crying while walking through a grocery store or listening to an advertisement about her favorite game show or anything to do with flowers. At other times, loneliness would enclose me like a tight sheet as I realized I would never hear her voice again on this earth. The only consolation I felt at times was I knew my mom had loved us all to the best of her ability.

Although she made a lot of mistakes during our childhood, she had done her best to make things right and change her life, by living each day in recovery. We were all proud of her accomplishment, but I still needed God to reassure me that Mom was indeed in Heaven with Him. *"Jesus said to them, I am the way the truth and the life, no one comes to the Father but through me." John 14:6*

As the hours rolled by, I continued to ask God for a sign. I had only been home one day when a beautiful autumn bouquet arrived from a co-worker of my husband who had never met my mother. I took a whiff of its delightful fragrance, and then placed it on the coffee table.

Later that evening I passed the arrangement and took a closer look. Tearing up, I showed my husband, "Look, there are six small red, orange, and yellow chili peppers mixed in with the bouquet. That's odd!" My tears turned into laughter as I remarked, "Mom would have loved this. JP didn't even know her affinity for chili peppers."

Early the next morning, after getting the kids off to school, I grabbed my New Testament and raced out of the house to my Bible study group. Sudden sadness overwhelmed me as I stepped inside. My thoughts were never far from my mom.

The worship leader said, "Take out your songbooks, and turn to page five. I hadn't planned on singing this one, but the Lord impressed this song on my heart this morning."

We began, *"And he walks with me and he talks with me and he tells me I am his own..."*

Immediately I began to cry as I realized it was the same poem, *In the Garden,* my sister and I had picked out for my mom's announcement and the very same song my Mom and aunt had sung as little girls.

Suddenly the words THREE SIGNS, popped into my head! God instantly opened my eyes. He was impressing on me, "I didn't give you one sign-I gave you three." He kindly reminded me of the song that had been chosen and it was no coincident the worship leader had picked it.

The chili peppers on the floral arrangement had also been a sign and seeing the deer at Mom's burial site confirmed it for me.

"Thank you, Jesus, for reassuring me. My mom is indeed with you in eternity." I never doubted again! *"The Lord redeems the soul of His servants, and none of those who trust in Him shall be condemned."* Psalm 34:32

43

My Big Brother

"The Lord is my strength and my shield; my heart trusted in Him, and I am helped; therefore, my heart greatly rejoices, and with my song I will praise Him." Psalm 28:7

All my siblings and I stayed devoted to one another as adults and saw each other whenever we could. On October 30th, 2006, just four years after my mom died, I received some news that would change my life forever.

"Darlin, I have something to tell you," Cary said. "Your brother Dave called to tell me, Mike was in an accident this morning and he's gone."

My heart turned cold, "No! No! Not my brother, Mike! What happened?"

"Mike was driving a cement truck and was going down a steep hill in a residential area when his brakes gave out. People heard him honking and waving his arm trying to alert them to get out of the way. Directly in from of him was a busy intersection and beyond that a row of houses. He must have been trying to miss them so he drove up on the curb and the truck flipped over. He died instantly."

No words could express the grief that I felt knowing I would never see my brother on earth again. The next couple days were a blur. Monica, Rob and I made arrangements for Mike's funeral. It was just too difficult for his widow to handle by herself. Cary, my brothers, and Mike's oldest son, Brandon, had gone to pick up Mike's ashes. As they walked up to the porch on an unusually warm autumn day, I stood outside waiting for them. Looking skyward, I noticed a red-tailed hawk soaring above, circling around and around Mike's house. "Brandon look," I pointed upwards.

"Aunt Deb, that is my dad's favorite bird. I still remember the story he told me about when he used to catch and train them as a kid. It is unusual seeing one in a residential area. I don't think I've ever seen one around here."

We watched as the remarkable bird continued to circle for a few minutes right above the house, before he turned and flew out of sight.

At Mike's memorial the next day, over 200 people attended, including a man named John Potter. Holding a child in his arms, he quickly ran up to the podium and grabbed the microphone. "This is my daughter, Aspen. She was in the house that day, the house that Mike, my Super-Hero, avoided driving into. I wanted to meet the family of the man who sacrificed his life for my daughter. If there is such a thing as a guardian angel, I believe Mike is one of them."

Friends and family stood up and shared stories about my wonderful brother. We talked about his childhood antics, his generous responsibility in helping out his neighbors and friends, and his great sense of humor. There was not a dry eye in the place. Roars of laughter erupted as we watched a video depicting Mike's short fifty-two years. Through his death, Mike became a hero, not only in the eyes of his family and friends, but also in the lives of those he had inadvertently touched in his untimely death. Even though Mike had not lived an exemplary life, God still allowed him to be remembered as a hero. He will always be thought of as a man who sacrificed his life for another.

Too soon we drove to the cemetery to bury my brother next to Mom. "Look," one of the nephews, pointed out. "There is a buck, a doe and a fawn standing on the hilltop." For some reason, we were all consoled at the sight.

A newspaper article came out the next day calling my brother a hometown hero. *"Mike Griswold tried to turn the cement truck around rather than run into a busy intersection and into a row of houses. He truly was a hero."* Mike had always been our hero and we were grateful others saw him as one also.

Back home in California I found myself crying all the time. To me it felt much worse than losing any other family member, fortunately, it kept me close to the Lord as I depended on him to get me through each day. I was so grateful those years before when Mike lived in California I thought back to when he shared his conversion with me. "Deb," he had telephoned me. "I know what John 3:16 means now come over I want to talk to you." *For God so loved the world He gave His only Son, whosoever believes will not perish but have eternal life."* The two of us sat together on his front lawn and talked about God's love. It had been an answer to prayer. Although, Mike was always quiet about his faith, he never failed to call and ask for prayer and share what God was doing in his life.

Throughout the days and weeks ahead, I often thought of his family and prayed earnestly for them to find comfort in the arms of Jesus. Every few days I would look up from whatever I was doing and I would always notice a red-tailed hawk soaring majestically overhead. It gave me comfort.

I began to reach out to Mike's young widow, who had been a part of our lives since she was seventeen, even though we lived almost a thousand miles apart from each other. I wrote to her frequently, called her, emailed her, and tried to encourage her. Lynn finally began to reach out to Jesus and found solace in accepting Christ as her Savior. Mike's daughter, Michele, was married on Father's Day just eight months after Mike died. A year later she and Jack had a beautiful little girl and eventually added another daughter to their union.

Mike's youngest son, Kellan was always quiet about his grief but finally learned how to live without his dad and found joy in his life once again. He was married in the Summer of 2017. Just nine months after Mike passed, Brandon's wife gave birth to a darling little boy. He joined his older sister Demi. "Aunt Deb," Brandon called. "We just had a baby, and we named him after my dad. Elijah Michael Thomas Griswold was born July 27 and he weighed five pounds, thirteen ounces."

"Brandon do you realize Elijah was born on my dad's birthday and 5/13 is Nanny's birthday. That is no coincidence, that is a God-incidence!" I remarked.

"That's so cool, Aunt Deb, it symbolizes all our loved ones who are in Heaven."

A year after my brother was killed the neighborhood association where he died called my sister-in-law. They asked if they could erect a permanent monument in honor of Mike. It would sit on the hill above the road where his cement truck had overturned. Since it was on protected land it would always stay there without being disturbed. Cary and I just so happened to be in town that week and we helped Lynn and her kids pick out a beautiful red stone. She had the words, *Mike*

Our Hero We Miss You, etched on it along with an eagle, a deer, and the Rocky Mountains. He truly was a hometown hero!

"You have turned for me my mourning into dancing." *Psalm 30:11*

44

Family Life

*"May you always be filled with the fruit of your salvation—
the righteous character produced in your life by Jesus
Christ—for this will bring much glory and praise to God."
Philippians 1:11*

Two years before my brother passed, we moved into another home only
a few blocks from our previous one. The house and I were nearly fifty
and we both needed some remodeling. I joined Curves and together my
husband, the contractor, and I worked on our home, painting, repair-
ing, and adding new rooms. Our new bedroom was much smaller than
our previous one. The outside patio was soon officiated as the new *family bed*. We transformed it to a place that could be used year-round,
with lovely, colorful flowers, lanterns, and even an outdoor heater.
It was here that the family continued to share laughter, prayers, and
sometimes tears. We welcomed friends and family as we sat together on
crisp spring mornings and warm summer nights. Throughout the years
when one of the kids went away; this is the place they would miss most
often. "Mom we miss having coffee on the patio with all of you," was

often remarked. Many life-changing decisions were made as a result of prayers at our "patio time."

With my children nearly grown, I began concentrating on my gardening. As I worked on my hands and knees, creating a living canvas, I thought of Mom often. I could almost feel her looking over my shoulder, pleased with the flowers and shrubs I had picked out. I even joked to my family that Jesus and Mom handpicked our house for us. We've had three weddings, two receptions and numerous birthday parties in our spacious and secluded front yard over the years, including Kristy's who was the first of our children to marry.

I had just turned 50 and celebrated with my family at a nearby restaurant. The following Friday we made plans once again to meet all the kids for dinner because my oldest had been unable to join us the week before. Kristy and Tyler left earlier to put in our name and wait while the rest of us rode in Jeremy's car to meet them.

On the way my oldest son said, "Can we stop at the Country Club? You remember Jorge, my old friend who used to work with me? He is working there now and he just carved his very first ice sculpture. He wants us to stop by and look at it. It would mean a lot to him."

"Sure," I said, "but I don't want Kristy and Tyler to be waiting on us."

"We're fine. We'll just go in for a minute," my husband said.

We knew Jorge pretty well since Cary was the one who first hired him and he and Jeremy had become best friends. We were proud of the way he had grown in his career.

Walking in, the kids and Cary strode in front of me. As we rounded the corner my husband opened the door when I realized the lights were off. Strolling into a darkened room, someone quickly switched on the lights, "Surprise! Surprise! Happy Birthday!"

When my eyes became accustomed to the light there standing before me were my closest friends, my cousins, and my brother and his kids who lived in Arizona. Even Steve, my youngest sibling, had come all the way from Colorado.

Tears flowed down my face, "Cary, what have you done?" I gratefully reached out to him.

There stood Kristy waving her arms erratically, standing next to Tyler. "Haw, and you thought you were going to meet us for dinner," they both roared with laughter.

Tyler proudly put his arms around me. "This time Dad included me. We all kept it a secret from you. Were you surprised?"

I tousled my youngest son's hair. "Yes, you guys are awesome."

Then Cary and the kids led me to the center of the room and at once a sea of colorful balloons were moved aside and there stood my sister and her youngest son.

"Monica, Levi, oh my gosh you guys came out from Colorado, too. Wow! I can't believe this." I looked fondly at my amazing husband and wonderful children. "Thank you for making my birthday so special."

Cary and the kids made a video telling me how much they loved me. "I love your faith, you taught me about God's love. We are so proud of you. You have been a wonderful mom and an awesome wife."

It gave me a chill. "How awesome to hear those words from you guys. I love you all so much. I am so grateful to be your mom and so proud to be your wife."

Later that night, after returning home, I held my husband close. "You never cease to amaze me. Thank you so much for all you do. I truly am a blessed woman."

"No, let me correct you I am the one who is blessed. You are my Proverbs 31 woman. I thank God every day for bringing you and the kids into my life."

"A wife of noble character who can find? She is worth far more than rubies. Her husband has full confidence in her and lacks nothing of value. She brings him good, not harm, all the days of her life. Her children arise and call her blessed, her husband also, and he praises her. Many women do noble things, but you surpass them all." Proverbs 31:10-12,28-29

The End

Epilogue

"I will repay you for the years the locusts have eaten. You will have plenty to eat, until you are full, and you will praise the name of the Lord your God who has worked wonders for you....." Joel 2:25-2

It's been several years since I started my memoir and a lot has changed. My amazing husband just surprised me with another party for my 60th birthday. Jeremy has recently married and continues to work for Bon Appetit' he lives about ten minutes from us. We see he and his wife, Alicia often. Kristy has been married to Tim for over ten years and has established herself as a successful artist. Painting ocean scenes and beaches is her specialty. She is featured in a local gallery in Palm Springs and Kristy hosts fun nights painting and sipping wine. Jeff is a great photographer, he has recently returned home after living in a foreign country for nearly five years. He is a close to all his siblings and his niece and two nephews. He has a great sense of humor and is enjoyed by all. Ashley has been married for over seven years to Adam and has given us three amazing grandchildren. Ellie who is six, Ezra 3 and baby Emory Brave just turned 1 and I am devoted to them. Thankfully, they live only 2 miles away. Tyler, our youngest just turned 24 he enjoys traveling and has made friends all over the world. He loves to visit foreign countries and has taken a 10,000-mile motorcycle ride from one end of the United States to the other with friends. All of our children live nearby and we gather together as often as we can, we continue to savor our "patio time." I see my siblings several times a year, we delightfully share in each other's lives through, Facebook, photos, letters, phone calls and visits.

"Darlin' there is something about those eyes and I am more in love with you today then the day we married," is a phrase I hear often from my beloved, adoring husband of twenty-seven years. We continue to marvel at all the amazing things God does in each of our lives. He has definitely restored all the lost years, all the painful experiences I've endured, all the tears, the fears the highs and lows of life and through them all, God has brought me Victory, Restoration and Hope. My Father in heaven has changed me through my relationship with Jesus Christ. I would not be where I am today without Him. Thankfully through the years He's revealed his unconditional love towards me, something I hope to share with others through my story.

Acknowledgments

My deepest thanks to my amazing husband without his support and inspiration and confidence in me, I would never have been able to write this book. I also want to thank my children and friends for believing in me and encouraging me to write my story and for helping me to press on to get my book published.

Thank you to my family members and many friends who read the book before it was in print and gave me feedback and the courage to get it published. Thank you for all those who wrote *Praises for:* and was a constant support and encouragement to me. Thank you to the people who helped me edit the book and to Book Baby for publishing my book.

I appreciate everybody who through reading, encouraging, and praying for me helped make this dream of mine a reality.

Pictures

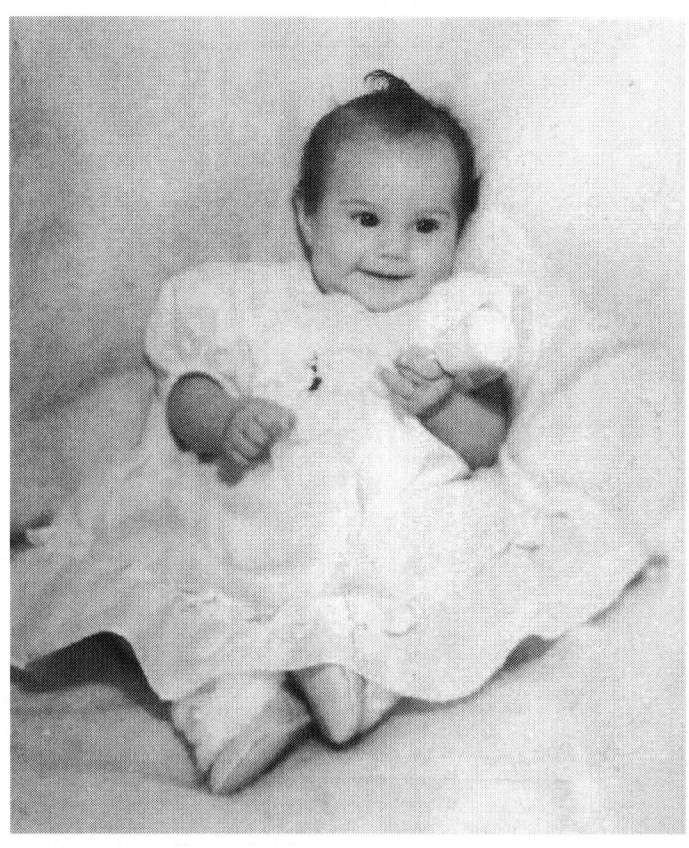

Debra Ann Griswold
September 11, 1955

Four-years-old living at the Spider house

Me and my sister, Monica holding hands, still best friends today

My oldest brother Mike, 5
Monica 3 and Me 4

My youngest brother, Steve 18 months
Rob 2 ½
Dave 3 ½ he and I were the only ones with blond hair

Making my first communion
At Saint Joseph's church in Fontana, CA

Mom and Dad shortly before or after they had just married

My love for horses started early

Mike training his red-tail hawk

Me at 16 shortly after Cary and I first met

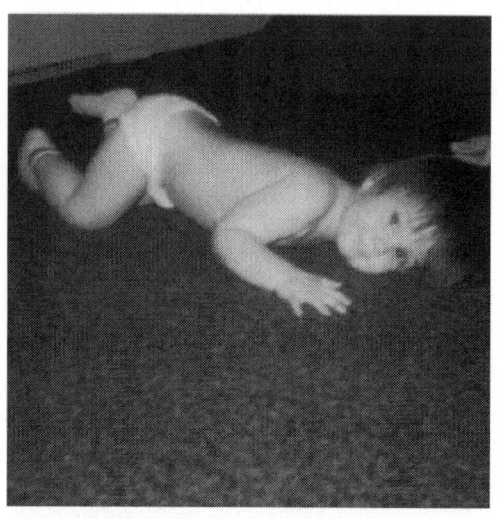

Jeremy born in 1973 in Colorado Springs, CO

Kristy born in 1977 in Colorado Springs, CO

Jeff born in 1979 in Colorado Springs, CO

My three kids in 1984 right before I married Lee

My siblings as adults and our Mom

Ashley born in 1987 in Colorado Springs, CO

Me and my growing family 1988

Cary at 23 years-old

Cary and me on our wedding day June 27, 1991

Our family in 1991 after arriving in California

Tyler born in 1994 in California

Dad in 1997

Me and my love 1992

Prince and me 2003

Mom and me 1999

Our family – my 50th Birthday 2005

Our Family 2015 at my 60ᵗʰ birthday party

All the kids 2017

Soul Mates 2018